✔ KU-517-129

LEEDS POLYTECHNIC LIBRARY

To Renew give the date due and this No.

206430

onal applicat

71 0140182 8

PEN

The savage in literature

International Library of Anthropology

Editor: Adam Kuper, University College, London

Arbor Scientiae
Arbor Vitae

A catalogue of other Social Science books published by Routledge & Kegan Paul will be found at the end of this volume.

The savage in literature

Representations of 'primitive' society
in English fiction 1858–1920

Brian V. Street

School of Social Sciences,
University of Sussex

Routledge & Kegan Paul

London and Boston

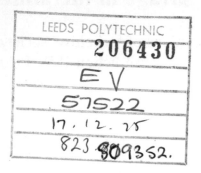
LEEDS POLYTECHNIC

206430

E V

57522

17. 12. 75

823.809352.

2 140182 -8

First published in 1975
by Routledge & Kegan Paul Ltd
Broadway House, 68–74 Carter Lane,
London EC4V 5EL and
9 Park Street,
Boston, Mass. 02108, USA
Set in Monotype Times
and printed in Great Britain by
Butler & Tanner Ltd, Frome and London
© Brian V. Street 1975
No part of this book may be reproduced in
any form without permission from the
publisher, except for the quotation of brief
passages in criticism

ISBN 0 7100 8110 3

To my parents

Contents

Preface and acknowledgments

I would like primarily to thank my parents, to whom this book is dedicated.

A great deal of the work for a book like this comes from hints, suggestions and references from friends and colleagues. In general, members of the Institute of Social Anthropology in Oxford have given me invaluable help over the years. In particular my tutor there during the period 1966–70, Dr Godfrey Lienhardt provided much in the way of inspiration and personal friendship, which I continue to value. The late Professor Sir E. Evans-Pritchard offered warm companionship and constant stimulation, and was largely responsible for the amenable atmosphere of the Institute in those years. The secretary, Barbara Alloway, and the librarian, June Anderson, have been both kind and helpful in the day-to-day details and problems of thesis-writing. A number of personal friends have provided help 'beyond the call of duty', so to speak, and have a considerable investment in what follows. I would like particularly to mention Andre Singer, Pauline Sutherland together with Claire and Rachel, Ken Hewis and Shirley Franklin.

The Social Science Research Council generously provided a grant from 1967–70 which enabled me to work on the thesis from which this book is drawn, and I would like to record my gratitude to them.

None of those mentioned above needs, of course, take any blame for the weaknesses of my work.

The publishers would like gratefully to acknowledge the following for permission to use copyright material:

Barnes & Noble Inc. for permission to quote from *Prelude to Imperialism* by Alan C. Cairns.
Macdonald & Janes Publishers for permission to quote from *The Far Interior* by Walter Montague Kerr (1886).
Thomas Nelson & Sons Ltd, London, for permission to quote from *Prester John* by John Buchan (1910).
Penguin Books for permission to quote from *King Solomon's Mines* by Sir Henry Rider Haggard (1885).
J. M. Dent & Sons for permission to quote from *A History of English Literature* (Vol. 2 *Modern Times*) by L. Cazamian and E. Legouis (1926).
Chatto & Windus for permission to quote from *The Great Tradition* by F. R. Leavis.
Peter Owen, London, for permission to quote from *Kipling and the Critics* by E. L. Gilbert.
Oxford University Press for permission to quote from *In the Power of the Pygmies* by Charles Gilson.
The Clarendon Press, Oxford, for permission to quote from *Theories of Primitive Religion* by E. E. Evans-Pritchard (1965), and *Social Anthropology* by R. G. Lienhardt (1964).
John Murray Ltd and Baskervilles Investments Ltd for permission to quote from *The Tragedy of the Korosko* by Sir Arthur Conan Doyle.
Hodder & Stoughton for permission to quote from *Uttermost Part of the Earth* by E. Lucas Bridges.
Associated Book Publishers for permission to quote from *Race Relations* by Michael Banton.
Edinburgh University Press for permission to quote from *Independent African – John Chilembwe* by G. Shepperson and T. Price (1958).
St Martin's Press and Macmillan for permission to quote from *The Imperial Idea and its Enemies* by A. P. Thornton.
Faber & Faber and Harcourt, Brace Jovanovich, Inc. for permission to quote from *The Waste Land* by T. S. Eliot.
Morton Cohen, Hutchinson Publishing Group and the Estate of Sir Henry Rider Haggard for permission to quote from *Rider Haggard—His Life and Works* by Morton Cohen and *She* by Sir Henry Rider Haggard.

Gerald Duckworth & Co. for permission to quote from *100 Years of Anthropology* by T. K. Penniman (1952).
Longman Ltd for permission to quote from *Not Worth Reading* by Sir George Compton Arthur.
Rupert Hart-Davis for permission to quote from *John Buchan* by Janet Smith.
Penguin Books for permission to quote from *The Founding Fathers of Social Science* edited by Timothy Raison and *Primitive Government* by Lucy Mair (1962).
Gyldendalske Boghandel for permission to quote from *Studies in Mid-Victorian Imperialism* by C. A. Bodelsen.
Pitt Rivers Museum for permission to quote from *The Origin and Development of the Pitt Rivers Museum*.
E. P. Dutton & Co. for permission to quote from *The Uttermost Part of the Earth* by E. Lucas Bridges.
Macmillan Publishing Co. New York for permission to quote from *Race, Culture and Evolution* by G. Stocking.
The Estate of Sir Henry Rider Haggard for permission to quote from *Allan Quatermain* and *Nada the Lily* by H. Rider Haggard.
Tavistock Publications Ltd, and Basic Books for permission to quote from *Race Relations* by Michael Banton.
Mrs George Bambridge and Macmillan Co. for permission to quote from *The Day's Work*, *Life's Handicap*, *Traffics and Discoveries*, *Plain Tales from the Hills* and *The Phantom Rickshaw* by Rudyard Kipling.
Mrs George Bambridge and Eyre Methuen Ltd for permission to quote from *Barrack Room Ballads* by Rudyard Kipling.
The Estate of Sir James Frazer for permission to quote from *The Gorgon's Head* and *The Golden Bough* by Sir James Frazer.
Trinity College Oxford and John Murray Ltd for permission to quote from *The Four Feathers* and *The Broken Road* by A. E. W. Mason.
Trinity College Oxford for permission to quote from *The Drum* by A. E. W. Mason.
The Tweedsmuir Estate for permission to quote from *The African Colony* by John Buchan.
The Estate of W. Somerset Maugham and Macmillan Co. for permission to quote from *A Choice of Kipling's Prose* edited by W. Somerset Maugham.
The International African Institute for permission to quote from *Lugbara Religion* by Professor J. Middleton.

Ibadan University Press for permission to quote from *Africa in English Fiction 1874–1939* by G. D. Killam.

New York University Press for permission to quote from *Anglo-Saxons and Celts* by L. P. Curtis Jun. (1968).

University of Wisconsin Press for permission to quote from *The Image of Africa* by Philip Curtin (1965).

Edgar Rice Burroughs, Inc. for permission to quote from *Tarzan of the Apes*, and *Jungle Tales of Tarzan*. Copyright © by Frank A. Munsey Company, 1912 and 1914.

Chapter 1

Literary themes and anthropological writings

In Conrad's romance *A Smile of Fortune*, Miss Jacobus, exiled from Europe on a small Far Eastern island, derives her impression of life at home from occasional newspaper reports:

> She had formed for herself a notion of the civilised world as a scene of murder, abductions, burglaries, stabbing affrays and every sort of desperate violence. England and France, Paris and London (the only two towns of which she seemed to have heard) appeared to her sinks of abomination, reeking with blood, in contrast to her little island where petty larceny was about the standard of current misdeeds, with now and then some pronounced crime – and that only among the imported coolie labourers on sugar estates or the negroes of the town. But, in Europe, these things were being done daily by a wicked population of white men. . . . It was impossible to give her a sense of proportion. I suppose she figured England to herself as about the size of the Pearl of the Ocean, in which case it would certainly have been reeking with gore and a mere wreck of burgled houses end to end. One could not make her understand that these horrors on which she fed her imagination were lost in the mass of orderly life like a few drops of blood in the ocean (Conrad, 1912, p. 67).

In an essay written twenty-two years later Professor Evans-Pritchard, from an anthropological standpoint, made a similar plea for attention to 'the mass of orderly life':

> Most specialists who are also fieldworkers are agreed that primitive peoples are predominantly interested in practical, economic pursuits; gardening, hunting, fishing, care of their cattle and the manufacture of weapons, utensils and ornaments and in their social contacts; the life of the household and family and kin, relations with friends and neighbours, with superiors and inferiors, dances and feasts, legal disputes, feuds and warfare. Behaviour of a mystical type in the main is restricted to certain situations in social life in such a way that to describe it by itself as Levy-Bruhl has done deprives it of the meaning it derives from its social situation and its cultural accretions (Evans-Pritchard, 1933, p. 42).

So some – but, as will be seen, not many – novelists, and some – but, as will be seen, not all – anthropologists have asked us to see what appears sensational in the wider context of what is ordinary.

Conrad here as a novelist and Evans-Pritchard, as a social anthropologist, indicate that the reading of reports on foreign people and the interpretation of them involve the selection of particular, often dramatic, features of their lives without regard to the total context which gives them 'a sense of proportion'. Part of the object of this work is to show how and to some extent why, particular aspects of 'primitive' life were seized upon by many English writers in the later nineteenth and early twentieth centuries and taken as representative of the whole. The representations of alien peoples in much of this literature were based on now outdated scientific theory and on the limited experience of travellers, many of them unsympathetic to other ways of life. Such descriptions thus tell us more about the Victorians themselves than about the people they purport to describe.

Background

The origin of these representations is to be found, in the nineteenth century, not only in popular literature but also in contemporary science and imperial politics, so that all three continually derive from and contribute to the changing image of 'primitive' man. During this period there was a dramatic increase in the concern with underdeveloped countries, led by commercial interests but closely followed by the politicians. Up until the 1870s relations with these countries remained informal, and while small business empires grew in parts of Africa and Malaysia, there was no attempt to exert political control, rather a dread of the responsibilities it would involve. But in the 1870s and 1880s began the 'scramble for Africa', and England found herself, to the surprise of some and the alarm of others, with an Empire which involved her directly in the political control of millions of people of different culture and 'race', most of whom the English did not understand. What knowledge there was of these peoples derived from literature and science.

Travellers' tales had been brought back from exotic lands since the Bermuda pamphlets and earlier, and during the early nineteenth century the supply increased. The information about other cultures had been incorporated into the contemporary framework of thought and scientists from various fields had used the information as it suited their particular interests. But during the middle years of the nineteenth century a group of scientists began to study this information in its own right and, in 1843, formed the Ethnological Society. Now the information was collected together and collated and future travellers could be given a guide as to what to look for. In 1846, Ethnology was given scientific recognition with a subsection at the British Academy (although it came rather heavily under the influence of biology and the natural sciences). In 1863, there was a rift over the attitude of some members to the American Civil War and to slavery, and a more politically conscious group formed a separate society called the Anthropological Society of London, whose membership and public recognition increased towards the end of the century. In addition to the influence of these learned societies, the particular study of 'primitive' peoples was given stimulus by the archaeological discoveries of the age, by Darwin's theory of evolution and by the acquisition of colonies in the 1880s, by which time a body of theory was available to those interested in the way of life of the people of the colonies. This theory became increasingly important in everyday social and political life.

The combination of scientific interest in primitive man with increased political and social contact with him, is reflected in the popular literature of the day. In the 1840s, publishing techniques were developed which enabled large quantities of very cheap fiction to reach the newly educated working classes. Novels were brought out in penny parts, the 'penny dreadfuls', and in 1847 the first successful attempt was made to produce cheap reprints of these serials in volume form. The themes of these first mass-produced novels were domestic, and conventions grew up which restricted the author to a stereotyped pattern of events and characters in limited contexts (James, L., 1963). By the 1870s writers were trying to break out of this strait-jacket. The growth of Empire at this time and the experiences of so many travellers in distant, exotic lands provided a ready-made alternative, and from the 1870s onwards fiction took up this theme. The 'ethnographic novel', estranged in time and space from the claustrophobic Victorian drawing-room, became popular. For the first time information on other cultures, expressed in vivid, exciting tales, was available to the mass public of England. Such romances, with their large circulation and appeal to a recently literate general public, are appropriately termed 'popular fiction'.

There is a unity in this period noted by students of literature: 'The end of the nineteenth and the beginning of the twentieth century make up a single literary period. This means that the relative unity of some predominant characteristics makes itself felt' (Cazamian and Legouis, 1926, p. 454).

There is a unity, likewise, in the particular kind of literature with which we are dealing; Dalziel, describing the early 'popular' novels, justifies her generalisations about it on the strength of a few examples by claiming: 'The descriptions of these novels and periodicals . . . are acceptable only on the assumption that one quality of mass-produced fiction at any date is its great sameness' (Dalziel, 1957, p. 3).

While Dalziel is referring to the domestic novel, the same is true of the 'ethnographic novel'. The mass-produced stories of far-off lands and their inhabitants, so popular during this period in England, are similar in style and content and, most significantly, in the assumptions they share with regard to 'primitive' peoples.

There is a unity in the scientific thought of the period, based on common interest in evolutionary and racial theory and the nature of 'armchair anthropology', and there is a unity in the political interests of the time, in the concern with overseas territory and the eventual emergence of an Empire.

Some significant aspects of this unity of consciousness can better be understood by a careful analysis of the 'popular' novels of the time and of the scientific theory on which they were based.

The image

'Imperialism' has customarily taken the blame for the distorted picture of 'primitive' life disseminated in the nineteenth century. The notion that 'primitive' peoples were inferior is assumed to be a political excuse for taking their lands. But many of the stereotypes had already hardened before the 'scramble for Africa', and imperialists tended to use theories already worked out by scientists and which lent themselves to political manipulation. Scientific theories of race provided a framework of thought with regard to primitive peoples which justified the actions of imperialists, but they arose, not out of an imperial situation, but in a pre-imperial world of science.

Cairns, in *Prelude to Imperialism*, analyses 'British reactions to Central African Society', in the period before direct rule from 1840 to 1890, and shows how many of the stereotypes assumed to come from the imperial situation, where white ruled black, in fact arose before:

In the pre-Imperial period, by contrast, the British lived and travelled in societies they did not control. These microcosmic, multi-racial societies were African dominated. Pioneer conditions and the poverty of whites evoked a greater degree of intimacy with, and dependence on, Africans than was the case with a later generation of colonists (Cairns, 1965, p. xi).

Yet, despite these pre-imperial conditions, Cairns finds many of the stereotypes which are so common in the literature of the 1890s and after and warns the reader of the dangers of uncritical acceptance of the earlier literature: 'If analysis is not to slide easily and completely into the mould of patriotism and racial pride, the value judgments which accompanied and sanctioned western expansion must be handled with discretion' (ibid., p. xiii).

Curtin, in *The Image of Africa*, pushes back the date of the hardening of the image even earlier, to the 1850s:

Thereafter, when new generations of explorers or administrators went to Africa, they went with a prior impression of what they would find. Most often, they found it and their writings, in turn, confirmed the older image – or, at most, altered it only slightly (Curtin, 1965, p. vi).

It is one of the contentions of this work that the development of a body of theory in academic anthropology at the end of the nineteenth century altered this image more than slightly. But the literature of the colonies did build largely on the past, as Bodelsen notes: 'The eighties gave literary expression to, and popularised, a movement already well under way' (Bodelsen, 1924, p. 8).

Killam, in *Africa in English Fiction 1874–1939* (where the emphasis is on social and political problems of Empire reflected in popular literature rather than on anthropological ideas), dates 'ethnographic fiction' from 1874 because in that year Henty published his first boys' books on the Ashanti campaign. He too agrees that the writers of this period perpetuated an older image:

> Addressing themselves to a general public caught up in the enthusiasm of the overseas venture in Africa, they knew what their readers wished to read and to that taste they catered.
>
> Thus the generality of authors adhere strictly in their treatments of the African setting to an image of Africa which was in large part formed before they came to write their books (Killam, 1968, p. x).

As we shall see later, the image was not confined to Africa. Since the ideas stemmed from nineteenth-century views of the world beyond Europe, it was easy enough to apply descriptions of African inferiority or 'savagery' to natives of South America, Asia or Malaysia, with the same lack of discrimination. The present work is concerned with the image of 'primitive' peoples in general, even though the bulk of the material concerns Africa.

By the mid-nineteenth century, then, the details of the image we have been discussing were fairly explicit. 'Primitive' peoples are considered to be the slaves of custom and thus to be unable to break the despotism of their own 'collective conscience'. Any custom 'discovered' among a 'primitive' people is assumed to dominate their whole lives; they are unconscious of it and will never change it themselves. This provides the basis for the analysis of many customs being reported back to nineteenth-century England by the growing number of travellers. And their reporting is already conditioned by the scientifically-backed metaphors of the chain of being and the ladder by means of which all other cultures were ascribed their place in a universal hierarchy. A people was given its appropriate rung on the ladder according to race. It was assumed that one's place in the hierarchy was determined by heredity; the ladder represented stages of social evolution with Anglo-Saxon at the top, and reporters looked for criteria by which to determine how far other races had climbed up it.

Since the races were thus divided up by various criteria and characteristics, a particular 'character' could be attributed to a whole people on the strength of casual personal observations; a 'race' might be gullible, faithful, brave, childlike, savage, blood-thirsty, noble, etc. and these qualities were assumed to be hereditary. Likewise, the Anglo-Saxon race had certain qualities which were inborn in all its members and it was these qualities which enabled it to dominate the rest of the world.

'Primitive' man, on the other hand, spent his whole life in fear of spirits and mystical beings; his gullibility was exploited by self-seeking priests and kings, who manipulated religion to gain a hold on the minds of their simple subjects; he worshipped animals and trees, tried to control the mystical forces of nature by means of ceremony, ritual, taboos and sacrifices, and explained the wonders of the universe in imaginative but 'unscientific' myths. Politically, the 'primitive' was in the grip of either anarchy or despotism; social control, if any, was exercised by the most savage tyranny, by the despotism of custom or by religious trickery. And his economic life consisted of either primitive communism in which everything was shared, or a system of each man for himself, 'grab and never let go' (Malinowski, 1922, p. 96). Life was a perpetual struggle against harsh nature and harsher men, and only the fittest would survive.

Much of this is, of course, 'true' up to a point, in the same way that what Miss Jacobus learnt of England was 'true'. But such descriptions lack the sense of proportion that can only be achieved by putting them in their full context alongside the mass of orderly life and alongside the many other, less exotic or dramatic, aspects of the religious, political and economic life of Englishmen and 'primitive' peoples alike. Needless to say, most popular reporting and novels dealing in such matters fail to do this, and their presentation is correspondingly distorted.

While the 'ignoble' side of 'savage' life tends to be thus distorted, so too is the 'noble' side. The tradition of the 'noble savage' was not entirely rejected in nineteenth-century thought, and many writers struggle with the conflicting theories presented by the literary tradition on the one hand and contemporary reporters and scientists on the other. In Rider Haggard, for example, the conflict between primitivism and progress causes inconsistencies within the novels and often affects the story itself; while he criticises many features of his own culture in contrast with the pristine goodness of primitive life, he ultimately subscribes to the doctrine of 'progress' and believes British influence will raise the native higher in the scale of being; thus the idyllic lands which his travellers struggle to find are left in the charge of enlightened Englishmen.

To some writers the 'native' is too unpleasant and dirty to correspond to the noble savage of literature, but they still subscribe to a romantic belief in the value of life near to nature, stripped of the artificiality of civilised society. The pastoral tradition in which the heirs of kings are abandoned on wild mountain slopes provides a technique which enables these writers to reconcile their faith in the superiority of the Englishman with their condemnation of urban superficiality by presenting an Englishman in the role of the noble savage. Tarzan and Tabu Dick combine the splendid physical qualities of the jungle native with the intellectual and moral superiority of an Anglo-Saxon heritage. The conflict is argued out within a common framework of thought which produces similar attitudes to the 'savage', whether he is considered 'noble' or 'ignoble'.

Similarly, the debates between the polygenists and monogenists and degenerationists and progressionists, which I shall examine more closely later, take place within a predetermined framework. Some writers emphasise the despotic character of 'primitive' political systems, others describe mere anarchy; some believe the 'native' must be treated firmly, even harshly, others subscribe to the 'soft' approach; some think 'primitive' man can be educated to their own 'superior' level, others believe his intelligence is circumscribed, his condition static. But these conflicts of opinion are limited by the collective representations of the period which provide the language, the categories and much of the imagery for describing 'primitive' man, whichever side individuals may take in the argument.

The perception of other societies and their way of life by nineteenth-century writers is thus conditioned by a common set of ideas, however much individuals may vary within the limits of the framework given them by their own society.

In the second half of the nineteenth century anthropological theory began to change, and the new ideas gradually influenced representations of 'primitive' peoples. The novels we shall be considering were all written in this latter period. While they express many of the assumptions that lay behind the earlier 'image' of 'primitive' peoples, they increasingly reveal the importance of the new ideas of scientists and scholars. Late nineteenth-century anthropological theory is to be found expressed in vivid, memorable terms in these popular novels, along with more general stereotypes of other societies derived from earlier times and different sources. The image of the native is given a specific colouring and a supposedly scientific respectability not common in representations of alien peoples.

In 1858 Darwin published his *Origin of Species*. Most histories of anthropology date from this work the interest in and development of the academic study of 'primitive' society. The image of such people, which Cairns claims had already hardened before *Origin of Species*, was both reinforced and altered by that work, and those of the expanding school of anthropologists such as Tylor, MacLennan and Robertson Smith. The image presented by the 'anthropological fiction' that started in the 1870s and increased rapidly at the turn of the century was not static, but rather developed as the academic subject developed.

Leo Henkin, in *Darwinism in the English Novel 1860–1910*, elicits some of the themes which the novels of the period derived from post-Darwinian science. The nearness of man to the apes, the struggle for survival, the portrayal of 'survivals' and prehistoric monsters, the disequilibrium brought about by loss of faith in the Bible, are only a few of the themes that were either new or treated in a new way because of *Origin of Species* and the discoveries of archaeology and anthropology at the same time.

While it is difficult to trace any consistent development in the image from mid-century to the early twentieth century, since some authors were in closer contact than others with anthropology, there are some recognisable trends. The inferiority of the native, so common in the earlier image, is reinforced by the popularity of evolutionary theory and the notion of the survival of the fittest. The use of race as a means of classifying mankind and the notion of the scale of value, with European man at the top and primitive at the bottom, are parts of the old image which lived on, strengthened further by post-Darwinian anthropology. But the detail with which native life is described increases as anthropologists pay more serious attention to what had previously been dismissed as irrational, trivial and superstitious, and authors occasionally attempt explanations of primitive customs in terms of current anthropological theory. Thus

D. H. Lawrence gives considerable significance to the symbolism of colours in Aztec ritual, where earlier authors dismissed face-painting as 'hideous distortions'. Theories of 'primitive' religion, of ancestor cults, natural mythology and 'animism', current in anthropological thinking, find their way into the popular novel and refine the image; and the discoveries of archaeology and palaeontology, providing man with a larger time span in which the evolution pointed out by Darwin can be shown to have taken place, gives the imaginative writer scope for creating worlds where ancient societies and customs are fossilised according to the pattern discovered by anthropologists in contemporary 'primitive' societies. 'Primitive' peoples were seen as representing earlier stages of European development, so that a particular group, on analogy with geological strata, could be seen as a 'survival' of a period through which the European had passed.

The period in which this image of 'primitive' peoples developed, from the publication of *Origin of Species* until the First World War, coincides to some extent with the rise and decline of the Empire, with the massive output of popular fiction about exotic lands, and with the scientific debates stimulated by Darwin and anthropologists. These three forces, then, politics, science and literature, served to form an image which by 1920 was as hardened as that which Curtin describes for 1850.

While the theories of anthropologists altered the image, it was also deeply affected by the way novelists treated it. Scientific and political ideas acquired a different character for the English public when they came to be expressed in the pages of popular fiction. Cazamian notes some of the more significant contributions of the writer, in attributing much of the mythology of Empire to Kipling:

> While statesmen grasped the possibilities included in a fact
> which their conscious will had never contributed to create,
> and were anxious to strengthen and develop it; while scientists
> explored it, studied its resources or told its progress, it was
> given to a man of letters to make it supremely and most deeply
> actual by implanting it among the familiar and intimate ideas
> of all men. It is from Kipling that, to the majority of the English,
> the existence of the Empire dates back (Cazamian and Legouis,
> 1926, p. 456).

Sometimes a writer knew anthropologists, as Rider Haggard knew Andrew Lang; sometimes he read deeply in anthropology, as did

D. H. Lawrence; and sometimes he owed his knowledge of the material and theory to his education and the 'general spirit of the age'. Some writers loved exotic lands and respected many of their inhabitants, as did Rider Haggard in Africa; some saw only pagan savages in need of conversion, as did R. M. Ballantyne in the South Seas; and some saw the natives as primarily imperial subjects, as did A. E. W. Mason in India.

The significance of all these writers for the anthropologist lies in that ability to make 'deeply actual' both the scientific theory of the day and these personal experiences and attitudes with regard to 'primitive' peoples. They helped to perpetuate and, at the same time, through their individual sensibilities, altered that image which Curtin, Cairns and Bodelsen consider was already hardened before such fiction began to appear.

The impact of this literature on the reading public of the turn of the century is told, most fittingly, by Andrew Lang, a reviewer whose word could sell or ruin a novel; who himself wrote one such romance in union with Rider Haggard, whom he influenced and helped in his writing; and who was also considered an anthropologist and wrote academic works of high standing. Lang writes in 1891:

> There has, indeed, arisen a taste for exotic literature: people have become alive to the strangeness and fascination of the world beyond the bounds of Europe and the United States. But that is only because men of imagination and literary skill have been the new conquerors, the Corteses and Balboas of India, Africa, Australia, Japan and the isles of the southern seas. All such writers . . . have, at least, seen new worlds for themselves; have gone out of the streets of the over-populated lands into the open air; have sailed and ridden, walked and hunted; have escaped from the fog and smoke of towns. New strength has come from fresher air into their brains and blood; hence the novelty and buoyancy of the stories which they tell. Hence, too, they are rather to be counted among romanticists than realists, however real is the essential truth of their books (Lang, 1891, p. 198).

A major concern of this work is the conflict between 'romance' and 'reality'. And, since the reality is the 'character' of other cultures, the enquiry is appropriately an anthropological one.

Popular fiction inevitably distorts the image it presents of 'primitive' man. For not only is the image derived from the scientific theories of the age, which have been rejected by science today as themselves distorted, but it is also conditioned by the nature of the medium itself. Such popular literature tended not to create 'rounded' characters but rather stereotypes, as it did with more domestic subject-matter. It was also directed at a mass audience and a big sale, so the exotic, exciting and savage side of 'primitive' life was emphasised at the expense of the everyday, commonplace and therefore dull. And the writer was usually describing a very limited experience in exotic lands in which the native was part of the backcloth and was often only met in the role of servant or warrior. A writer describes only that of which he has experience; Kipling, for instance, writes of Anglo-Indian society in detail and native society only superficially, since the conditions of his seven years in India make this inevitable. But often these limitations are forgotten, and it is assumed that a writer is providing a valid picture of native society as it is lived. Somerset Maugham, in an introduction to his *Choice of Kipling's Prose*, notes that 'Kipling seems to have been intimately acquainted only with the North West'. This, however, is not a criticism and he adds: 'Like any other sensible writer he placed the scene of his stories in the region he knew best' (Maugham (ed.), 1952, p. v). He writes favourably of Muslims but scornfully of Hindus, and is limited in many other ways, as indeed were most colonial civil servants in India: 'This is a pity, but it was Kipling's right, as it is of every author, to deal with the subjects that appealed to him' (ibid., p. vi).

Maugham is right, and the reasons for Kipling's limitations are another matter, which will be dealt with later. But what is harmful is when the selective process and the limitations are ignored and, often to increase the sale of an author, it is claimed he presents a total picture. Maugham, having pointed out the selective process, falls into the trap himself, when he later praises Kipling for putting 'before the reader with extreme vividness the crowded Indian scene in all its fantastic variety' (ibid., p. xxvii). Maugham has previously noted that India is not a country, it is a continent. No-one can know it all. Yet the reference to Kipling's portrayal of all its 'fantastic variety' suggests that Kipling 'knew' the whole of India and expressed it in his novels. The 'tang of the East' and 'the smell of the bazaars' may well be found in Kipling's work but the generality these phrases suggest is not, indeed cannot, be there. It is in accepting that one writer represents for England the nature of India or Africa or Australia that the image becomes further distorted as descriptions of part of a country are taken as typical of the whole.

Likewise, Rider Haggard's adventure stories, set in South Africa and based on a few years there, are given wider significance. Morton Cohen, in his biography, writes: 'For many Englishmen Africa became the Africa of *King Solomon's Mines*' (Cohen, 1960, p. 95). And these Englishmen included those to whom it was 'read in the public schools, even aloud in class-rooms' and who eventually became the administrators of provinces in Africa. The impact of Haggard's work was partly due to the public's disillusionment with the domestic novel and the life of the towns. 'It let the reader turn his back on the troublesome, the small, the sordid; and it took him on a journey to the Empire's frontier to perform mighty deeds he could believe in' (ibid., p. 96). *King Solomon's Mines* sold 31,000 copies during the first twelve months and all the major literary figures of the day praised it (ibid., p. 95). That it deserved this praise as an exciting adventure is hardly deniable and, compared with much 'anthropological fiction' which its success gave rise to, it deals in considerable detail with African life. But it still perpetuates many of the scientific theories of the time, and further adds to the distortion of the image of 'primitive' man the limitations of Haggard's own experiences and the exigencies of the popular novel. So that for the reviewers and public alike to accept it as a valid picture of 'Africa' meant that the public was putting unwarranted weight on the fiction and accepting as 'real' what was presented as 'romance'.

To analyse in full the 'impact' of such literature on the reading public would be another study. The significance attributed to Kipling by Lang and Maugham, and to Haggard by Cohen, suggests the lines along which such an enquiry might go; and the present study of the assumptions writers shared with their public might throw some light on the impact they themselves expected their work to have. But the main concern here is with the ideas themselves, with the way in which they are presented and with the constraints of popular fiction likely to affect them.

For this purpose it is important, also, to distinguish the individual novelist from his work, to focus on the ideas that he uses rather than trying to attribute them to the man himself.

An author, for instance, may attribute certain views to a character 'to express an ulterior design without necessarily subscribing to them himself'. Rider Haggard portrays the 'character of the average hunter/explorer as a man describing only superficially and without analysis'. He often employs a persona as 'editor' to interpolate foot-notes that show up the limitations of Allan Quatermain's descriptions of African life. This puts many of the value-judgments that are made into perspective. The attitudes are not necessarily those of Haggard himself. Such situations are significant anthropologically, however, for the insight they provide into some of the attitudes of the period, for the importance they show being attributed to them and to the anthropological theory of the day. Haggard's own position is secondary. Popular fiction gave such views wider currency, whatever the writer's personal stand.

However, Haggard and many other writers of the period do present, in a favourable context, ideas about 'primitive' peoples which a modern anthropologist would consider distorted and even debasing. Allan Quatermain is presented as a hero and many of his views are given as those expected of an English gentleman, a posited ideal for many readers. Indeed, in his condemnation of most hunters he implicitly excludes himself. Thus his attitudes to the natives, while not necessarily those of Haggard himself, are presented in such a favourable light that the reader is likely to accept them as valid. Quatermain is sympathetic to some Africans but he still subscribes to the 'received notions' of the day – the Chain of Being, the use of the racial model for ascribing peoples a place in the hierarchy, the judging of 'internal' by 'external' characteristics. By being presented through the eyes of an idealised hero such views are likely to be perpetuated.

Similarly, John Buchan presents a character, Davie (in *Prester John*), as expressing certain ideas on English rule of South African natives with which the reader is expected to sympathise:

> I knew then the meaning of the white man's duty. He has to take all the risks. . . . That is the difference between white and black, the gift of responsibility, the power of being in a little way a king, and so long as we know and then practise it, we will rule not in Africa alone but wherever there are dark men who live only for their bellies (Buchan, 1910, p. 88).

Buchan is not presenting these views in a way likely to make his readers critical of them. Davie is the hero of the novel, he is presented in a positive way, his views carry some weight. There is no suggestion of irony, no hint that they are the rash exaggerations of a young boy. Moreover, our knowledge of Buchan through his other writings, fictional and non-fictional (e.g. *The African Colony*) and the facts of his own career (member of the 'Milner Kindergarten', etc.) confirm that he himself would be unlikely to refute the views expressed by his character. The identity gap between writer and character is very narrow here, as it is in much of the writing with which we shall be concerned. While this fact remains secondary, from an anthropological point of view, to the importance of the ideas themselves, it probably contributes to the writer's ability to make such ideas 'deeply actual'. To deny that these writers often did identify with the views presented by characters in their novels would be as mistaken as to suggest that such identification was always the case.

In some instances the character who presents a 'harsh' view of native life is presented in an unfavourable light. Bertram Mitford presents the conflict between 'hard' and 'soft' approaches to the 'natives' in terms of two English characters in Matabeleland and makes clear his own preference for the 'softer' character. Forster in *A Passage to India* uses Ronny's unfair criticism of an Indian to put him in an unfavourable light. Wallace, on the other hand, evidently prefers Sanders's 'hard' approach. Such writing is mainly significant anthropologically and historically in demonstrating what attitudes were current at the time and the extent to which they were based on contemporary anthropological and scientific theory. I would add, though, that attitudes which we would today consider 'harsh' and 'unfair' to the dignity of other ways of life were most often presented by such writers in a favourable context. As we shall see, many of the writers of popular novels in the late nineteenth and early twentieth centuries use their characters as mouthpieces for their own ethnocentrism.

Kipling and Haggard, for instance, were writing about very different parts of the world, yet, despite occasional acknowledgments of local difference, they share common attitudes of superiority to 'primitive' races that had been made respectable by anthropologists. The extent to which the theory that had been developed to deal with 'primitive' man made all 'primitive' men seem the same, is evident from the similar preconceptions with which the inhabitants of Borneo, Matabeleland and the Punjab are approached by English writers. There is a common body of expectations, a common mythology on which to draw, and differences of detail are subsumed beneath a common structure. Thus the unity of the scientific framework is also to be found in the style of the novels which use it. Hence this work does not attempt to be comprehensive, but rather attempts to deal with a small selection of the material in close detail, on the assumption that this selection, apart from differences in the character of authors and local idiosyncrasies, represents the general features to be found in most novels of this genre. Killam's bibliography lists over 1,000 novels which deal with Africa alone, and this does not include many listed here; old bookshops are full of such works and the public libraries still find a demand for many of them, besides the better-known works of Kipling, Haggard and Buchan. All a work such as this can hope to do is to point to general features common in novels of the genre and indicate to what extent they derive from the science of the day, selecting examples from the most famous and the unknown, from Africa and Malaysia, from 'good' literature and 'bad', to demonstrate the extent to which these works share so much in common.

After the First World War Malinowski, continuing and refining the methods of direct observation of 'primitive' peoples dramatised by the Torres Straits Expedition in 1898 radically altered anthropological thinking in England. The principal change was in the adoption of a more relativistic attitude to other societies and in the development of the 'field work' method, by which anthropologists lived among alien societies for a number of years, learned their language and studied their way of life from 'within'. As a result, the attempt to 'place' others on a universal hierarchy, by such criteria as 'intelligence' or 'degree of monotheism', was abandoned in favour of the study of their institutions and the function these served in the total life of the society. The use of racial, biological models for determining a society's 'internal' characteristics such as 'morality', as though they were passed on 'through the blood', has been superseded by models which attempt to interpret the total context of institutions and values. Likewise the metaphors of the Chain of Being and the Ladder have been put into historical perspective. Anthropologists do not expect any more to place a society in its appropriate niche in the world order. The search for origins was seen as ultimately of little value, since the thought of early man could not be re-created out of his physical traces. Moreover, contemporary 'primitive' societies were seen to have developed along their own paths for as long as western society, so that they could not be used as examples of 'early' man, as 'survivals' of customs which western man held centuries before. The development of society is not like that of the rifle, which was used by Pitt Rivers as the basis of his museum; there is no necessary order of development from polytheism to monotheism, from kingship to republicanism, as there is a necessary development from flint-lock to repeating rifle. So anthropologists began to study the institutions of other societies in their own right, to take them seriously, however strange they might seem by the standard of the observer's society. Putting aside his culturally induced distaste for such practices as cannibalism, for instance, the anthropologist attempts to understand what it means to the people involved, how it fits into their patterns of thought, their shared system of symbols, their political and religious and economic institutions. Where the Victorian anthropologist wondered how he, as an Englishman, would think and act in a 'primitive' society, the modern anthropologist attempts to interpret how the members of that society themselves see the world – their categories of thought, the ways in which they divide up the world around them, the values and norms which give meaning to their lives and the institutions through which they act. Whether such a task is possible is currently being debated by philosophers and anthropologists, who are jointly analysing the problems of translation, of 'rationality' of understanding 'in their terms' and 'in our terms'. But the approach presupposes respect for other modes of thought and action, an immediate response to alien experience which says 'what does it mean to them?' not 'how strange it seems to me'.

In attempting to apply greater scientific rigour to the study of other societies, anthropologists aim to be 'objective', at least to the extent of not making value-judgments and of assessing their own bias.

The scientific ideas represented in nineteenth-century popular fiction are here analysed in terms of these current anthropological standards. Such standards are themselves embedded in the values of a particular society and will themselves be analysed in the same way by future scientists. They provide, however, a starting-point for interpreting fictional representations of 'the mass of orderly life' in other places with a greater 'sense of proportion' than that evident either in Miss Jacobus's notions of the 'civilised world' or in the nineteenth-century 'civilised' world's notions of 'primitive' people.

Chapter 2

The English abroad

The collective representations of the Victorian with regard to the members of 'primitive' societies derive, in general, from the scientific philosophical and literary traditions of nineteenth-century England and, in particular, from the experiences of those who travelled in alien lands and whose attitudes were conditioned by their purpose in being there and by the specific events of the time. The sort of people who brought back reports about 'primitive' life and their attitudes to the peoples they met are themselves portrayed in the very novels which testify to their influence. We can thus discern the basis of some of the stereotypes in popular fiction from the examination of European characters in that fiction. 'Primitive' man is seen by the novelist through their eyes, and it is they who indicate the barriers between the European and the 'savage' which provided the popular image of savages later examined.

L. P. Curtis, discussing the racial pride of the English in the nineteenth century, defines the concept of Anglo-Saxonism on which it was based as:

> The belief that the glory of English civilisation as it had
> evolved over the centuries in the British Isles . . . was no accident
> or freak of nature but the result of a set of skills and talents
> which were the unique inheritance of a people bound together

by common ancestry or blood, who were conventionally known as Anglo-Saxons. The tangible success of those who claimed this Anglo-Saxon heritage in ordering their own political, social and economic affairs, as well as those of other races, their sterling achievements in literature, the arts and science and their prowess in seafare and warfare provided incontrovertible proof that the Anglo-Saxon genius was no figment of a chauvinistic imagination (Curtis, 1968, p. 8).

Such ideas, as we shall see later, were supported by the scientific racism of the day. The superiority of the Englishman and his heritage was constantly being 'proved' by the inferiority of other races such as the Negroes and their lack of an equivalent history. As L. P. Curtis remarks, this racial pride was thought to be justified by scientific enquiry, chauvinistic as it also was:

> The Victorian Anglo-Saxon – to indulge in something of a stereotype – found his explanation for the rise of the British Empire not in Divine Providence, not in 'British luck' and not in the universal laws of political economy, but in the distinctive racial attributes of the English people (ibid.).

He further shows (ibid., p. 12) how the historians of the day (Kemble, Green, Stubbs, Freeman, Charles Kingsley and Froude) constantly referred to this racial heritage to explain current history and created genealogies of English royalty, English families and English customs to support their claims. Popular fiction was able to give dramatic life to these claims by presenting them in terms of concrete characters, whose abilities and actions brought home to the reader just what it meant to be an Englishman. These qualities are brought into vivid contrast with the 'baser' actions and qualities of the 'inferior' races of the world, and the descriptions of the Englishman in these novels demonstrate how and why they developed the picture of other races that they did.

Rider Haggard's heroes, particularly Allan Quatermain, exemplify those qualities which have raised the Englishman above the rest of the world and made it so difficult for him to understand other peoples. The heroes of popular fiction, like Quatermain, are gentlemen, 'the highest rank that a man can reach on this earth' (Haggard, 1887a, p. x).

As the travellers in *Allan Quatermain* move towards more unknown

and s, Haggard reflects on the English character: 'The Englishmen
are adventurers to the backbone, the colonies which will in time
become a great nation, will testify to the value of this spirit of adventure which seems at first sight mere lunacy' (ibid., p. 108). Likewise,
in *King Solomon's Mines* Sir Henry Curtis continues both to represent and mould the image of the English gentleman; he is 'honest,
trustworthy and brave', he refuses to accept payment for his help
since 'a gentleman does not sell himself for wealth' (Haggard, 1885,
p. 117). But he also represents the merging of the accepted intellectual
superiority of the Englishman with great physical qualities; the
natives acknowledge his courage and strength in battle, and when
he dons the dress of the 'savages' for fighting he looks as noble and
ferocious as their own leader, Umbopa. He thus joins Edgar Rice
Burroughs's Tarzan in reconciling English superiority with romantic
primitivism by representing what is noble in the savage as being also
British; he is courageous and, as his semi-nakedness reveals, with
an inherent natural gentility which conforms to the Arcadian tradition. Such 'noble Britons' are no more corrupted by industrial
civilization than are the noble savages. They have the best of both
worlds.

But, if these nineteenth-century English gentlemen of fiction are
sometimes related to the noble savage, they also recall the literature
of Christian chivalry. The latter-day Sir Galahad braves the dark
terrors of Africa, often physically similar to those of fairyland with
its hidden entrances and abundant vegetation, with the same moral
and physical superiority. The gentleman, with his courage, honour
and chivalry, resembles the Arthurian knight, and his journey through
strange lands peopled with uncouth beings resembles that of the
knight through fairyland. The creatures of fairyland were like the
primitives, different from the knightly heroes, with unusual powers
and customs and standards other than the reader's own.

Thus the popular literary tradition of chivalry contributed, on
the imaginative level, to the acceptance of such differences in the
real world of Africa and provided a ready-made framework of
fictionally inspired attitudes towards these real people, Africans and
others, helping to keep them, to some extent, unreal to the English
public. The differences between whites and blacks, already emphasised by the nature of much of the reporting, were imaginatively
reinforced by the superiority of the knight of chivalry to the unnatural opponents he met in romantic literature.

English gentlemen abroad, then, had as one of the models before them the knight of chivalric romance. For example, the three boys in Ballantyne's *The Coral Island* set out to rescue a maiden in distress when they hear that a native girl they have befriended is being forced by her chief to marry a man she doesn't love:

> Besides, having become champions for this girl once before, it
> behoves us, as true knights, not to rest until we set her free;
> at least all the heroes in all the story books I have ever read
> would count it foul disgrace to leave such a work unfinished
> (Ballantyne, 1858, p. 196).

And, when they are captured by the natives, it is this thought which sustains them:

> Yet I must say that I have great hope, my comrades, for we
> have come to this dark place by no fault of ours – unless it
> be a fault to try to succour a woman in distress (ibid., p. 227).

Like the Red Cross Knight and others, they turn to the Christian God to pray that their mission may succeed.

The dream-like quality of many lands visited by the latter-day orders of chivalry is also paralleled by the sense of unreality which pervades many descriptions of exotic lands and their inhabitants. So, when Tarzan first sees the natives, he is made to appear to doubt their reality: 'Surely no such creatures really existed upon earth; he must be dreaming' (Burroughs, 1917, p. 184). And the desert wastes in Conan Doyle's *The Tragedy of the Korosko* look like 'another planet' (Doyle, 1898, p. 63). It is significant that both Edgar Rice Burroughs and Conan Doyle also wrote science fiction. There is something in common between creating an alien society in remote parts of this earth and on distant planets.

Conan Doyle also emphasises the dream-like quality of a European's experience in 'primitive' lands. The adventures of a group of Europeans captured by the Dervishes seem to them like 'a nightmare': 'Indeed, it had much of the effect of a dream upon the prisoners.' And when they have escaped and look back on the journey across the desert one comments: 'How far away and dream-like it all seems. . . . All this feels to me as it if had happened in some previous existence' (ibid., p. 49).

It is, of course, a technique of any adventure story to create this sense of unreality, but its significance in the context of popular literature about exotic lands is that it contributes to the sense of alienation the European reader feels from the lands and peoples he reads of, and this is likely to affect his own relations with those people and the reports he sends home when in turn he himself travels abroad.

Buchan's hero in South Africa remarks, 'The clear morning sunlight, as of old, made Bleauwildebeestfontein the place of a dream' (Buchan, 1910, p. 68). And he places himself specifically in the role of a knight when he meets Laputa, the powerful inciter of savage hordes, and Henriques, the seedy trickster, in combat:

> There is a story of one of King Arthur's knights – Sir Percival
> I think – that once, riding through a forest, he found a lion
> fighting with a serpent. He drew his sword and helped the lion
> for he thought it was the more natural beast of the two.
> To me, Laputa was the lion and Henriques the serpent and,
> though I had no good will to either, I was determined to spoil
> the serpent's game (ibid., p. 23).

The unreality of the land through which the knights ride, related both to paradise and to the strange terrains of science fiction, is specifically associated by Edgar Wallace with the strange events an Englishman may expect to encounter in Africa. In *Sanders of the River*, the hero, a 'firm' district officer in West Africa, further alienates African life from European experience:

> There are many things that happen in the very heart of Africa
> that no man can explain; that is why those who know Africa
> best hesitate to write stories about it. Because a story about
> Africa must be a mysterious story and your reader of fiction
> requires that his mystery shall be in the end X-rayed, so that
> the bones of it are visible. You can no more explain many
> happenings which are the merest commonplace in Lat 2°N.
> Long. (say) 46°W., than you can explain the miracle of faith
> or the wonder of telepathy (Wallace, 1911, p. 166).

Much of the literature on exotic lands at the turn of the century thus over-emphasises the difference between European life and that in the so-called 'primitive' countries. This appears in symbolic terms in Buchan's *Prester John*. The story starts with a black man coming to a white community where he is seen as an interloper; from here the white man goes out to the black's land and penetrates to his deepest hideout, where, as an alien himself, he sees native customs in their natural environment and faces 'the loneliness of an exile'.

Buchan's picture of the black man practising his 'black art' by the Scottish sea and dancing naked round the fire is 'desperately uncanny', stressing from the start the strangeness of the black man, putting him outside the limits of known experience. He is, thus, characterised as dangerous, unsafe. There follows a description of native drums as representing a different, unnatural world: 'Neither natural nor human it seemed, but the voice of that world which is hid from men's sight and hearing' (Buchan, 1910, p. 67).

When the setting changes to South Africa, the land itself empha-sises the distinction between primitive and civilised. Davie escapes from his native captors and returns from danger to purity; the sight of trees and ferns 'gave me my first earnest of safety. I was approach-ing my own country. Behind me was heathendom and the black fever flats. In front were the cool mountains and the bright streams and the guns of my own folk' (ibid., p. 140). He crosses a rise as dawn breaks and his new security expresses itself in a familiar quotation from Shakespeare: 'Night's candles are burned out and jocund day walks tiptoe on the misty mountain top.' Thus the dawn, the freshness of the land and sophisticated poetry combine to represent civilisation as opposed to the dark and feverish lands and inarticulate cries of savagery.

Davie himself represents the use of geographical boundaries for symbolic purposes in his likening of the new land he has escaped to, to 'a water-meadow at home, such a place as I had in boyhood searched for moss-cheepers' and corncrakes' eggs' (ibid., p. 145). That land is thus brought back within the boundaries of known experience. And when, later, he escapes from a cave where he was held prisoner, the point is made again. He looks at the bracken and sweet grass, fresh with the dawn, and feels new hope that savagery can be overcome:

> Here was a fresh, clean land, a land for homesteads and
> orchards and children. All of a sudden I realised that, at last,
> I had come out of savagery. Behind me was the black night
> and the horrid secrets of darkness. Before me was my own
> country, for that loch and that bracken might have been on a
> Scottish moor (ibid., p. 206).

The 'darkness' that he is leaving behind is that of native culture, or 'savagery'. This symbolism recurs throughout the book, most notably in a phrase frequently used as shorthand for preconceptions about Africa, when Davie refers to the native ceremony in the cave: 'Last night I looked into the "heart of darkness" and the sight terrified me' (ibid., p. 119). The incomprehensibility of the 'natives' and their lack of enlightenment are seen in terms of night-time and darkness. That is, as contrasted with the certain light of dawn and the familiar landscape of one's homeland. Africa represented for many Englishmen a 'dark immorality', and if some writers like Conrad could use the phrase 'heart of darkness' as a metaphor for the condition of Europeans too, most, like Buchan, grounded it on the assumption of the moral anarchy of Africa and the Africans.

Cairns (1965), p. 68), writing about the missionary's fears that the 'debased' culture in which he must live is contagious, notes that many reports from mission stations in Africa use this imagery of light and dark. The loneliness of the European in the midst of the black masses is described by Elliott in *Gold from the Quartz* (1910) as a fear of falling 'into their disgusting slough'. And Moffat writes, just before leaving Africa: 'I am like a man looking forward to getting back to the sweet air and bright sunshine after being in a coal mine (Cairns, 1965, p. 68). Cairns adds:

> Africans were darker than other tribal peoples, a factor which probably seemed to indicate greater biological difference.
> The symbolism of colour itself was undoubtedly detrimental to favourable European attitudes. The white/black dichotomy in Western thought has equated whiteness with cleanliness, the light of day, moral purity and absolution from sins. Black has implied sin, dirt, night and evil. The colour contrast was also apparent in the frequent use of metaphors of light and darkness in missionary literature. The coincidence of racial divisions with the moral distinction implicit in these metaphors helped to make skin colour an identification mark for differing levels of moral and religious attainment (ibid., p. 75).

He adds that the motto on the first postage stamps in the British Central Africa Protectorate was 'Light in Darkness' (ibid., p. 265).

Conan Doyle in *The Tragedy of the Korosko* adds further to these symbolic contrasts. His story is of a group of passengers on a Nile steamer captured by a band of Dervishes and carried across the desert into the heart of savagery. When they approach Wady Halfa a young girl, Sadie, comments: 'We really are on the very edge of civilisation and with nothing but savagery and bloodshed down there where the Southern Cross is twinkling so prettily, why it's like standing on the edge of a live volcano' (1898, p. 21). The Southern Cross comes to signify for travellers at this time not only that they have arrived in the Southern hemisphere, but also that they are in 'uncivilised' lands, and Sadie's remarks set the tone for frequent reference to the symbolic line between savagery and civilisation.

Conan Doyle himself went to Egypt for a few months' holiday in 1896 and took a Cook's tour to Wady Halfa. Here, he imagined to himself what it would be like if a band of Muslim fanatics appeared, and from this idea arose the story. Standing at Sarras, he thought 'it wonderful to look south and to see the distant peaks said to be in Dongala, with nothing but savagery and murder lying between' (Pearson, 1943, p. 123).

His characters faithfully reproduce these feelings. What shocks them particularly is that the division between civilisation and savagery is physically so narrow. Explaining the local geography, Colonel Cochrane states that from where they stand 'there is nothing between us and them' and, likewise, when they have been captured and taken into the desert the contrast between physical and temporal proximity and psychological distance is stressed: 'What a chasm gaped between their old life and their new, and yet how short was the time and space which divided them' (Doyle, 1898, p. 91). By evening, however, they can look back on the morning's events with surprise: 'Yes, it had been this morning and it seemed away and away in some dim past experience of their lives, so vast was the change' (ibid., p. 103). They almost expect to find themselves in another world, yet when they look up to the sky they see 'the same thin crescent of moon – but what a chasm lay between that old pampered life and this' (ibid., p. 130).

These statements, of course, enhance the sense of adventure and strangeness necessary to any romantic tale, but they are also part of the general tendency of the time to exaggerate the difference between these strange lands and the comforting, known world of Europe. This exaggeration could not but make it more difficult for the European reader to appreciate possible similarities between native and European life.

Conan Doyle's travellers are romantics. The desert wastes look

like 'another planet' (ibid., p. 63) or like some 'forgotten primeval
sea' (ibid., p. 50) and their beauty belongs to another medium, one
which words cannot tell but which finds expression in music:

> There is a movement in one of Mendelssohn's songs which
> seems to embody it all – a sense of vastness, of repetition, the
> cry of the wind over an interminable expanse. The subtler
> emotions which cannot be translated into words are still to be
> hinted at by chords and harmonies (ibid., p. 31).

No doubt the sight of the desert may give rise to such feelings
towards the sublime, but in this context the appeal to media other
than language, the reference to other planets and primeval seas,
provides emotional confirmation of the unreality of native lands
which, as we have seen, makes the inhabitants themselves appear
more unapproachable and difficult to understand. By emphasising,
in this way, the gap between European and native, England and (in
this case) Africa, the popular writers created an emotional barrier
against the understanding of 'primitive' peoples which affected the
response and reports of future travellers.

Yet there is also an effort to bridge the gap at points, to find some
link for the traveller with the country from which he came, the culture
to which he belongs. Mendelssohn's music provides a point of reference by which the strangeness of Africa can be partly incorporated
into familiar European experience, as does the nostalgic appeal of a
Scottish moor for Davie. A. E. W. Mason, too, demonstrates how
the gap may be bridged. In *The Four Feathers* he describes rapid
movement from England to the Sudan, thus making the foreign
land less permanently alien, and he shows how what happens
thousands of miles away may affect individual lives at home. Thus
distant countries are brought within the world view of those who
have never seen them, so that they no longer seem to belong to a
totally different planet. Durrance, an army officer vying with Feversham for the hand of Ethne, reads an account in a London newspaper of the discovery of some of Gordon's letters in the Sudan and
dismisses it as of little interest. The author adds: 'There was nothing
more untrue. In the same spot where he had sought for news of
Feversham news had now come to him, only he did not know it'
(1902, p. 103).

This technique of anticipation and cryptic hints is used to sustain
interest while the focus is on England and the hero away in the

Sudan, but it also serves to demonstrate that everyday life in England is not so divorced from those far-off events. Feversham's discovery of Gordon's letters, in fact, cancels out the first white feather he has been given for cowardice and will reinstate him in the eyes of Ethne and mar Durrance's chances of winning her hand.

The idea of a bridge is made explicit later through a piece of music. Ethne plays her favourite overture for her lover, who is across the sea in Africa, and she suddenly fancies that he also can hear it: 'The music became a bridge swung in mid-air across the world, upon which just for a few minutes she and Harry Feversham might meet and shake hands' (ibid., p. 164). She awaits an answer and expects it from across the sea she is gazing at. But it comes from another source. For Durrance tells her that he last heard that music in Wady Halfa, played by a Greek who turned out to be Feversham in disguise: 'So the answer had come – Ethne had no doubt that it was an answer. . . . It seemed to her that he had spoken to her as she to him. The music had, after all, been a bridge' (ibid., p. 165).

Thus people in far-off lands communicate through various symbols and the lands no longer seem so far apart. Love and personal relationships bind those at home to those in the wilder parts of the Empire. Physical separation could be overcome far more easily than the moral and psychological separation between Europeans and the native inhabitants of those distant lands.

This separation from the local inhabitants is sustained by memories of loved ones at home, enabling the traveller to cut out of his mind the land he is actually in. The emotional link is only with his own culture which he thus brings with him to the alien environment. The point is brought home strongly by the practice of juxtaposing descriptions of foreign scenery with those of more comforting and familiar features of the English countryside. This technique enables the voyager in strange lands to live in a cocoon, psychologically isolated from his physical discomforts by carrying with him, in his mind, his own environment. Stanley noted this in Livingstone:

> He has lived in a world which revolved inwardly, out of which
> he seldom awoke except to attend to the immediate practical
> necessities . . . then relapsed again into the same happy inner
> world, which he must have peopled with his own friends,
> relations, acquaintances, familiar readings, ideas, associations;

so that wherever he might be, or by whatsoever he was
surrounded, his own world always possessed more attractions
to his cultured mind than were yielded by external circumstances
(quoted Cairns, 1965, p. 69).

From an anthropological point of view, this is what prevents
travellers from extending to the country and people they visit that
sympathy necessary to a full understanding. It is the source of the
social exclusiveness of British colonial society with its Victorian
habits, parties and tiffin, attempting to externalise those memories of
home which sustain them in a foreign land, and which obviate the
need for them to come to further terms with what they characterise
as alien.

In *A Passage to India* (1924), one of the most sophisticated novels
in this genre, E. M. Forster uses the theme of the barrier between
the English and the 'natives' as a symbol of the wider issue of human
relationships at all levels. The theme of a 'separateness', of barriers
between individuals, between the sexes, between the members of
the same race and between members of different races and cultures,
is represented most dramatically in the portrayal of the relationship
between the English colonist and the native Indians. Thus at the
immediate level, this particular historical situation is described in
close detail and with more attention to the problems for both communities than in the works of Kipling and other writers on India,
to whom the Indians remain, to a large extent, part of the scenery.
Forster, in his concern to portray the difficulties of communication,
creates a number of Indian characters whose attempts to establish
relationships and to overcome the problems of 'separateness' are as
difficult as they are for the English. Aziz, for instance, an Indian
doctor, feels a conflict between his cultural background and his
personal friendship with Fielding, a sympathetic Englishman, former
principal of a Government college, and their relationship becomes
the most intense example of the theme of the book.

The situations in which English and Indian meet are realised in
some detail in their own terms, but they are also used as part of the
more universal problem of whether any two people can understand
each other. Various set pieces represent the tensions between English
and Indians – an unsuccessful bridge party in a forced atmosphere
(op cit., p. 35); a tea party at Fielding's house in which the momentary harmony is shattered by the arrival of Ronny, the narrow-

minded Englishman who is also City Magistrate (ibid., pp. 50–63);
a court proceeding (ibid., ch. 24) in which Aziz is accused of molest-
ing Ronny's fiancée and which causes a deeper rift between the
Indian and English communities and between Aziz and Fielding;
and a meeting in Aziz's room when he is ill, in which the disclosure
of personal secrets fails to bridge the gap between the individuals
(ibid., ch. 9). In all these scenes Forster is concerned to render a
credible and detailed portrayal of life in India at the time, and to
indicate the particular problems faced by all who lived there. But
he uses them also for his wider theme. Self-conscious attempts at
communication, he believes, are doomed to failure, and the tensions
in these situations derive as much from universal human characteristics as from the problems of imperialism. In Forster's novels,
moments of communication are achieved by accident and spon-
taneously and seldom last long. Aziz, playing polo with an English
subaltern, establishes a relationship with him while they are playing
which is put into perspective by his companion's later condemnation
along with the rest of the English community except Fielding of 'the
man who attacked Adela' (ibid., p. 149). Ronny and Adela become
engaged and forget their previous arguments after they have been
thrown together in a car accident. Fielding and Aziz, discussing
their relationship in the context of British imperialism, come together momentarily when their horses bump against each other and
this scene, the last in the novel, represents Forster's position as to
the possibility of communication not only between England and
India but between any human beings:

> But the horses didn't want it – they swerved apart; the earth
> didn't want it, sending up rocks through which the riders must
> pass single file; the temples, the tank, the jail, the palace, the
> birds, the carrion, the Guest House, that came into view as they
> issued from the gap and saw Mau beneath; they didn't want it,
> they said in their hundred voices, 'No, not yet', and the sky
> said, 'No, not there' (ibid., p. 256).

This is the situation depicted in many novels of the time. The
English abroad find it well-nigh impossible to overcome the barrier
between themselves and 'alien' peoples. This novel deserves more
detailed attention than the space available makes possible, but it is
important to note that Forster, along with Conrad and Lawrence,
is one of the few writers of this period who treats the members of a

'backward' country with the seriousness and sympathy considered necessary for an anthropological understanding by modern standards.

The English preserved their identity amidst alien cultures by adhering to the fashions, customs and idiosyncrasies of home to the extent that these features were transformed into a total system with its own ritual and mythology, and new arrivals from England could quickly adapt themselves to the scheme. Many of the elements of this culture are reflected in the popular literature of the time, where, as we have seen, symbols are shown to be of vital importance for the white man amongst the natives. Thus Tarzan, and again the boys on Ballantyne's Coral Island, take cold baths every day, a ritual which recalls the values of the home society. And when the travellers on the Korosko find themselves in the middle of the desert, they recall the steamer, 'their saloon, with the white napery and the glittering glasses, the latest novel and the London papers' (Doyle 1898, p. 92). Like Livingstone, as described by Stanley, they try to live in a safe cocoon of home:

> One was in a green Irish valley and another saw the long
> straight line of Commonwealth Avenue and a third was dining
> at a little round table opposite to the bust of Nelson in the
> Army and Navy Club and, for him, the swishing of the palm
> branches had been transformed into the long-drawn hum of
> Pall Mall. So the spirits went their several ways, wandering
> back along strange untraced tracks of memory, while the weary,
> grimy bodies lay senseless under the palm trees in the Oasis
> of the Libyan desert (ibid., pp. 169–70).

So also, the education of a young English boy in the Sudan in Henty's *With Kitchener in the Sudan* involves his keeping up his games, not only for their physical value but also so that he will grow up like an English public school boy. A considerable amount of time is devoted to teaching him how to wear his breeches, how baggy to have his knickerbockers and how to use a cheque book.

Such rituals of British colonialism are most stylised in the Anglo-Indian society chronicled by Kipling. The women attend balls and intrigue, the men play school-boy japes on each other, attribute a profound significance to the regimental symbols and do their duty as occasion calls. Kipling emphasises the dependence of the English on each other in 'By Word of Mouth'. In this tale a couple cut themselves off and learn the hard way: you 'can't afford to play Robinson Crusoe' (Kipling, 1888, p. 318), there are too few in the land and all are dependent on each other. The conviction that the native is too inferior to be of any help in the grand task of ruling India forces the English back into their own narrow circle. The point is made in 'A Bank Fraud': 'If a man's English subordinates fail him in India, he comes to hard times indeed, for native help has strict limitations' (1888, p. 189).

In a later story 'At the End of the Passage', four Englishmen ride long distances from their work each week to meet each other at a hot, broken-down station, where they play whist 'crossly' and complain of the difficulties of their weekly work: 'The players were not conscious of any special regard for each other. They squabbled whenever they met; but they ardently desired to meet, as men without water desire to drink' (Maugham (ed.), 1952, p. 70). They also go through the same ritual when they are there every week, to stave off their sense of loneliness amidst the vast land and peoples they do not fully understand:

> The company yawned all together and betook themselves to an aimless investigation of all Hummel's possessions – guns, tattered novels, saddlery, spurs and the like. They had fingered them a score of times but there was really nothing else to do (ibid., p. 71).

The white man felt that he was alien in this strange land and that he could only survive by perpetuating his image of life in England, which recalled the seemingly trivial ritual, the tea parties, the balls, the dinners and the ceremonies. Kipling represents this society in his novels with a sharp and critical eye for detail. In 'William the Conqueror' the heroine returns from a famine to her station to find 'men and women coming in for the Christmas Week, with racquets, with bundles of polosticks, with dear and bruised cricket-bats, with fox-terriers and saddles' (ibid., p. 230). After the hardships of her job, the ritual, its significance pointed up by the familiarity of 'dear' and 'bruised', is a blessed relief. As the band strikes up 'Good King Wenceslaus' her lover whispers comfortingly: 'It's like home, rather . . . I remember . . .' (ibid., p. 231).

Critics in England objected to the triviality of Anglo-Indian life and Maugham writes: 'The life described was empty and frivolous. The self-sufficiency of these people is fearful to contemplate' (ibid.,

p. ix). Lang accepts, to some extent, the 'reality' of Kipling's picture
of this society:

> The seamy side of Anglo-Indian life: the intrigues, amorous or
> semi-political, the slang of the people who describe dining as
> 'mangling garbage', the games of tennis with the 'seventh
> commandment', he has not neglected any of these. Probably
> the sketches are true enough and pity tis true (Gilbert, 1966,
> p. 3).

But there is another side: 'Mr Kipling is too much a true realist
to make their selfishness and pettiness unbroken, unceasing.' Their
triviality is relieved for him by their 'consistency in the face of
various perils – from disease and from the "bullet flying down the
pass" ' (ibid., p. 4).

Kipling's picture may not be entirely balanced, then. It may over-
emphasise certain aspects of colonial society, though it probably
represents a greater 'sense of proportion' than his picture of native
Indian society. As a novelist he selects the 'subjects that appeal to
him'. Nevertheless, his stories do help the modern reader to feel
some aspects of life as it was lived then. Kipling provides us with
some fairly accurate and 'deeply actual' insights into the way in
which colonial society cut itself off from the inhabitants of the
country it ruled. The natives are represented as incidental to the
rulers – if social life has to stop to put down an uprising or to help
in a famine, then the civil servants are disgruntled and Kipling
satirises them for it. In 'William the Conqueror', when a man is
called down to replace Scott, who is detailed off to help in a cholera
outbreak, Scott chuckles: 'He thought he was going to be cool all
summer. He'll be very sick about this'. (Maugham (ed.), 1952,
p. 208). But he himself complains that his pet project will have to be
put off: 'I hoped to be put on the Luni protective works this cold
weather but there's no saying how long the famine may keep us'
(ibid., p. 211); while William is more optimistic: 'But of course this
ought to be a good thing for us all, departmentally, if we live' (ibid.),
and in 'The Brushwood Boy', Cottar is glad of a native uprising,
since it provides him with an opportunity to try out his troops:
'Cottar almost wept with joy as the campaign went forward' (ibid.,
p. 155).

Kipling shows how the natives are seen through the eyes of Anglo-
Indian society and their activities evaluated according to the influence

they are likely to have on that society. The Indian is not conceived as an equal human being. In another tale, 'In Error', an engineer who spent four years in a native village had little human contact with the people: 'In the four years he was utterly alone' (Kipling, 1888, p. 180). And the surveyor in 'At the End of the Passage' rides a long way for his weekend of cards because, among the Indians, 'I'm altogether alone, y'know' (ibid., p. 73).[1]

Although Kipling's tales tell also of some aspects of native life, his picture of Anglo-Indian society, however limited, shows in what way the members of that society were likely to 'understand' the Indians and suggests the limitations of his own image of them.

If the Englishman has this image of native society and of his own, it becomes important for him to keep the two apart, never to 'weaken' in front of the native or go down to his level. His work demands the qualities of the Anglo-Saxon gentleman and so he must preserve the dignity and aloofness characteristic of this ideal. Hence the 'stiff upper lip'. Hence, when Stanley meets Livingstone, he addresses him as though they were meeting for the first time in an English drawing-room or an Anglo-Indian mess.

Cornell, describing Kipling's background in Anglo-Indian society, notes that he himself was sent back to England at the age of six because of that society's fears of its children succumbing to native influence and thus losing those 'English standards of rectitude, self-denial and honesty'.

> But all these concerns were symptoms of a thinly disguised
> fear and hatred of India herself, a dread lest children raised
> in the country become acclimatized to it and lose their national
> and racial identity. The following passage from *The Son of His
> Father* reveals how this dread could overcome even the
> unwillingness of parents to send their children so far away, for
> so long a time (Cornell, 1966, p. 4).

> 'It's awful', said Mrs. Strickland, half-crying, 'to think of his
> growing up like a little heathen.' Mrs. Strickland had been
> born and brought up in England and did not quite understand
> Eastern things.
> 'Let him alone', said Strickland, 'he'll grow out of it all or it
> will only come back to him in dreams.'
> 'Are you sure?' said his wife.
> 'Quite. I was sent home when I was seven and they flicked it

out of me with a wet towel at Harrow. Public schools don't
encourage anything that isn't quite English' (ibid., p. 5).

And Cornell adds:

For the English, we must recall, never considered themselves
colonists. To adapt to Indian conditions was to conform to an
inferior standard. It was better to be alien and incompatible
than to incur any suspicion of becoming like the natives of the
country (ibid.).

The fence with which Anglo-Indian society surrounded itself is
similar to that in Kipling's own childhood games: 'The magic, you
see, lies in the ring or fence that you take refuge in' (ibid., p. 13).
By such techniques the outside world is made manageable, whether
it is the terrifying Aunty Rose whose world of piety rejected Kipling's
boyhood flights of imagination or the inscrutable Indian with his
strange beliefs and customs and who, however, in practice did not
always remain in his place within the British framework of thought.
   The Englishman who 'went native' in Kipling's tales always pays
the penalty. 'A man should keep to his own caste and breed' he
writes in 'Beyond the Pale', and the hero of that tale who 'took too
deep an interest in native life' will never do so again. Other tales such
as 'To be Filed for Reference', tell of men of low caste (Kipling used
this term for Englishmen as well as Indians) who go downhill through
drink and association with natives, eventually becoming Hindu or
Mussulman (Kipling, 1888, p. 235). Hence his Anglo-Indians, the
soldiers, administrators and civil servants, however trivial they may
seem to English society, are preserving its identity abroad.
   George Orwell analyses this characteristic in himself in a difficult
situation in Burma, in 'Shooting an Elephant'. He was divisional
police officer of a small town, where he felt he was the butt of all
the local sneers and jibes against Europeans. He was divided between
a sympathy for these people's complaints against British imperialism
and a feeling for his own background. One day an escaped elephant
ran wild in the town. Orwell was obliged to deal with the situation.
Although he took a rifle with him he did not want to shoot it, since
an elephant represented a 'huge and costly piece of machinery'. But
a large crowd gathered behind him, wanting him to kill it for their
entertainment. At this moment, he realised that the white man's
domination in the East was merely apparent.

'He becomes a sort of hollow, posing dummy, the conventionalized figure of a sahib. For it is the condition of his rule that he shall spend his life in trying to impress the 'natives' and so, in every crisis, he has got to do what the 'natives' expect of him. He wears a mask and his face grows to fit it. I had got to shoot the elephant' (Orwell, 1936, p. 95).

He is not a very good shot, but 'A white man mustn't be frightened in front of "natives" ' (ibid., p. 96). His main concern is less with his own safety than with the fact that, if he were trampled by the elephant, the crowd would laugh: 'That would never do.'

He kills the elephant and is criticised by some of his colleagues for doing so. Though he was justified in law by the fact that it had killed a 'coolie', his real reasons had not been based on the law but on the obligations of the Englishman abroad, and he wondered afterwards 'whether any of the others grasped that I had done it simply to avoid looking a fool' (ibid., p. 99).

Other travellers had also noticed that the self-image of superiority often caused the white man to act against his better judgment, in a belief that, by fulfilling the image, he was impressing the native. Selous, in *Travel and Adventure in S.E. Africa*, published in 1893, notes that the traditional Englishman who (as in Noël Coward's song) 'walks in the hot sun, bare-armed and often bare-legged, carrying his own rifle and running after game', does not always impress the natives. Rather 'they think he only does so because he is poor and cannot afford to pay men to hunt for him and porters to carry him in a palanquin, sheltered from the heat of the sun by an awning or an umbrella' (Cairns, 1965, p. 37). Cairns adds: 'It immediately becomes apparent that, psychologically speaking, much of the white man's burden was found in a demanding, self-imposed standard of conduct' (ibid., p. 38).

In the popular literature, English heroes are always gentlemen, and this involves them in many dramatic exhibitions of the obligations of a gentleman. Thus in *A Boy's Adventures Round the World* a group of sailors shipwrecked in the East Indies keep up a show of racial pride and courage amidst a crowd of cut-throat natives by singing the 'Death of Nelson':

> Along the lines the signal ran
> England expects every man
> This day will do his duty

which duly rouses the patriotic spirit of the Englishmen and over-
awes the natives (Higginson, 1919, p. 123).

And when, in Mason's *The Drum*, the native hordes are seething
outside the English Commissioner's house in Northern India, the
man and his wife maintain their customary sang-froid. She powders
her nose for dinner and, during the meal, they talk about the art of
cooking as though the native uprising were unimportant.

E. M. Forster describes the conditions of life in India for the
British as part of wider interests. Living in an alien environment,
they find it difficult to make contact with the Indians and turn,
instead, to each other, overcoming their internal differences in the
face of a larger conflict, as the Hindus and Muslims resolve their
conflicts and unite against the 'invaders'. During the trial of Aziz,
the English community reveal that self-conscious concern with keeping up appearances in front of the natives, noted by Orwell, by filing
in with a condescending air: 'Their chairs preceded them into the
Court, for it was important that they should look dignified' (Forster,
1924, p. 171), and they follow this up by moving onto the platform:
'A platform confers authority' (ibid., p. 175). But the Indian judge,
showing considerable courage, asks them to move down again.
Forster, like Orwell, is not impressed with this side of English colonial
life and he satirises it subtly. Aziz, attempting to become friendly
with Fielding, lends him his own collar stud when the latter is without one at a tea party. Ronny, whose lack of sympathy with the
Indians Forster repeatedly condemns, notices that Aziz has no collar
stud and draws a moral from it: 'Aziz was exquisitely dressed, from
tie-pin to spats, but he had forgotten his back collar stud, and there
you have the Indian all over; inattention to detail; the fundamental
slackness that reveals the race' (ibid., p. 64). Ronny represents the
worst kind of colonial in Forster's eyes: 'The only link he could be
conscious of with an Indian was the official' (ibid., p. 60). He doesn't
'like to see an English girl left smoking with two Indians' (ibid.,
p. 61), and the worst aspects of his character have been brought out
by his life in India: 'His self-complacency, his censoriousness, his
lack of subtlety, all grew vivid beneath a tropic sky' (ibid., p. 63).

Forster, however, shows the other side of the picture; he describes
the advantages brought by the British to India, such as law (ibid.,
p. 39) and food in times of famine and he sets up the character of
Mr Fielding in opposition to Ronny; he 'was a hard-bitten, good-
tempered, intelligent fellow' (ibid., p. 48) whose sympathy with the

Indians alienated him from the English community, a situation that Forster analyses in detail: 'He had discovered that it is possible to keep in with Indians and Englishmen but that he who would also keep in with Englishwomen must drop the Indian' (ibid., p. 49).

The sophistication of Forster's descriptions of Anglo-Indian life is unusual in the novels of the time, and he is one of the few writers to analyse 'race relations' in their own right. But for him, this social commentary is part of a more universal theme of human communication; he transcends the stereotypes of most 'anthropological fiction' not only in the detail with which he describes the contact of different races and cultures, but also in the use he makes of it.

In most novels of the time, however, both the writer and the English heroes they portray merely remain fearful of what they cannot understand in other societies. Nor does this fear of foreign places and their inhabitants apply only to Africa or India. To the Irish heroine of Mason's *The Four Feathers*, England is a 'strange land' and she yearns for the security of her native heather 'upon the hillsides of Donegal. Great sorrows and great joys had this in common for Ethne Eustace – they both drew her homewards, since there endurance was more easy and gladness more complete' (Mason, 1902, p. 161). The significance of this characteristic in the context of literature about exotic lands is that it demonstrates that barrier between the fictional traveller and the people among whom he travelled which was part also of the real traveller's reports on exotic peoples. By thinking of home, re-creating home customs and cherishing their inward-looking world, the English abroad could not but see the natives through ethnocentric spectacles. Popular fiction both presents the consequences of this viewpoint in dramatic manner and depicts the situation which gave rise to it. Whereas the descriptions of the natives are often distorted, those of English society are likely to be more accurate since the writers themselves belonged to it.

If this fiction displays in detail the cast of thought which led to an unfavourable view of the native, it also presents characters whose framework of thought might be expected to lead them to a favourable view. But both those who arrive having rejected their own culture and expecting to find the terrestrial paradise, and those who expect unmitigated savagery, see the exotic land and people through equally distorting spectacles. Durrance, in *The Four Feathers*, 'came to the wild uncitied places of the world with the joy of one who comes into an inheritance, a man to whom these desolate tracts

are home and the fireside and the hedged fields and made roads
merely the other places' (Mason, 1902, p. 114). We saw, in discussing
the conflict between primitivism and progress, that writers had difficulty in reconciling the noble savage of the literary tradition with
the wild, dirty creature of the travellers' tales. In the same way, a
conflict arose with regard to the land they inhabited, whether it was
indeed the terrestrial paradise, the fruitful land which made the
traveller yearn for home. In both cases, the fictional traveller has
arrived with preconceptions derived from his own culture and
mythology, and his expectations create a barrier between him and the
people among whom he is living.

These travellers and adventurers who figure in nineteenth-century
popular fiction are clearly often stereotyped and may not exactly
represent what the real Victorian traveller was like, but they show
what the Victorians thought the European 'traveller' was like, and
are certainly nearer the reality than the descriptions of the foreign
peoples among whom they travelled.

The range of such English characters abroad and their roles there
once they arrive are described with care in the fiction of the period.
In *The Four Feathers*, Feversham goes to Africa to prove himself
after receiving four white feathers accusing him of cowardice. It is
a commonly held view in the writings of the period that underdeveloped countries provide scope for character training and physical toughness, an idea of which modern 'outward bound' courses
are perhaps a survival. The obstacles to be overcome on the course
were not only the terrain but the natives themselves. Thus, in *The
Tragedy of the Korosko*, a city man finds his real identity through the
adventure in Africa, actually enjoying the privations of capture by
the Dervishes because they reveal to him the pettiness of his former
life. Sadie, in the same novel, also finds 'It has taught me more than
all my life put together' (Doyle, 1898, p. 253). In *Greenmantle*, John
Buchan demonstrates the value of the hero's experiences as an
African hunter for preparing him to succeed in the British secret
service in Europe. Hence, the African environment is supposed to
have built up his character: 'A man's temper has a lot to do with his
appreciation of scenery' (Buchan, 1916, p. 169). This is one reason
why some men went to Africa; its 'scenery' and inhabitants provided
a challenge to their personality and might affect their 'temper'
favourably.

In Bertram Mitford's novel of South Africa, *The Weird of Deadly*

Hollow (1891), the hero has come in the first place to reject his home culture (which had, in fact, rejected him) and to this end he lives in a reputedly haunted kraal to cut himself off from society (including the local English community) and live alone with nature. But he gradually moves back from his primitivism towards the community, finally representing the view of living in Africa as an opportunity for character training and self-knowledge. He occasionally goes hunting with his white neighbours and the exhilaration of the sport, the pursuit of springbok across the beautiful veldt against a back-cloth of dramatic mountain ranges, serves to rejuvenate the broken man. He has lived through the storm on the heath that Africa can represent to the foreigner, and 'found' himself again.

Rider Haggard, too, presents the scenery of South Africa as a testing ground for English character. Allan Quatermain represents the ideal of an outdoor man, both skilful and honourable in his hunting, respected by natives and whites alike as a 'real man', suggesting to the reader at home the tough and exhilarating nature of life in Africa for the virile Englishman. And in *The Broken Road* Mason parodies the British officer who thought India was a large tiger park and became disillusioned when he couldn't find one to shoot (Mason, 1907, p. 67).

But other fictional characters suggest that such tales must have encouraged some to go to Africa who had neither the character nor ability to endure its hardships. It is these would-be Quatermains, perhaps escaping some failure at home, whom District Commissioner Sanders in Edgar Wallace's African tales so despises. He meets one who he knows will only make trouble for him and objects:

> Man, I know this country and you're a newcomer; you trekked
> here because you wanted to get away from life and start all
> over again. If you had wanted to commit suicide, why come
> to Africa to do it? (Wallace, 1911, p. 93).

Some representations – or misrepresentations – of native life derive from the different viewpoints of the District Commissioners, humanitarians and philanthropists, missionaries, occasional scientists and traders who visited outposts of Empire. The missionaries went out with the preconception that savage 'superstition' had to be replaced by the 'superior' values of Christianity, that the native was inferior from this point of view. In order to encourage recruits for the field, missionary reports tended to emphasise the aspects of native life most abhorrent to the Victorians, thus justifying their task of conversion. In Ballantyne's *The Coral Island*, the advantages of Christianity are compared to the 'dirty chaos' of idolatry; the villages that have been Christianised are neat and tidy with colourful gardens and attractive cottages, while those of the idolators are filthy and chaotic, at which Peterkin exclaims: 'What a convincing proof that Christianity is of God' (Ballantyne, 1858, p. 202). This attitude naturally understates any value that native ritual and custom might have, and the missionaries impose it on people back home to persuade them to come out: 'Tell them of the blessing that the gospel has wrought *here*' (ibid., p. 208). But the missionary was not always as successful as Ballantyne implies, and could be duped by the native and his teachings twisted. Sanders, Edgar Wallace's District Commissioner, finds that idealistic missionaries make his job more difficult and he often has to rescue some well-meaning preacher from the clutches of a pagan congregation. Thus a woman missionary appears in his district and sets up a station with the help of some natives she believes to be converts. At the appropriate time, they carry her off into the bush to the meeting-place of their secret religious cult, which has been using the cover of Christianity to prepare for a native uprising. Sanders saves her just in time and she returns home disillusioned. An important feature of missionary work used to encourage new recruits was the challenge of the task, the personal character training to be acquired by living alone in the middle of Africa. Cairns amply documents this feature of colonial life, showing also how a misguided optimism led to many deaths from carelessness (Cairns, 1965, p. 15). Sanders contrasts the idealistic and the realistic missionary approaches: the Protestant, he says, puts his faith in God; the Jesuit has 'four Martini-Metford rifles, and three thousand rounds of ammunition, and his house is built of stone' (Wallace, 1912, p. 185).

Whether a missionary's approach was more idealistic or more practical, his basic assumptions had already been formed before he reached his jungle settlement. Christianity was the superior religion and native 'superstition', with its fetishes and numerous gods, represented an earlier form from which monotheism had evolved over the centuries. Lang satirises this attitude in his sketch *In the Wrong Paradise*. The Rev. Peter McSnadden, a member of the mysterious 'U.P. Kirk', has been preaching among the Canadian Indians for years, 'trying to win them from their fearsome notions about a place where they would play at the ba' on the Sabbath, and such like shameful heathen diversions' (Lang, 1886, p. 119). Now he finds that at his death he has gone to their paradise instead of his own Heaven and there he provides the Indians with their ultimate pleasures, such as continually scalping him. Lang refers this to the Christian doctrine (as he understands it) that, in Heaven, 'the pleasures of the blessed will be much enhanced by what they observe of the torments of the wicked' (ibid., p. 118).

Scientists, too, come in for their fair share of satire. Conan Doyle's Professor Challenger, in *The Lost World*, stalks around the plateau in a completely impractical way, disputing learnedly with Professor Summerlee about the nature of life and whether a bird they saw was a pterodactyl or a stork, while other members of the expedition spend all their time keeping the two men out of trouble. And in *Tarzan of the Apes*, two professors wander into the jungle disputing a nice philosophical point while a roaring lion waits to pounce. Hearing his roars, they comment on the inefficiency of the local zoo allowing 'felis' to escape and then wander blissfully off in the direction of Cape Town when their camp is a few hundred yards away in the other direction. Learned professors were then much in the public eye, and in fiction they, like the 'idealistic' missionary, appear as being out of touch with the hard facts of colonial life.

Those who claim to be involved in the hard drudgery of colonial duties and to 'understand' the native tend to be scornful of the ignorant new arrival from England. The literature of exotic lands satirises a wide range of such people in order to present its own heroes in a stronger light. Thus, Kipling emphasises the adroitness of the Indian civil servant or soldier compared with the ignorance of 'experts' from home. In 'Without Benefit of Clergy', an MP from England is indulged but ignored:

> The Member for Lower Tooting, wandering about India in top-hat and frock-coat, talked largely of the benefits of British rule. . . . His long-suffering hosts smiled and made him welcome and, when he paused to admire with pretty picked words the blossom of the blood-red dhab-tree that had flowered untimely for a sign of what was coming, they smiled more than ever (Maugham (ed.), 1952, p. 300).

In 'The Tomb of His Ancestors', a man sent to vaccinate the hill tribes is captured by them and rescued in the nick of time by a knowledgeable soldier (ibid., p. 56). In 'Aurelion McGoggin', a thinker who has read Spencer and Comte and who doesn't believe in God or in the necessity of taking orders is distrusted by the men on the spot for holding views which may apply in foggy towns but are hardly relevant to 'open, brown, naked India' (Kipling, 1888, p. 108). And in 'A Bank Fraud' a clerk from Huddersfield, sent out for his lungs, becomes a burden to his fellows and eventually dies (1888, p. 186).

Although the constant appearance of such characters is meant to emphasise the ability of Kipling's heroes, for some they merely serve as a further indictment of the sort of people who ruled the Empire and the untrustworthiness of their image of the native, which they provided for people at home. Somerset Maugham condemns Kipling's heroes in the colonial enterprise as savagely as Kipling had condemned these newcomers:

> And what sort of people were they? They were ordinary,
> middle-class people, who came from modest homes in England,
> sons and daughters of retired government servants and of
> parsons, doctors and lawyers. The men were empty-headed;
> such of them as were in the army or had been to universities
> had acquired a certain polish, but the women were shallow,
> provincial and genteel (Maugham (ed.), 1952, p. ix).

Everyone involved in the colonial enterprises inevitably was prevented by the nature of his work and English background from being objective. Teachers, farmers, tourists, traders and humanitarians were all distracted by their personal interests from paying sufficient attention to the native and his environment to take a fully balanced view (by modern standards) of either. And the District Commissioners and the like, who are represented frequently in fiction as the experienced, practical, knowledgeable heroes, had their own bias. One main distinction between them, to judge by the picture of them in popular literature, was in the 'hard' and the 'soft' approach to the natives.

Sanders represents the 'hard' approach – he is a District Commissioner in West Africa, whose experience of the tribes he rules is that they respond only to tough treatment, and his reaction to any humanitarian objections is that he knows the natives, whereas idealists at home do not. His attitude is justified by Wallace's notions of African 'character':

> He governed a people three hundred miles beyond the fringe
> of civilisation. Hesitation to act, delay in awarding punishment,

either of these two things would have been mistaken for
weakness among a people who had neither power to reason
nor will to excuse, nor any large charity (Wallace, 1911, p. 8).

Thus when a young king becomes recalcitrant, Sanders takes 'a
hundred men, a Maxim and a bundle of rattan canes' and marches
on the chief's village. He grabs the king 'by the scruff of his neck'
and proceeds to cane him, while his riflemen hold back the angry
subjects. This very chief later dies willingly for Sanders, proving
that the natives themselves respect such firmness.

The Maxim gun is the backbone of Sanders's rule, and whenever
there is trouble he steams up the river in an old paddle boat with a
detachment of soldiers, justified in his massacre of the natives by
their own bloody customs. Indeed, the process becomes almost
tedious to him as the descriptions of the battles evince: 'The man
behind the gun polished a dull place on the brass water jacket with
the blue sleeves of his coat, then looked up. . . . Ha-ha-ha-ha-ha
laughed the little gun sardonically' (ibid., p. 187), and a whole village
ceases to exist. If Sanders were not there to keep the 'peace', we are
told, the natives would be at each other's throats all the time:

> Chiefest of the restrictions placed on the black man by his
> white protector is that which prevents him, when his angry
> passions rise, from taking his enemies by the throat and carving
> them with a broad curved blade of native make. Naturally,
> even the best behaved of tribes chafe under this prohibition the
> British have made (ibid., p. 180).

There is no indication that Wallace could see (as a comparative
anthropologist or a more sensitive novelist might) that the British
merely replaced the 'curved blade of native make' with the Maxim
gun.

Another justification for firm rule is that there are weak tribes
who need protection, such as the 'shy Acholi people, who lived too
near the Akasava for comfort and, moreover, needed nursing' (ibid.,
p. 47). Sanders's solution is to set an escaped convict up as chief to
'make men of these people'. The Victorian emphasis on games and
physical prowess is thus transferred to the African scene and used as
moral guide for dealing with the native. Hence the Zulu tribes are
praised for their magnificent physique and martial abilities, while the
weaker tribes are scorned as inferior. Attitudes learned on the

playing fields of Eton are given practical expression in the relations of white and black in the African jungle.

Ballantyne's heroes, too, believe in 'coming strong over the blacks' (Ballantyne, 1858, p. 201), and even Tarzan acquiesces in the idea of punitive expeditions. A band of French sailors in Tarzan's bit of jungle lose one of their comrades and immediately set out in an armed band to exact vengeance on the natives. Their friend, in fact, has already escaped but, when they arrive and see the remnants of his clothes, the natives cannot persuade the irate Frenchman of their innocence:

> Only excited gestures and expressions of fear could they obtain
> in response to their enquiries concerning their fellow, and at
> last they became convinced that these were but evidence of the
> guilt of these demons who had slaughtered and eaten their
> comrade two nights before (Burroughs, 1917, p. 193).

So they kill the whole male population of the village in reprisal, justified according to the author by the savagery of natives in general and by the need to maintain the superiority of the white man. There is no suggestion that Burroughs is making a comment on French 'savagery'.

The necessity for this type of assertion is explained by John Buchan, himself once in the Colonial Office and later Governor-General of Canada. In *Prester John*, he shows how hard the white man had to work to prevent the native getting out of hand. Davie helps in the settlement of the Zulu armies which had been poised against white rule in South Africa and afterwards reflects:

> I knew then the meaning of the white man's duty. He has to
> take all the risks, recking nothing of his life or his fortunes,
> and well content to find his reward in the fulfilment of his task.
> That is the difference between white and black, the gift of
> responsibility, the power of being in a little way a king,
> and so long as we know this and practise it, we will rule not
> in Africa alone but wherever there are dark men who live only
> for the day and their own bellies. Moreover, the work made me
> pitiful and kindly. I learned much of the untold grievances of
> the natives and saw something of their strange twisted
> reasoning (Buchan, 1910, p. 215).

We shall see later the origin of some of these conceptions of native 'character'. For the moment, the passage reveals the justification or British rule and the preconceptions on which District Commissioners would act towards the natives once that rule had been established. Both 'harshness' and 'kindliness' involve a belief in the superiority of the white man and the inability of the native to govern himself responsibly. The novelist, by presenting such views in a favourable light, makes them more acceptable to the reader and, to that extent, helps to perpetuate them.

The need for the white man is reinforced by statements attributed to the natives themselves. Don Ignatio, in Haggard's *Heart of the World,* notes that Strickland was the leader on their journey 'as, to speak truth, among companions of a coloured race a white man of gentle birth is always acknowledged to be by right of blood' (Haggard, 1896, p. 186). When they arrive at the Indian city, however, Zibalby, the native leader, takes control and Strickland is seen as an alien warrior admitted on sufferance and subject to the local laws. The implication might seem to be that within its boundaries each culture has its own autonomy. Such an acknowledgment of native rights had been made in West Africa at first, during the early nineteenth century (Curtin, 1965, Part II). But the growth of imperialism gave the white man power even within native culture as the century progressed. The native was not thought fit to rule himself and his laws were not binding on whites.

> A basic aspect of the imperial frame of mind was general assumption of British moral superiority, with the accompanying belief that the possession of the virtues of responsibility, trust and integrity legitimized intervention and the seizing of power over the backward peoples of the earth (Cairns, 1965, p. 238).

This is how the situation develops in the *Heart of the World* and in other inland states approached by white travellers in Haggard. Strickland is soon accepted and asked to be ruler, as the native rulers are incompetent. The same happens to Curtis in Zu-Vendiland where Haggard draws attention to the strange reversal by which, within a year of arriving as a stranger, Curtis the English gentleman is accepted as a king. Such examples, while confirming white superiority, also reflect the growing myth, emphasised by the popularisation of the discovery of Livingstone, of white travellers who would be accepted as kings or gods among 'savages'. Thus the three boys in *The Coral Island* expect fairly shortly to take over control of the native inhabitants, since 'white men always do in savage countries' (Ballantyne, 1858, p. 21).

All the ramifications of the 'civilising mission' are argued out by the passengers on the 'Korosko'. The Frenchman argues that, far from fulfilling their moral destiny by giving laws and civilisation to the world, the British are merely searching for power, and invent native uprising to give them an excuse to send in troops. The Mahdi and his Dervishes are a figment of Britain's imperialist imagination. These arguments are swiftly destroyed when the Frenchman is challenged about Algeria and claims 'Algeria belongs to France' (Doyle, 1898, p. 29), and when actual Dervishes appear to whisk away their would-be rulers. Thus the adventure itself becomes a justification for British imperialism.

The men who actually put these ideas into practice are not always like Sanders. Bertram Mitford describes a Commissioner in South Africa at the time of the Matabele uprising, who had been born there, learned the native languages and 'had all the idiosyncrasies of the native character at his finger ends, a phase of useful knowledge which a few years spent at an English public school had failed to obliterate'. The bane of his life is less the natives, with whom he is on reasonable terms, than his police chief, an Englishman who came out merely to clear his debts and who has no knowledge of nor interest in natives. John Ames tries to 'humour' and understand his charges, whereas Inglefield, the police chief, prefers the 'hard' approach: 'Oh, you go on the coddling plan', he scorns:

> For my part – well – a nigger's a nigger, whether he's an induna or whether he isn't and he ought to be taught to respect white men. . . . A dirty snuffy nigger with a greasy black curtain ring stuck on top of his head. Pooh! Fancy treating such a brute as that with respect (Mitford, 1900, p. 11).

John Ames's reply is that used by Sanders to those who advocate the 'soft' approach: 'Perhaps when you've had a little experience you may be in a position to form an opinion' (ibid., p. 86). Thus 'knowledge' of the natives can be used to justify either approach, and the scorn of those on the scene for those at home does not necessarily mean that they are any better equipped to understand the complexities of 'primitive' life.

Mitford's unfavourable portrayal of the 'harsh' approach to natives provides a clear example of how a novelist may present a character as holding certain views in order to make some comment on those views. They are not necessarily those of the writer himself.

The main significance of such writing for the anthropologist is that, whatever the writer's position, it reveals the currency of such views during that period and, as we shall see, the wide use made of anthropological theory in work directed at the general public. However, as noted before, the 'harsh' view of native life is, in the novels being dealt with here, most often presented favourably. The heroes of the stories present those views of the native which would today be considered unsympathetic or biased, and the writer must thus take some responsibility for the distorted image of 'primitive' life presented uncritically in his work.

Many novelists satirise the kind of travellers whose reports of 'primitive' life are likely to be unrealistic. But the reports presented by such writers' heroes are just as likely to be unrealistic. Wallace presents Sanders's views as reasonable. To the modern reader they are as unreasonable as those of the woolly-minded 'do-gooders' of whom he is so scornful.

Wallace is very concerned with criticising these 'unrealistic' adventurers in order to show his own hero in a better light. He describes, for instance, how some people decide on an expedition to Africa. A conversation in Maida Vale leads to the choice of a good title for the expedition, 'The Isisi Expedition'. The adventurers then find out where Isisi is. And finally they choose as leader a man who, having nearly shot a lion once in Uganda, is considered an expert on Africa (Wallace, 1912, p. 51). Similarly an American in Kipling's 'The Captive' is astonished at the way an English officer 'chooses stray continents for Adrian to drink his coffee in', from the map of the world (Kipling, 1904, p. 22).

Philanthropists are even more laughable. Wallace describes a Miss Clinton Galbraith who, inspired by sentimental accounts in a newspaper, goes to Isisi to 'mother' the infant king. She takes packing cases full of 'school paraphernalia paid for by the tender readers of "Tiny Toddlers"' (Wallace, 1912, p. 12), but becomes disillusioned when she finds that 'he lives in a mud hut and wears no clothes'. 'A child of nature', said Sanders, blandly, 'you didn't expect a sort of Louis Quinze did you?' (ibid.). She goes home sadly and writes 'Alone in Africa, by an English Gentlewoman'. Likewise Dickens's strictures on 'telescopic philanthropy' in *Bleak House* must have helped to discredit some approaches to Africa; not every report would be taken as gospel.

But a great many were, and the picture which the Victorians

received of 'primitive' life derived from the mass of popular writing on the subject which was the main source of information for most of them. We have seen, in this chapter, how many popular impressions of exotic places and native character arose from the interests of particular travellers, as they are represented in the fiction. The European fictional characters, based upon some aspects of real travellers and administrators, erect for a wider public than the real travellers would command, barriers to an objective understanding of the facts that lie behind their reports.

Having seen how some preconceptions were given currency in popular fiction, we now discuss the relation of these preconceptions to wider Victorian moral and scientific debate.

Chapter 3

Evolution and race in popular literature: classification, scientific and fictitious

Introduction

Among the Lugbara, strangers – people outside the boundaries of Lugbara society – are conceived of as representing the exact opposite, morally and physically, of the in-group:

> The . . . pattern, with normal members of society at the centre, then a fringe of quasi-members of society who possess some super-human powers and, beyond them, the rest of the world, peopled with inverted, asocial beings, can be seen in Lugbara socio-spatial categories (Middleton, 1960, p. 236).

Such stereotypes of 'outsiders' are commonly based not only on lack of knowledge but on a positive desire to accentuate the unity of the in-group by emphasising the differences and particularly the vices of other groups (Allport, 1954, chs. 3, 4, 7). L. P. Curtis describes this phenomenon in nineteenth-century England with regard to Victorian stereotypes of the Irish:

> The almost mechanical way in which Anglo-Saxonists assigned to the Irishman those very traits which were most deplored or despised among the respectable middle and upper classes in Victorian England leaves little room for doubt that the gentlemen who relied upon this stereotype were merely projecting onto an

extrapolate.

assumedly inferior group all those emotions which lay buried within themselves and which the English social system encouraged – and at times compelled – them to repress. Projection is one of the common consequences of repression (Curtis, 1968, p. 64).

A study of Victorian stereotypes of other cultures, particularly of the 'savage', shows that the medium through which the stereotype is presented to the general public – popular literature and periodicals – has an important influence on the stereotype itself. To understand this one must know something of academic preoccupations at that time – the Victorian and pre-Victorian view of the 'savage' did not begin with popular romance. It derived from academic discussion over several centuries, which percolated through to all levels of Victorian society with the assistance of popular literature. This chapter attempts to follow some of the tributaries of Victorian thought about race, as they flowed into the mainstream of nineteenth-century imagination and as they are represented in the pages of contemporary fiction.

Michael Banton has suggested how, in Europe, the popular image of other races originated in academic circles:

> Discrimination against strangers and particularly against dark-skinned people is probably of antiquity. But 'race' as it is known today is a relatively new idea. Only in the last two hundred years has an ideology of race claiming scientific validity been added to the rhetoric of national, economic and social conflict (Banton, 1967, p. 12).

The ideas used to express 'national, economic and social conflicts' in Victorian England were derived, in large measure, from biology and physical anthropology, and the attitudes to other cultures expressed in popular fiction were derived from these same sources.

Classification

Margaret Hodgen in *The Doctrine of Survivals* traces many Victorian ideas back to the medieval system of classification. 'The Great Chain of Being', in particular, provided a useful model for nineteenth-century scientists. Every aspect of nature, from the highest to the lowest, was placed in a particular category in a universal hierarchy and the scientist was to 'examine, classify and arrange the whole order of nature in a rational pattern' (Curtin, 1965, p. 36). The eighteenth-century biologists incorporated man, and the divisions within mankind, into this hierarchy and concerned themselves with the classifying, and with the criteria for such classifying, of man. These two concerns became fundamental to nineteenth-century racial studies, and were the elements of academic study that most dramatically filtered through to the general public. Once the notion that a man could be classified 'scientifically' had been accepted, it could be used for any social, political, economic and religious ends.

Linnaeus, in his *Systema Naturae* (1735), provided the basis for future classification in the field of biology. He attempted to place the whole of nature in a universal framework, and put man on the same scale as (though much higher than) the animals. Bendyshe, an important member of the Anthropological Society of London, emphasised the importance nineteenth-century anthropologists attached to this work: 'Man, for the first time, was classed as one with the rest of the animal creation' (Bendyshe, 1865a, p. 335). Man was divided into 'Homo sapiens, homo frus, americanus, europaeus, asiaticus, afer and monstrosus' (Penniman, 1935, p. 54). Many of these divisions, including Homo monstrosus, were still being used, with modifications, in nineteenth-century anthropology.

By 1795, Blumenbach was able to record at least twelve different authors besides himself, who had attempted some such classification of mankind:

> The first person, as far as I know, who made an attempt of
> this kind, was a certain anonymous writer who, towards the
> end of the last century, divided mankind into four races;
> that is, first, one of all Europe, Lapland alone excepted, and
> Southern Asia, Northern Africa and the whole of America;
> secondly, that of the rest of Africa; thirdly, that of the rest
> of Asia with the islands towards the East; fourthly, the Lapps
> (Blumenbach, 1795, p. 267).

Michael Banton, with the help of Bendyshe's 'History', unwittingly supplies the name of Blumenbach's anonymous author:

> The first time race was used as a basis for a taxonomy of
> mankind was in an essay by the French traveller and
> physician, François Bernier, published anonymously in 1684.
> He writes of 'four or five species or races of men in

particular whose difference is so remarkable that it may properly be used as the foundation for a new division of the earth' (Banton, 1967, p. 16).

Blumenbach, after citing Linnaeus's division into four, refers to Buffon, 'who distinguished six varieties of man:

1. Lapp or polar
2. Tartar (by which name, according to ordinary language, he meant the Mongolian)
3. South Asian
4. European
5. Ethiopian
6. American' (Blumenbach, 1795, p. 267).

And he adds another eight such systems to the list, varying in their classification from two races to seven. The taxonomies are: 'Governor Powell, 3; Abbe le Croi, 2; Kant, 4; John Hunter, 7; Zimmerman, 4; Meinen, 2; Klugel, 4; Metzger, 2' (ibid.).

Criteria for classification

As the lists suggest, the criteria for classification vary. Linnaeus 'followed common geography' (and skin colour), Buffon added 'such features as hair, colour, stature and features' (Penniman, 1935, p. 54), and Governor Powell was 'the first to pay attention to the racial form of the skull as connected with the subject' (Blumenbach, 1795, p. 267). Blumenbach himself, however, first made the study of craniology widely accepted, and started a tradition that became one of the most important elements in physical anthropology in the late nineteenth century. He classified mankind into five divisions (four in the first edition of 1775), the Caucasian, Mongolian, Ethiopian, American and Malay, the latter two representing stages between the other three respectively (ibid., p. 264). His criteria included hair, colour, bodily structure and most important, skull form. Penniman writes: 'His classification and collection became world famous and it was for a long time the fashion to visit his museum to view the various cranial types' (Penniman, 1935, p. 56). And he suggests that one reason why this aspect of the study of man received such general attention was the clarity and definition offered by Blumenbach, 'the majority of people prefer to work within limits' (ibid.).

The application of such precise terms of reference to the complex details of social life had the obvious attraction that it enabled the vast amount of data on other societies being brought back to Europe to be neatly classified and tabulated. Greene notes that Darwin's theory, far from demonstrating the limited value of this approach, actually helped to spread it:

> It is an interesting problem in the history of thought why the question of origins or race formation should have attracted so much attention in the period before Darwin's *Origin of Species* and the problem of classification so much after that event (Greene, J. C., 1954, n. 3, p 40).

Banton suggests an answer: since Darwin had seemed to solve the problem of origins and provided a methodology that could be used in the laboratory, he favoured the sort of classification which was better suited to laboratory conditions where skulls and human anatomy could be preserved and measured. And the findings of such measurements were supposed to indicate something about the social life and values of the person measured.

Pieter Camper (1722–89) had already devised a system of measuring skulls which could be used to classify the different races:

> One line was drawn from the meeting of the lips to the most prominent part of the forehead and another from the opening of the ear to the base of the nose. The crucial angle was formed where these two lines met. . . . Camper claimed that if this angle were measured for men of different races . . . the measurements would fall into an ordered series from Greek statuary as the ideal form, through the European races, to Negroes as the lowest human variety and finally to the lower animals (Curtin, 1965, pp. 39–40).[1]

A correlation could thus be postulated between skull shape, physical appearance, and intellectual and moral capacity. Camper's description brings into the scientific account of races the notion of quality and value-judgment. Likewise, Meiners had referred 'all nations to two stocks, (1) handsome, (2) ugly, the first white, the latter dark' (Blumenbach, 1795, p. 268), and Blumenbach himself describes the Caucasian race according to similar criteria: 'I have taken the name of this variety from Mount Caucasus . . . because its neighbourhood, and especially its southern slope, produces the most beautiful race of men' (ibid., p. 269); and he quotes travellers in support of this, for example Chardin: 'I have not observed a single ugly face in that country' (ibid.).

The addition of such qualities as beauty and of psychological characteristics to the classification of races was noted by St Hilaire in summarising Blumenbach's achievement:

> It is apparent that Blumenbach was more or less aware of three truths whose importance no-one can dispute in anthropological taxonomy, that is to say: the plurality of the races of man; the importance of characteristics deduced from the conformation of the head; and the necessity of not placing in the same rank all the divisions of mankind, which bear the common title of races, in spite of the unequal importance of their anatomical, physiological and, let us also add, psychological characteristics (St Hilaire, 1835, vol. 1, p. 129).

This addition, the 'psychological', is the factor which allowed the non-scientist, the traveller, the politician and the trader to give their own views of other cultures as though they were scientific propositions. The scientists themselves set the example by giving their own chauvinism an air of scientific respectability.

Cuvier could, for example, write in *The Animal Kingdom* (1827–35) of the Caucasian race as the one

> to which we ourselves belong [and which] is chiefly distinguished by the beautiful form of the head, which approximates to a perfect oval. From this variety have sprung the most civilised nations and such as have most generally exercised dominion over the rest of mankind, while of the negro, the hordes of which this variety is composed have always remained in a state of complete barbarism (quoted Curtin, 1965, p. 231).

And Sir William Lawrence, trying in a lecture in 1819 to establish the gulf between the European and other races, likewise correlated external qualities with 'internal' ones: 'The distinction of colour between the white and black races is not more striking than the pre-eminence of the former in moral feelings and in mental endowments.' The Negro is debauched, sensual and insensitive to others, lacking the 'elevated sentiments, manly virtues and moral feelings' of the white man (in Curtin, 1965, p. 232).

The link between race and culture, physical and mental qualities, having been established, any subjective feelings with regard to the 'character' of other races can be given scientific backing.

If the criteria for distinguishing between the races of man depended upon such subjective considerations, Voltaire and Rousseau could claim that Negroes were naturally inferior to Europeans in mental ability, and Hume that 'there never was a civilised nation of any other complexion than white' (ibid., p. 241), with as much justification as Blumenbach could claim that the Caucasian was the most beautiful. That chauvinism was rendered in 'scientific' terms in the late nineteenth century is asserted by Curtis in his analysis of Anglo-Saxonism and anti-Irish prejudice:

> The Victorian Anglo-Saxon – to indulge in something of a stereotype – found his explanation for the rise of the British Empire not in Divine Providence, not in the universal laws of political economy, but in the distinctive racial attributes of the British people (Curtis, 1968, p. 8).

Similarly, the character attributed to savage races can be traced to this racial model: 'He tried to explain the failure of other nations to match that achievement by the absence of those same racial traits or features' (ibid.). Just as the desirable qualities of the English gentleman are lacking in primitive races, there are, conversely, many undesirable qualities which, likewise, have their origin in a racial heritage.

Popular literature, with its tradition of oversimplification of characters and interpreting internal qualities from physical appearance (cf. James, L., 1963), adopted the principles of nineteenth-century racism and gave them life in terms of the characterisation of members of other races. Woven into the very fabric of the romantic tale are the suppositions that the 'savage' is faithful, gullible, child-like and cannibalistic and often ugly; that friendship between the races is difficult, and only possible if a native shows the qualities of an English gentleman and that intermarriage is distinctly harmful; that some races are so low on the scale of humanity that their use as a music-hall joke is fully justified; and that the author may foist any characteristic on a whole race if it serves the purposes of the story and provides a motive for the actions of an individual member of that race.

George Orwell has pointed out such stereotypes in boys' weekly comics:

The assumption all along is not only that foreigners are comics who are put there for us to laught at, but that they can be classified in much the same way as insects. That is why in all boys' papers, not only the 'Gem' and 'Magnet', a Chinese is invariably portrayed with a pigtail. It is the thing you recognise him by, like the Frenchman's beard or the Italian's barrel-organ. In papers of this kind it occasionally happens that, when a setting of a story is in a foreign country, some attempt is made to describe the natives as individual human beings, but as a rule it is assumed that foreigners of any one race are all alike and will conform more or less exactly to the following patterns:

Frenchman: Excitable, wears beard, gesticulates wildly.
Spaniard, Mexican etc: sinister, treacherous.
Arab, Afghan etc.: sinister, treacherous.
Chinese: sinister, treacherous, wears pigtail.
Italian: excitable, grinds barrel-organ or carries stiletto.
Swede, Dane etc.: kind-hearted, stupid.
Negro: comic, very faithful (Orwell, 1940, p. 188).

Perhaps the best known native 'character' in this tradition in nineteenth-century English novels is Rider Haggard's faithful Negro Umslopogaas, who served as a model for countless other 'savages'. Umslopogaas is first presented in *Nada the Lily* (1892) as a heroic figure in the noble savage tradition. He is a son of Chaka, the great Zulu king, who had ruled that all his sons be killed, but was tricked in this case by a wily witch-doctor. His rise is told in the classical tradition of the cast-out heir. He is adopted by an enemy of the king and is lost in the woods, where he is reared by a wolf and becomes a member of the pack. He then returns to a human village, where he engages the chief in the annual leadership battle, is inevitably victorious and wins a great battle-axe, which he carries with him from then on into many a heroic battle. He is known as the Slaughterer and the tales of his deeds are told around many a camp-fire in Southern Africa. He is praised by the white men for his great physique and for his manly virtues of courage and fair fighting, which he might almost have learned on the playing fields of Eton. He lives for killing and believes that man loses his dignity if he does not kill: 'Man is born to kill. He who kills not when his blood is hot is a woman and no man' (Haggard, 1887a, p. 44). But the method of fighting must be fair: 'May my shadow be accursed and chilled to the bone for ever if it should fall to murdering like a bushman with poisoned arrows' (ibid.). Indeed, he prefers not to use the large blade of his axe, but rather the 'punch' on the other end, since 'he considered the punch a neater and more sportsmanlike tool!' (ibid., p. 41).

Although his idea of sport may be a trifle bloodier than that of the Victorian public school, it stems from the same sense of honour and dignity. Haggard defends it by comparing it with less honourable values in Victorian life: 'It is better to slay a man in fair fight than to suck out his life's blood in buying, selling and usury' (ibid., p. 230). Umslopogaas is being used by Haggard, as are most noble savages in the literary tradition, in order to condemn the values of the writer's own society. He represents the 'physical' and 'natural', as opposed to the intellectual and the cultural, attributes which were applied by the Victorian to 'primitive' and 'civilised' respectively.

The apparently enlightened description of an individual native is thus tempered somewhat by the fact that it is rendered within the framework of a particular European convention; Umslopogaas is being used to prove a point, rather than to be admired as an individual. And the reason that the Englishmen accept him is that he has many of the qualities of an English gentleman – honour, dignity and courage. Thus even Umslopogaas is something of a caricature, and the patronising condescension with which he is treated puts him and his fellow 'savages' firmly in their place. When Quatermain praises him, the praise is qualified by the racial assumptions of nineteenth-century science: 'He is, in his savage fashion, the finest general I have met' (Haggard, 1887a, p. 74). And, although he refuses to be a servant, he still has all the faithfulness usually attributed to the native servant. He never leaves Quatermain, he fights with and for him and he eventually dies in a heroic defence of Quatermain's friends.

He thus serves to reinforce Haggard's primitivism while, at the same time, he supports the theme of progress by acknowledging the ultimate superiority of the white men he meets. But, whereas the characters of romance fiction modelled on Umslopogaas tend to perpetuate these elements of the stereotype, the original Umslopogaas is based on a character whom Haggard actually knew. He was a Swazi aide-de-camp of Shepstone's while Haggard was in South Africa:

> He was a tall, noble fighter, a lithe black Achilles, handsome in spite of his sixty years. . . . Early in the journey, Haggard

and Umslopogaas became friends and often they would sit together, Haggard's attention caught as the warrior told stories of his youth and of his people (Cohen, 1960, p. 35).

It is this personal experience which makes Haggard's character come to life in a way that few such figures in romance fiction do. Although Umslopogaas perpetuates the racial ideas of Haggard's period, he transcends the limitations of the popular representations by his individuality, his sense of life and the heightened imagination which Haggard brings to bear on descriptions of him. The final scene where he holds the steps against a whole army before dying a Horatian death has been praised by many commentators as one of the outstanding set pieces of imaginative fiction.

Umslopogaas's faithfulness unto death is emulated, though seldom so imaginatively, by many a native character in the pages of Victorian romance, as well as in Haggard's other novels. Khiva, in *King Solomon's Mines*, dies for his master beneath the feet of a mad elephant, which would have otherwise killed the white man; and in *Jess*, Jantje serves his master like a dog, though less is expected of him as a Hottentot.

G. A. Henty seldom sees the 'savage' in any other role than that of a servant, unless it be as the doughty warrior in a Sudanese or South African army. His stories of the various campaigns of the British Army in Africa concentrate on the political background and on the deeds of derring-do undertaken by stalwart British youths. The native of the country concerned remains in a hazy background, either brewing tea for the return of his adventuring master or fighting in the ranks as a savage warrior or a brave comrade. In *With Kitchener in the Sudan*, for instance, a young English boy joins the campaign against the Mahdi, which is seen as restoring the land from barbarism to civilisation and wiping out the stain to British honour caused by the desertion of Gordon by the British Government. When he sets out towards Wady Halfa the advice he receives from fellow officers sounds like a boy scout's manual – what sort of underpants to wear, how to prevent his knickerbockers looking baggy and, in the same breath, how to hire a native servant.

Those in Cairo are lazy, so he is advised to wait until Dongola, where they 'may not know much but are ready enough to learn and, if well treated, will go through fire and water for their master (Henty, 1902, p. 92). He chooses one who is physically weak but looks intelligent, and the native's face lights up at being so chosen: 'I will be faithful, bey' (ibid., p. 93). While this worthy works away industriously in the background, his master wanders around the camp to assess the situation and is pleased to see the Sudanese troops 'as full of fun and life as a party of school boys' (ibid., p. 95). They all have a splendid physique, they love fighting, and their womenfolk, who follow to cook for them, urge the stragglers into war with bellicose taunts. On the whole, he concludes, a merry, tireless crew, proud to be fighting with the British. Thus, the physical prowess and warlike character of Umslopogaas, together with the faithfulness of him, Khiva and Jantje, are perpetuated in the Sudan in Henty's characterisation of primitive peoples, as sweepers-up and fighters.

Carlyle, in his 'Occasional Discourse on the Nigger Question' (1849) had suggested that the savage was not a servant merely because of the social situation but through scientific necessity:

They had been created inferior in order to serve their European masters.

'That you may depend on it, my obscure black friends, is and always was the Law of the World, for you and for all men. To be servants, the more foolish of us to the more wise' (quoted in Curtin, 1965, pp. 380–1).

The natives are so often servants in popular literature because the authors believed it was scientifically ordained that natives should be servants. And an author's personal experience often reinforced this attitude. Louis Cornell traces the origin of Kipling's attitude towards his Indian servants to the fact that he spent the first six years of his life in India:

Thus, the Anglo-Indian child spent his early years as part of a natural and accepted pattern of Indian life. Unconcerned with the implications of their position, the children in Kipling's stories treat their Indian servants as both friends and inferiors and the Indians respond with a combination of deference and affection. Though many of his Indian tales present the bewildering complexity of the Indo-English relationship, Kipling never fully outgrew the innocence of his first six years. In a sense the loyal and affectionate servant remained for him the prototype of the admirable Indian native (Cornell, 1966, p. 3).

In 'The Tomb of His Ancestors', John Chinn, whose grandfather had 'made men of the Bhil', returns to the native regiment in which his grandfather's servants still serve, and is treated with the same deference as his ancestor, of whom they believe he is the reincarnation. Chinn walks into the darkness of his hut and is greeted by Bukta:

> A faint light burned in his room and, as he entered, hands clasped his feet and a voice murmured from the floor. . . . I bore you in my arms, Sahib, when I was a strong man and you were a small one . . . I am your servant, as I was your father's before you. We are all your servants (Maugham (ed.), 1952, p. 44).

This is a special case, as Chinn's ancestor was so beloved and he is believed to be a reincarnation, but it represents the British ideal of a native prince voluntarily becoming a British servant. Even the major of the regiment, though, is a little taken aback when he actually sees it happening:

> . . . for the spectacle of the senior native commissioned officer of the regiment, an 'unmixed' Bhil, a Companion of the Order of British India, with thirty-five years spotless service in the army and a rank among his own people superior to that of many Bengal princelings, valeting the last-joined subaltern, was a little too much for his nerves (ibid.).

More typical is the treatment of an English child by native servants represented in 'Tods' Amendment':

> Tods was the idol of some eighty 'Jhampanis' and half as many 'saises'. He saluted them all as 'O Brother'. It never entered his head that any living human being could disobey his orders and he was the buffer between the servants and his Mamma's wrath (Kipling, 1888, p. 198).

Such tales have their origin in Kipling's own upbringing and his attitudes to native servants. In the context of Victorian racist thought, these incidents further reinforce the belief that it is the natural role of the 'inferior' races to be servants to the white.

Mphalele, writing of later English fiction in which the African is represented as a servant, notes that the British attitude leads to 'moral corrosion' and that the servant becomes 'menacing' (Mphalele,

1962, p. 134). The British masters are disturbed by never knowing
what is going on in the minds of their black servants, 'a seeming
black automaton', and their failure to enter into the servant's
private life leads to a variety of clashes. In one instance a white
woman, objecting to her servant's refusal to meet her eyes, allows
one of them to undress her in order to establish some relationship
with him (ibid., p. 139). In others, the white people are forced back
on each other's company and they 'feel the world around them
narrowing and crowding in on them' and, while the servants remain
an unperturbed catalyst, their masters become tense and disturbed.

But these later works deal with black/white relations directly as
a social problem and Mphalele is justified, to some extent, in his
heavy emphasis on character studies and on whether the natives
portrayed are 'round' or 'flat'. Such a treatment of 'native' servants
represents a change from that possible in the period we are dealing
with, up to the First World War, when the stereotypes of natives
derived from a less self-conscious tradition and when the myths of
racial superiority, social evolution and the white man's burden were
more deeply rooted in the ideology of writers and readers alike.
During this period, it was more usual to characterise the 'savage'
as inherently simple, child-like, gullible or faithful than to analyse
the problems of 'race relations'.[2]

Gullibility is a feature which enables British sovereignty to be
maintained by the use of western knowledge and technology to
frighten the simple native into submission. Perhaps the most famous
and memorable example is the use of an eclipse to overawe the native.
In *King Solomon's Mines* the travellers take advantage of an eclipse
to reinforce the natives' belief that they are gods. Good notes from
his diary that an eclipse of the moon is due. If he and his fellow
travellers can make the natives believe that it is through their power
that the face of the moon is darkened, then the natives will abandon
the evil witch-doctor, Gagool, and follow the white men. The eclipse
occurs and the natives are duly overawed, but a conflict arises for
Haggard between the demands of his story and the 'character' which
he is accustomed to attribute to the native. For while many are
convinced, many others are not, and Gagool claims to have seen
such natural phenomena before. But those who are sceptical – about
half the population, since it is divided for the battle – are cast on
the side of the evil rulers, and their scepticism is devalued by selfishness and ambition, by the strength of Gagool and by the story's

requirement that a large group should oppose the white men in an exciting battle. So the final impression is not of a considerable degree of scepticism among the natives but of their gullibility, superstition and stupidity. The sceptical ones are rebellious and cunning. The exigencies of the story have obscured the wider implications of the event and contributed another 'factual proof' to the current image of primitive man.

Another example of this use of an eclipse occurs in Bertram Mitford's *John Ames* (1900). While the commissioner is falling in love with a flirtatious Englishwoman in Cape Town, the rumblings of native discontent are to be heard back in Matabeleland. The witch-doctors have gathered the people together on a moonlit night and worked them to a pitch of frenzy in which they will accept the eclipse of the moon as a sign from the gods. The oracle tells the crowd to look upwards at the darkening heavens as the eclipse begins and 'in silent awe the superstitious savages gaze blankly upon the phenomenon'. Mitford goes on to explain why they should be so awestruck, and does not merely attribute it to the 'superstitious' character of their race: 'There are those among them who have beheld it before and to such under ordinary circumstances it would be looked upon with little concern, now, however, worked up as they are, it is different' (ibid., p. 67).

The stereotype of the awestruck native is thus filled out with explanations in terms of mob psychology, a practice not so common in the travellers' tales and novels of the time, which often preferred to account for all such events in terms of 'superstition' alone. Mitford, instead, subscribes to another popular theme, that of the witch-doctor as a wily politician, playing on the susceptibilities of his people, taking advantage of their gullibility. Thus the witch-doctor here realises that some of his people will recall that the sun darkened before the Zulu race rose against their white enemies and he uses this to add force to the present augury: 'For the children of the Zulu the sun grew black. For the children of Matydone the moon' (ibid., p. 68). And it is not just any unnatural event that is being used by the witch-doctor. He is able to use the particular features of an eclipse to symbolise the political situation he is concerned with – the link is not merely fortuitous:

So, the blackening of the moon is the hiding of the nation, crushed, blackened, beneath the might of Makiwa [white

people]. But the blackness does not last. So is the foot of
Makiwa removed from the neck of the people of Matydone.
Behold (ibid.).

As he points, the moon begins to reappear and the whole multitude
burst out into excited chanting at this forceful symbol of their coming
release. Thus Mitford uses the same physical situation as Haggard.
The disbelievers in Haggard's account are persuaded by their own
political hopes and by the strength of their leader, herself a witch-
doctor. In Mitford's tale, they are carried away by the excitement of
the situation and the aptness of the symbol. Both suggest the same
basic explanation: that religious leaders use superstition and gullibility for their own ends, but, whereas in Haggard the white men
also use it to take advantage of the overawed native and the fact
that many are doubtful is passed over lightly, in Mitford the allaying
of doubts is explained more reasonably and the use of the eclipse as
a symbol makes it a more integral part of the whole situation and
less of a *deus ex machina*.

Once the eclipse had been established as a means of frightening
the natives, it became for the romance writer a convenient and
dramatic symbol of the gullibility of primitive peoples. Captain
Charles Gilson, nearly thirty years after *King Solomon's Mines*, uses
the technique in an almost cursory, offhand manner. Captain
Crouch, a seasoned campaigner in Africa, decides at the end of an
adventure that he wants to maintain his hold over the natives for
future use, so he looks up his *Old Moore's Almanack* to find an
eclipse. He gathers the natives in the moonlight, chants a Victorian
nonsense poem solemnly and, at the appropriate time, using a watch,
tells the moon to disappear. The natives are terrified: 'As one man
they rushed forward and flung themselves at the feet of the White
Wizard, whose servant was the moon' (Gilson, 1919, p. 276).
Crouch's friends ask him why he did it and he replies:

In this benighted country I have a reputation to keep up.
The story of tonight's performance will travel hundreds of miles
across the grassland. It is as well to have friends, or at any
rate admirers, in the heart of a continent like this (ibid., p. 278).

Haggard's heroes had used the technique to save themselves from
death, and Mitford's 'villains' to start a native uprising. Gilson, so
many years later, uses the same technique in an unimportant situation, as though it were merely necessary to put it in somewhere as

part of the tradition. Haggard put down native awe at eclipses to 'superstition', while Mitford tried to explain their use by crowd psychology. Gilson, with more anthropological material and ideas to draw on, presents another academic theory as his explanation of native mentality and character. As the Bongos regard the eclipse in amazement, he explains their thoughts:

> It was as if the incomprehensible and mystic words which had been uttered by the White Wizard had conjured up one of the spirits of the sky, which even then was passing slowly across the face of the moon (ibid., p. 275).

We shall deal later with that phase of anthropological thought which believed all primitive religion to be the superstitious peopling of the universe with spirits. It is enough, for the moment, to note how the theories of anthropologists are used in popular fiction to provide various explanations for primitive attitudes to situations which become traditional themes in fiction. The ease with which the native can be deceived is brought home to the reader by the vivid use of eclipses, and academic theory is used to 'explain' the natives' reaction.

The gullibility of the native is also emphasised in many other situations. When Allan Quatermain wants his rifles guarded by a man whom he describes as 'a thief of a savage with greedy eyes' on the strength of a passing glance, he tells him there is a devil in the gun and that, if he touches it, the devil will come out with a bang (Haggard, 1885, p. 54). The native touches it and the 'devil' knocks him off his feet. Such explanations of fear and the reasons for it tend to emphasise the gullibility and 'superstition' of the native reaction rather than the practical understanding of the power of weapons which many soon acquired. The image portrayed of blind superstition takes no account of native ability to use firearms once their initial fears of the unknown are conquered. Only in such later works as Forester's *The Sky and the Forest* (1948) does the image change. Here, the first superstitious fears are balanced by the way in which Loa, the native chief, comes to use guns himself and to adapt the white man's inventions to his own ends, instead of remaining in awe as do most of Haggard's natives.

Haggard, however, is not alone in demonstrating how white superiority was asserted by the ostentatious use of the rifle before those to whom it is an object of wonder. Thomson, a famous traveller and writer on Southern Africa, remarks that the exhibition of a rifle 'never failed to produce a decided impression on the natives' (Thomson, 1881, p. 130), while Petherick describes this impression among the Azande:

> I seized a fowling piece . . . and, pointing to a vulture hovering over us, I fired. But, before the bird touched the ground, the crowd was prostrate and grovelling in the dust, as if every man of them had been shot. The old man's head, with his hands on his ears, was at my feet, and when I raised him his appearance was ghastly and his eyes were fixed on me with a meaningless expression (Petherick, 1861, p. 458).

But the traveller in fiction does not always shoot only birds. In *The Lost World*, the professors are rescued from their ape-like captors by a volley of rifle fire from the rest of the party, whereupon 'the dense mob of ape-men ran about in bewilderment, marvelling whence this storm of death was coming' (Doyle, 1912, p. 163). And Lord John later reflects: 'I don't believe they ever understood how the fellow I shot came by his hurt' (ibid., p. 157). This display of force gives the Indian population hope that, with these white gods to protect them, they can rid the plateau of the apes, so they prostrate themselves before the white men in the traditional posture of such accounts, and their leader explains: 'They are great fighters. They command the thunder and the lightning' (ibid., p. 174).

A native chief in Ballantyne, overcoming his initial awe of similar events, decides he wants the thunder and lightning for himself. He is given a demonstration of the fire-power of an English schooner's gun:

> The chiefs were directed to look at a rock about two miles out to sea and the gun was fired. In a second, the top of the rock was seen to burst asunder and to fall in fragments into the sea. Ramata was so delighted with the success of this shot that he pointed to a man who was walking on the shore and begged the captain to fire at him, evidently supposing that his permission was quite sufficient to justify the captain in such an act (Ballantyne, 1858, p. 161).

Thus, when the reaction of the native to firearms is not portrayed as superstitious awe, it is seen instead as bloody-thirsty desire to exploit their potential. If the native is not always gullible, it is because he is also savage.

In this the Europeans who introduce the gun are in fact usually the best guide to its indiscriminate use. Sanders uses the Maxim liberally to keep order, in keeping with Belloc's sentiments:

> Whatever happens, we have got
> The maxim gun
> And they have not.

Michael Banton uses this quotation to show how the biological theories of the age assumed a political significance. In the natural world, only the fittest survived, and they survived by winning an often bloody battle against those less fit, on the principle that 'Might is Right'. Banton suggests that a new beatitude was written into Victorian morality, 'Blessed are the strong, for they shall prey upon the weak' (Banton, 1967, p. 48). This philosophy justified the white races fighting the black, as it justified the same harsh methods that Nature 'red in tooth and claw' applied. The attitude is reflected in the indiscriminate use of the gun by such heroes of popular fiction as Sanders.

The ease with which threats of the use of firearms could deceive and terrify the native further reinforced the image of his gullibility and stupidity. Such episodes are represented in the fiction to add tension to a tale and to provide light relief at the expense of the naïve native. In *A Boy's Adventures Round the World*, some British sailors arrive at an island *en route* for Singapore from Batavia and are met by a group of 'savages'. They take one aboard and show him two 'formidable-looking brass-mounted eight-pounder guns', which are, however, 'only put there for show, since being very old they dared not be discharged' (Higginson, 1919, p. 115). Inevitably, they have the desired effect and the Malay exclaims in awe, 'Ho, ho! You plenty men and gun cappee' (ibid.). In many other tales, their fear of firearms is taken for granted as proving how easy it is to deceive superstitious primitive peoples.

The power of the rifle is obvious, but the European also took advantage of native ignorance of more harmless technology. As Cairns comments: 'Awe was also fostered by deliberately playing on African ignorance with respect to much of the gadgetry of western civilisation, such as mirrors, watches and umbrellas' (Cairns, 1965, p. 46). The fright of an African who attempted to catch the second hand of a watch 'was unmistakable – limbs actually trembled' according to Duff MacDonald. It was such exhibitions of fright which led Samuel Baker to assert that 'savages' could be ruled by either force or 'humbug' (Baker, 1898, p. 202). 'Humbug' is a common means of control. One native chief in Sanders's domain proudly exhibited a piece of notepaper with Sanders's handwriting on it, supposedly confirming the chief's cordial relations with the great white ruler. In fact, it says 'Arrest and detain bearer if found in any other territory than the Isisi' (Wallace, 1911, p. 161). Another tribe, terrified of their neighbours, are given a sign whose 'devil marks' keep them safe. The 'marks' read, 'Trespassers Beware'. And, on another occasion, an 'enlightened' native (in fact, an escaped convict from Liberia) terrorised a tribe by a telescope which they mistook for a gun (ibid., p. 43).

Ramata in *The Coral Island* is, likewise, unsure of the real nature of a musket and 'asked where the white man got hatchets hard enough to cut the tree of which the barrel was made!' (Ballantyne, 1858, p. 160). But this simple native's chief delight was the ship's pump:

> He never tired of examining it and pumping up the water.
> Indeed, so much was he taken up with the pump that he could
> not be prevailed on to return on shore but sent a canoe to
> fetch his favourite stool, on which he seated himself and spent
> the remainder of the day in pumping the bilge-water out of
> the ship! (ibid., p. 161).

The exclamation mark, of course, emphasises that a chief who takes such childish pleasures in pumping bilge-water cannot be taken seriously.

An equally trivial event excites the natives in *King Solomon's Mines*. When they surprise the travellers, Good is half-undressed. Only half his face is shaved, his legs are bare, he is wearing an eyeglass and his false teeth continually disappear into his mouth. When the travellers eventually leave Kukuanaland, they learn that legends have grown up about this strange figure, and people travel miles just to gaze at his legs.

Many travellers, like Curtis and his companions in *King Solomon's Mines* took glittering beads with which to smooth their way. The ivory or diamonds for which the travellers often scornfully exchanged these beads was then taken to Europe where it was made into beads for Western women.[3] The natives of Kukuanaland, to whom beads are brought, have lived for centuries over an open diamond mine, whose gems they have ignored. For the authors of this period, ivory and diamonds were so obviously more valuable than glass that the willingness of natives to exchange the 'more' for the 'less' valuable merely reinforced ideas of their simple-mindedness.

Most anthropological fiction of the time has some such example of the use of 'humbug'. In Gilson's tale, Captain Crouch terrifies the pygmies who surround him, by repeatedly changing his false eye for one of a different colour (he carried a box of them for this purpose). The chief is overawed: 'His little eyes grew rounder and seemed in danger of springing from his head', and he flees back to his companions 'to one of whom he clung for protection, trembling from head to foot'. Crouch follows up by making explicit to the natives what their reaction should be:

> You have seen yourself . . . that I am a man of many eyes. I am
> known as the White Wizard . . . if you and your people remain
> my friends, it will be well for you. If you declare yourselves our
> enemies, witchcraft will not spare you (Gilson, 1919, p. 57).

The exigencies of the story, however, demand that the pygmies do remain hostile, since this provides the main excitement; so the pygmies reject Crouch's request, despite their fear of his 'witchcraft'. Once again, however, it is the natives' childish awe at white gadgetry, rather than their ultimate rejection of it, which is the most memorable part of this incident.[4]

The antecedents of the child-like savage lie in the English romantic writing (cf. Fairchild, *The Noble Savage*, 1928) where the 'noble savage' is often identified with the child, freely receiving the influences of nature and free from the corruptions of civilised life. Such flights of fancy were rudely dispelled by later nineteenth-century accounts of 'savages' and the Darwinian struggle of primeval man, but the comparison of the savage with the child lived on with a new meaning. If, as anthropological theory held, the primitive races represented a previous stage in the development towards 'civilised' man, then the model of a child growing into a man could be applied to human evolution, with the European races as the mature and fully developed men and the primitive races as 'children'. Thus, the 'parent' races are obliged to treat their child-like charges with the care and control of a Victorian father. Paternalism and trusteeship are validated by anthropological theory and literary tradition.

Tylor, in *Primitive Culture* (1873), for instance, attempted to explain the theory of animism to his 'civilised' audience by asking them to recall their own childhood attitudes to inanimate pheno- mena. As the child saw a life force in everything and had to unlearn this attitude later, so the 'savage', not having developed beyond the stage of the child, saw spirits all round. And the theory of 'survivals' was and still is supported by comparing primitive customs and children's games. Elements of activities, which were once serious and which still are for many primitive peoples, live on in fossilised form in the games of civilised children, whose play with bows and arrows, finger counting and so on, has outlived the serious practices that are being imitated. This was and often still is made to bear the further inference that savages are like children.

With such authoritative support, the popular writers could con- fidently compare savages with children. Haggard, interested in anthropology through a long friendship with Andrew Lang, often echoes the anthropological comparison. Near the end of *Jess* there is a glimpse of the Hottentot servant's cave, where bits and pieces of clothing have been collected from many sources, magpie fashion, the whole suggesting to Jess a comparison with 'the most aboriginal of our primitive ancestors' (Haggard, 1887b, p. 299). The Hottentot Jantje is a member of one of the child races. He lurks between the trees in a way 'which is doubtless bred in him after tens of centuries of tracking animals and hiding from his foes'. He is indulging his 'natural instincts' for 'he needed periodical recreation of this sort' due to the inactive nature of life on the farm: 'Like a civilized child, he longed for wild beasts and enemies and, if there were none handy, he found satisfaction in making a pretence of their presence' (ibid., p. 109). In his everyday life, the Hottentot thinks in the same way as the civilised child when playing games.

Sanders, already frequently mentioned, bases his job on the assump- tion that the native is child-like:

> He trusted all natives up to the same point that you trusted
> children, with a few notable exceptions. The Zulu were men,
> the Basuto were men, yet child-like in their grave faith . . .
> living so long with children of a larger growth it follows that
> he absorbed many of their child-like qualities (Wallace, 1911,
> p. 7).

Whenever he visits them and sees their love of glister, the chiefs dressed in tinselled robes or stolen army redcoats, and observes their

SIL—

simple ways, he feels even more avuncular and realises 'they are all like children' (ibid., p. 78).[5] John Ames, too, realises that a district commissioner is 'expected to act the part of a benevolent uncle all round' (Mitford, 1900, p. 59), and the use of the term 'boy' in addressing full-grown native servants perpetuates the distinction in Kipling and Henty.[6]

But if these writers see the native somewhat benevolently as a child, they are also aware of 'savage' nature and of the 'atrocities' the native would commit if unrestrained. Indeed, the whole picture in Ballantyne's *The Coral Island* is of barbarous and blood-thirsty cannibals attempting, with uncontrolled frenzy, to tie every white man to the stake. The boys first see the 'savages' engaged in a ferocious battle in which both sides fight like demons until the conquerors prepare to roast their victims for the evening meal. At this, and the sight of the chief hurling a woman's baby into the sea before turning to her with his knife, the boys can stand no more and rush forward to the rescue.

Having saved some of the 'savages', they are then able to chat with them on friendly terms, to restrain them from eating their erstwhile conquerors, and to conclude that 'among these cannibals we had seen many symptoms of a kindly nature'. But the most powerful memory is still of having their 'paradise suddenly broken in upon by ferocious savages, and the white sands stained with blood and strewed with lifeless forms' (Ballantyne, 1858, p. 134). This side of native life is emphasised by 'Bloody Bill,' a lusty pirate who attempts to dispel the 'myths' about natives being pleasant people which were circulating in humanitarian circles in England. He tells dreadful tales of native atrocities, of roasting victims alive and feeding live babies to a hideous snake, stories which he fears the good people at home would not believe. But, he asserts, 'I've seed it with my own eyes' (ibid., p. 163). The missionary, too, is concerned because folk in England blind themselves to the reality of native horrors and he urges the boys to disillusion them on their return, partly in order to recruit more missionaries for the field:

'I trust that, if you ever return to England, you will tell your Christian friends that the horrors they hear of in regard to these islands are *literally true* and that, when they have heard the worst the half has not been told them. For there are perpetuated here foul deeds of darkness of which man may not speak. You may also tell them', he said, looking around with a smile, while a tear of gratitude trembled in his eye and rolled down his coal-black cheek, 'tell them of the blessings that the gospel has wrought here' (ibid., p. 208).

Ballantyne revels in detailed descriptions of native atrocities, which 'prove' his missionary to be right. A ship is launched over live, squirming bodies, the natives fight bloody, ferocious battles, they tie the Englishmen to a stake and dance gleefully round suppers of human flesh. When the boys first saw the savages 'their thoughts had been instantly filled with all they had ever heard or read of wild beasts and savages, of torturings at the stake, roastings alive and such-like horrible things' (ibid., p. 37). Since *The Coral Island* became a children's classic, one may suppose that such details were not, by Victorian standards, to be denied the young and therefore upset no-one's preconceptions.[7]

The natives in Wallace's tales can also be cruel. The Akasava prefer to torture their enemies, 'killing them very little but rather burning them'. They 'put hot embers in their hands and bound them tightly' (Wallace, 1911, p. 26). And, if Sanders is continually firing his Maxim gun at them, they are always thinking of new, sadistic ways of getting at him. His servant puts glass in his food and a tribe who capture him make him walk on hot stones barefoot. The Dervishes in Doyle's *The Tragedy of the Korosko* have their inherent cruelty written on their faces. The Baggara Arabs are 'small, brown, wiry, with little vicious eyes and thin cruel lips' (Doyle, 1898, p. 81). And a Negro whose face is pitted with smallpox looks 'good-natured compared with his arab comrades' (ibid., p. 99). These men are fanatical, bigoted and savage and look little different from the warriors depicted in 'a seventh-century frieze': 'The East does not change and the Dervish raiders were not less brave, less cruel or less fanatical than their forbears' (ibid., p. 80).

This fear of the undercurrents of violence in the Sudan was given wider expression with the defeat of Gordon by the Mahdi: 'Fanatical Dervishes flocked to his banner and after a series of petty successes this truculent and crafty ruffian defeated and annihilated, in October, 1883, an Egyptian force under Hicks Pasha' (Arthur, 1938, p. 103). Affected by such accounts, Englishmen went to the Sudan feeling that they were bringing civilisation to a land more overtly savage than many in Africa, 'a callous country inhabited by a callous race' according to Mason (1902, p. 220). He describes acts of cruelty in the dreadful prison at Omdurman, including the practice of swelling with water the palm fronds binding a man's wrists, so that, as they dried, they could contract and cut into his skin (ibid., p. 190).

The only comparable activities that the writers can think of in their own society are those of criminals. Davie, in *The Coral Island*, wonders who will tame the 'white savages' when a band of pirates massacres the natives (Ballantyne, 1858, p. 138). And Burroughs, describing a white prisoner being tortured by cannibals, remarks that white pirates are even crueller (Burroughs, 1917, p. 187). The comparison of the whole of a primitive society with the criminal elements of 'civilised' society implies that primitive peoples are congenitally more criminal and 'evil' than 'advanced' races. And the popular writers, by emphasising the sadistic side of the people they are describing, sustain this image, so that the words 'savage', 'primitive', 'Negro', 'barbaric' and 'cruel' can often be used interchangeably.

Some writers acknowledge that some people are more 'savage' than others, though again the epithet is applied to whole races. Thus Henty makes a distinction between the fanatical Arabs and the more peaceable black tribes of the Sudan. The blacks seem 'gentle and peaceable', while there is a 'deep fanatical feeling in every Musselman's nature' (Henty, 1902, p. 23), which drives them to conquer and to massacre. The tribes only put up with the Dervish from fear, a wish for survival, a love of fighting and a distrust of each other, and they prefer the British Egyptian army and the treatment they get from British officers. With the right British training these men could defeat the Mahdi. In Doyle's novel, as in reality, they do indeed fight with the British against the Dervishes.

Doyle, too, refers to differences between the blacks and the Arabs. When the natives, mostly Dinka and Shilluck, meet each other they grin and chatter foolishly, whereas the Arab ritual is more dignified and, while the former have a sense of humour, the Arabs tend to take everything seriously. Here the technique of giving a 'character' to a whole race is perpetuated but the differences between native tribes are recognised. They are not all (as in some writers) lumped together as 'savages'. This is partly because the Arab and the duskier Nilotes do look and behave very differently and partly because the blacks are fighting with the whites and so are seen by them in a different light. Whereas the Arabs retain the cruelty of their seventh-century ancestors, the blacks have been 'tamed' and retain only traces of their past. Their war cry, 'a wild inspiriting yell . . . brought with them from their central African wilds' (Doyle, 1898, p. 241) is used to help the British. It is, therefore, less detestable or 'savage' than the cries of those natives who present a threat, as in *The Coral Island*, where it becomes 'a yell that seemed to issue from the throats of incarnate fiends' (Ballantyne, 1858, p. 125). Thus, the degree of cruelty of the native is largely determined by which side he is fighting on, and by the particular expectations and experiences of the relator himself.

Similarly, many writers use the licence and example of scientific theory to attribute other particular features to the native. Wallace's hero, Sanders, for instance, believes that the native has no memory:

> If he was quick to punish he acted in accordance with the spirit of the people he governed, for they had no memory and yesterday, with its faults, its errors and its teachings, was a very long time ago and a man resents an unjust punishment for a crime he has forgotten (Wallace, 1911, p. 145).

However, if he forgets the crime, he soon forgets the punishment too: 'You may be sure that the Akasava memory is very short and the punishment which attended their last misdoing is easily forgotten' (ibid., p. 180). But these statements are contradicted elsewhere in the novel: 'The Isisi people keep extraordinary records in their head, handed down from father to son' (ibid., p. 127). Such inconsistencies are inevitable when a writer tries to attribute to a whole race characteristics he has observed in individual members of it, but the example was being set at the highest academic levels, where irreconcilable scientific explanations of the 'character' of particular races were also purveyed.

Discussion in the Anthropological Society of London about Negro intelligence had suggested that the Negro child developed until the age of twelve; then the 'sutures' closed and his intelligence stultified; he could not develop white man's qualities of combination and memory (*Anthropological Review*, II, 1864, p. 386). Popular writers perpetuated these ideas by putting them in fictional form. Wallace relates the native's lack of memory to the political situation a district commissioner has to deal with. And Patrick Greene, in *Tabu Dick*, adapts it to enable his hero to escape conveniently from difficult situations. When Tabu Dick is chased by a horde of savages, he evades them by going beyond the jungle edges. Instead of lying in wait, they return to their camp fire and: 'Presently . . . the incident was forgotten. The memories of savages are short-lived about some things. The warriors made merry with wild songs and wilder dances' (Greene, L. P., 1935a, p. 42).

The embodiment of these theories in fictitious characters planted them more firmly in the popular mind than abstract debates by scientists could ever do, though the scientists themselves sometimes resorted to similar methods in order to make a point. The habit of associating physical characteristics with 'internal' mental qualities, while a matter of lively debate in scientific circles, passes into popular literature as an accepted 'fact' and provides the novelist with respectable backing for his own generalisations about 'primitive peoples'.

Once it becomes possible to relate qualities like intelligence and memory to 'race', the traveller and writer can also introduce remarks about friendliness or a sense of humour, as Doyle did in comparing Arabs and Nilotes. An 'old Oxonian', in an article on practical jokes at Oxford, turns to the savage to broaden the scope of his enquiries:

> The utter and unmitigated savage never plays practical jokes upon his fellow man. He has so much of the principle on which practical joking generally depends that he can inflict pain and enjoy a fiendish gratification at the sight of suffering. But the sense of humour, which is needed for a joke of any kind, is totally absent, possibly because the whole working life of a thorough savage is occupied with the tasks of procuring food and guarding himself from violence. He perpetuates no practical jokes because he has not yet attained the intellectual power of comprehending them (Henty (ed.), n.d., p. 111).

Wallace, on the other hand, concludes that this very concern with violence which is supposed to characterise savage life is what contributes to the sense of humour of the savage. When Sanders finds his bed in a native village sewn with poisoned spikes he puts it down to the 'grim sense of humour' of the native (Wallace, 1912, p. 130).

There is a consistency in all these representations, which, despite the idiosyncrasies of individual authors, reveals a common core of ideas, which at the time might have seemed to be 'given' and inevitable but which seem, from a later vantage point, to be culturally conditioned. This common core can be recognised even when individual authors add personal details to the stereotype.

Greene adds to the usual stereotypes of faithfulness and super-stition more particular ones: that natives can't make logical short cuts (Greene, L. P., 1935a, p. 21), that savage people and jungle beasts alike have an ability to sleep at will (ibid., p. 35), that natives have cunning infantile minds (ibid., p. 61), that they are fatalistic (ibid., p. 127), and have a sixth sense (ibid., p. 171). Likewise, Buchan mentions in passing that 'a Kaffir cannot wink' (Buchan, 1910, p. 127), his skin is 'insensible to pain' (ibid., p. 117)[8] (proved by a Zulu standing on red-hot iron), he is always 'mortally afraid of a white man's dog' (ibid., p. 152), and his thought processes involve 'strange, twisted reasoning' (ibid., p. 216). And Wallace describes the natives Sanders encounters as 'having the gift which every native possesses of pigeon-holing his grievances' (Wallace, 1912, p. 54), as having a liking for forbidden fruit (ibid., p. 127), a pen-chant for triviality (Wallace, 1911, p. 145), a prescience 'which is every aboriginee's birthright' (ibid., p. 154), and a sense of telepathy (ibid., p. 179).

Kipling in 'The Gate of 100 Sorrows' mentions in passing, in an authoritative tone, that opium affects yellow and white men differ-ently: 'The yellow man is made different, opium doesn't tell on him scarcely at all; but white and black suffer a great deal' (Kipling, 1888, p. 279). In 'Beyond the Pale', while admitting that much that is written of 'oriental passion' is exaggerated, he affirms that it really does exist and that, when an Englishman finds it, 'it is quite as start-ling as any passion in his own proper life' (1888, p. 176).

If such cultural differences can be put down to racial heritage, then even cannibalism, supposedly one of the greatest distinctions between a gentleman and a savage, can be cited as a hereditary characteristic of inferior races. The Englishman, it is assumed, doesn't practise it because his instincts, passed down to him through his race, revolt against it. Thus Tarzan, with no cultural training in an English environment, nevertheless has inherited the instinct which tells him that the cannibal breaks a natural law: 'Hereditary instincts, ages old, usurped the function of his untaught mind and saved him from transgressing a world-wide law of whose very existence he was ignorant' (Burroughs, 1917, p. 78). The natives, of course, have no such inhibitions and proceed to break natural law with relish, revelling in meals of human flesh. Sanders, too, believes that it is unnatural to eat one's own kind and tells the cannibalistic N'gombi, 'Only hyenas and crocodiles eat their own kind' (Wallace,

1911, p. 142). Haggard uses the threat of cannibalism to spice the adventures of the travellers in *She*, where the enlightened ruler punishes his people for reverting to such decadent habits. Sitting at a feast and casually observing a row of earthenware pots beside them, they suddenly notice that one is being heated in the fire and realise that these are 'The people who place [red-hot] pots upon the heads of strangers' to cook them ready for eating (Haggard, 1887c, p. 85). That cannibalism is natural to primitive people is implied by Gilson in a description that links it with their physical appearance. They are 'bestial, gorilla-like creatures, with exceptionally powerful jaws and teeth like fangs, hunting human flesh' (Gilson, 1919, pp. 108, 123, 157).

Some anthropological writers were less prone to attribute cannibalism so liberally to primitive peoples. T. Winterbottom, who wrote enlightened ethnographies on West Africa at the beginning of the century, tried to check the myth about the prevalence of cannibalism. He concluded that 'aside from ritual cannibalism, there was not a single authentic account by a reliable witness!' (quoted in Curtin, 1965, p. 210). The prevalence of the myth arose in fact because most Africans 'appear struck with horror when questioned individually on the subject, though at the same time they make no scruple of accusing other nations at a distance and whom they barely know by name, of cannibalism' (quoted in Lienhardt, 1964, p. 11).[9] This is borne out by a writer in Tierra del Fuego who followed up the accounts of cannibalism there brought back by Darwin's expedition. He suggests that the natives 'started to give the answers they thought were expected':

> We are told they described, with much detail, how the
> Fuegians ate their enemies killed in battle and, when there were
> no more such victims, devoured their old women. When asked
> if they ate dogs when hungry, they said they did not, as dogs
> were useful for catching otter, whereas old women were of no
> use at all (ibid.).

Some accounts suggest the natives on the coast of Africa were frightened of their inland brothers and really believed they practised cannibalism, while others acknowledge that they were merely trying to terrify the white traveller. Whatever cannibalism may have been practised, it was not on the scale suggested by popular fiction and was not the inherent feature of primitive life suggested by accounts of savage hordes seeking human flesh and dancing gleefully round boiling pots.

Popular mass-produced literature inevitably describes minor characters in 'flat' terms without 'rounding out' the details of their personalities, but this practice was supported at the turn of the century by the way the anthropologists themselves proceeded. Thus the writer could refer in passing, with a background of 'scientific' authority, to primitive people's inherent 'laziness', 'childishness' or 'cruelty' or to the white man's 'honour', 'intelligence' or 'democratic principles' as though these features were 'natural', given by racial background and inheritance to all members of a particular race. These descriptions failed to disturb the reader's preconceptions either of primitive life or of English character. The distinction that they drew between races provided an intellectual and emotional context which determined how many of the actions of different races, with regard to each other, were represented. These national distinctions are made to seem inevitable and permanent because they were the product of racial inheritance and were passed on 'in the blood'. They are given wider credence and publicity in their casual acceptance as facts by writers of popular fiction. The collective representations of other cultures are strengthened through the medium of popular fiction but grounded in the scholarship of the period.

Chapter 4

Evolution and race in popular literature: hierarchy and racial theory

The attribution of a 'character' to the different races of mankind was not merely a means of static classification – it was used to determine the place, even the value, of each race in a universal hierarchy. E. B. Tylor, for instance, the 'father of English anthropology', uses 'internal' criteria of classification to determine the degree of advance of a particular culture:

> The principal criteria of classification are the absence or presence, high or low development, of the industrial arts . . . the extent of scientific knowledge, the definiteness of religious belief and ceremony, the degree of social and political organisation and so forth (Tylor, 1865, pp. 23–5).

Stocking quotes a writer in the *Contemporary Review* who argued against the application of scientific principles to these cultural aspects of life: 'Spiritual progress is a very different thing from material and can only be comprehended by the light of very different laws, which lie beyond the jurisdiction of science' (Stocking, 1968, p. 78). Stocking claims that E. B. Tylor's *Primitive Culture* was written to refute such arguments and to show that natural laws could be applied to cultural as well as material development. By showing the evolution of such cultural phenomena as religious belief, Tylor hoped to demonstrate that a 'Science of Man' was possible and he claimed that the ethnographer could test 'progress' more precisely than the naturalist could:

> He [the naturalist] cannot know whether a theory of development from species to species is a record of transitions which actually took place or a mere ideal scheme serviceable in the classification of species, whose origin was really independent. But among ethnographers there is no such question as to the possibilities of species of implements or habits or beliefs being developed one out of another (Tylor, 1871, pp. 14–15).

It was in the light of this that the items in the Pitt Rivers Museum, Oxford, were arranged. General Pitt Rivers was interested in the history and development of firearms, and it had occurred to him 'that this sort of evolutionary progress might, with advantage, be studied not only in all kinds of weapons but also in other arts and industries and he enlarged the scope of his private collection accordingly'. When he presented his collection to a museum he ordained that the specimens be laid out 'so as to trace, as far as practicable, the succession of ideas by which the minds of men in a primitive condition of culture have progressed from the simple to the complex and from the homogeneous to the heterogeneous' (*The Origin and Development of the Pitt Rivers Museum*, pp. 2–3).

It was assumed that the religion and beliefs of a whole race could be studied as a unit, evolving in sophistication and complexity in the same way as firearms and material culture had evolved. So the ethnographer not only studies culture; he also uses the details of a people's cultural life as evidence for their place in the hierarchy of mankind. Frazer, in *The Golden Bough* (1890), postulated a development of thought from magic, through religion to science, which corresponded to the development from 'primitive' to 'civilised'. And Spencer, even before Darwin applied the principle of evolution to natural species, used an evolutionary approach to mental phenomena. The basis for Pitt Rivers's ideas was provided by Spencer's theory that the whole universe, including human societies went 'through a process of increasing differentiation on the one hand and increasing integration on the other. The unevolved structure was internally homogeneous . . . the evolved was heterogeneous' (Goldthorpe, 1969, p. 78).

The notion of a universal hierarchy had been inherited, as we earlier noted, from the medieval concept of the Great Chain of

Being. Margaret Hodgen points out how the architectonic framework of the chain became a chronological one in the late nineteenth century. The static hierarchy gave way to a time sequence in which, while everything was still given its appropriate category, it was now held that the categories developed from each other in chronological order. This evolutionary structure was given scientific support by Darwin's biological discoveries; the various races could now be given their place in the chain of development that ultimately led to European 'civilised' man. For when nineteenth-century biologists rejected the principle of fixity of species implicit in the theory of the Great Chain, they retained the notion of hierarchy. Andrew Lyons in 'The Genesis of Scientific Racism' (*Journal of the Anthropological Society of Oxford*, vol. 1, no. 2, 1970, p. 99) refers to Winthrope Jordan's observation on this: 'the popularity of the concept of the Chain in the eighteenth century derived in large measure from its capacity to universalise the principle of hierarchy' (Jordan, 1969, p. 228), and Godfrey Lienhardt shows how this principle was still important in the social life of nineteenth-century England:

> They [ethnographers] were themselves reared in a strongly
> hierarchical society, taking for granted great and seemingly
> fixed distinctions of rank, wealth and privilege and, in surveying
> the peoples of the world, they saw them also as hierarchically
> arranged in a scheme of evolution or creation in which
> 'higher' and 'lower' races, 'higher' and 'lower' customs and
> beliefs formed a gradation between the apelike and godlike
> or the infant and the adult in Man (Lienhardt, 1964, p. 7).

In studying other cultures, the unit studied was that of 'race'. The criteria for classifying this unit involved both 'internal' (intellectual and moral) and 'external' (physical) features on the assumption that there was some natural link between them; and the main object of this classification was to place the racial unit in a chronological hierarchy where the top place had been reserved for the student himself.

The English popular writers here discussed gave imaginative life to these theories by presenting them through vivid characters and exciting adventures. The exploits of Allan Quatermain, Tarzan and Sanders, when they confront such native characters as Umslopogaas and Bosambo, bring home to the general public what such theories meant 'on the ground', in the everyday lives of those Englishmen who actually met 'primitive people'. And the writers, drawing upon 'scientific' information in the creation of native characters, pay attention not only to their race but to their place in the hierarchy, according to such criteria as religious development, intelligence and artistic skill.

H. Rider Haggard follows closely the anthropological model. Having discussed Zu-Vendi ethnography in considerable detail in *Allan Quatermain*, he turns to the question whether they are 'a civilised or a barbarous people'. He discovers, as Tylor did,[1] that a culture may be 'advanced' in one respect and 'backward' in another, so which feature is used as a criterion for 'civilisation' determines what rank on the scale the culture is promoted to.

First, he takes art as the criterion and finds:

> . . . in some branches of art they have attained the very highest
> proficiency. Take, for instance, their building and statuary.
> I do not think that the latter can be equalled either in beauty
> or imaginative power anywhere in the world. . . . But, on the
> other hand, they are totally ignorant of many other arts
> (Haggard, 1887a, p. 156).

They cannot make glass, their crockery is rather primitive, 'they know nothing about steam, electricity or gunpowder'. Haggard is undecided where to place them on the scale, since they are good at some things and bad at others. As for their religion, he is more sure of his ground and more prepared to ascribe them a place on the strength of it:

> As regards their religion, it is a natural one for imaginative
> people who know no better, and might therefore be expected
> to turn to the sun and worship him as the all-Father, but it
> cannot be justly called elevating or spiritual. It is true that they
> do sometimes speak of the sun as 'the garment of the spirit'
> but it is a vague term and what they really adore is the fiery
> orb himself (ibid., p. 157).

Since spirituality and a belief in the after-life are requisites for an 'advanced' religion, high on the scale, he is forced to ascribe them a lower place: 'So, on the whole, I cannot say that I consider this sun-worship as a religion indicative of a civilised people, however magnificent and imposing its ritual' (ibid.).

We shall see later (Chapter 7) how the notion of the hierarchy and of stages of development from primitive to civilised were applied to comparative religion. Frazer, for instance, summarises Robertson Smith's theory that the Christian religion developed out of, and was foreshadowed by, primitive ones in similar terms to Haggard's assertion that the mark of civilised religion is the degree of spirituality, of ethical content: 'It was foreshadowed, indeed, in a very crude and materialistic form and without any of those ethical ideas which the Christian doctrine of Atonement derives from a profounder sense of sin and divine justice' (Frazer, 1927, p. 289). One criterion by which a society's place on the scale was to be decided was thus the 'ethical' and 'profound' character of its religion, which the observer could judge merely by watching a ceremony and without a knowledge of the language.

Another criterion was skill in building, which again could easily be observed by the traveller and which, again, depended on subjective and ethnocentric standards. The Flower Temple of the Zu-Vendi is so magnificent that Quatermain feels 'that even highly civilised art might learn something from the Zu-Vendi masterpieces' (Haggard, 1887a, p. 34). The temple is used, however, for bloody human sacrifice and the travellers are nearly dropped through a trap-door there into a raging furnace, and so its use qualifies its value as evidence for high development.

The classification of races in terms of artistic skill is used in *The Tragedy of the Korosko* to emphasise the low position of 'Mohammedans' in the scale. The British are in Egypt to protect its artistic treasure from the Dervish hordes, claims Colonel Cochrane, for:

> There is no iconoclast in the world like an extreme Mohammedan.
> Last time they overran this country they burned the
> Alexandrian library. You know that all representations of the
> human features are against the letter of the Koran. A statue
> is always an irreligious object in their eyes. What do these
> fellows care for the sentiment of Europe? The more they could
> offend it, the more delighted they would be – down would go
> the Sphinx, the Colossi, the Statues of Abou-Simbel (Doyle,
> 1898, p. 34).

Thus, the Mohammedan objection to the depiction of the human form and to images of any kind (despite their other contributions to art) argues that they must be barbarous savages and be placed low on the scale. Likewise, the Zu-Vendi ability to build palaces enabled Haggard to raise them a few rungs on the ladder, while Kipling judges how low the Indian border tribes are by the fact that they have not 'yet produced a poet' (Kipling, 1888, p. 78).

Another criterion, especially popular in fiction, seems to be military organisation and physical strength, with overtones of the noble savage. In Haggard the Zulu race and the Masai are considered superior to the Hottentots and Bushmen and so regard themselves. Bertram Mitford's Zulu characters of the same period likewise assert that faith in their physical superiority which fits so neatly with European ideas of a universal hierarchy. They assume it to be natural that they will conquer the other tribes in their country and the Zulu witch-doctor, who tells the story in *The King's Assegai* (Mitford, 1894a), scorns the hill dwellers and cannibals as much as do the white men. To him the cave dwellers' lives seem as 'nasty, brutish and short' as Hobbes would have described them, even to the details. They have dirty camps in contrast with the order and cleanliness of a Zulu kraal, and their wizened physique, 'short and broad with crafty faces', compares unfavourably with the majesty of the Zulu warrior. Moreover, the Baputi fire poisoned arrows and then retire to the safety of caves, a procedure the Zulus consider 'unmanly' in comparison with their own open warfare.

Thus examples of ethnocentricism among primitive peoples are used to support the ethnocentricism of the European. And the criterion of physical prowess, which fits so well with European concepts of chivalry and which the Zulus apply to their neighbours, is described as though the Zulus too subscribed to European concepts of social evolution, the Great Chain and a universal hierarchy.

Other writers introduce more unusual criteria, demonstrating how deeply the principle of social evolution permeated Victorian thought. One quaint example comes from the article 'Some Harmless Practical Jokes' already quoted. Though not concerned with primitive man at all, but with recording a few of the best practical jokes that an 'old Oxonian' can remember from his Oxford days, the author nevertheless draws on the hierarchy theme to widen the scope of the enquiry:

> It is a remarkable fact that Practical Jokes belong only to intermediate stages of civilisation. The English gentleman is above it and the savage intellectually incapable. Likewise, children at school move into a practical joke stage and then mature out of it. Boys, who are necessarily but partially

reclaimed savages – I hope that my young readers will pardon
me for these observations, which I could prove to be true if
time and space were afforded – are always given to such practical
joking. . . . When lads leave school to go to college, they
cannot be expected to change their natures so entirely that the
love of practical jokes is altogether eradicated. It still exists,
though it is of a milder nature, because they have advanced a
step in civilisation (Henty (ed.), n.d., pp. 111–12).

All these criteria tended to have some consistency, despite the
idiosyncrasies of particular authors, since the criteria were those of
Victorian society. Similarly, the interest in anthropology at the turn
of the century meant that writers, as well as inventing their own
fictitious tribes, frequently represented the same few actual peoples
who were being used in scientific circles as examples of how the
theory of hierarchy could be applied. Thus the Bushmen, the Hottentots, Pygmies and the Zulus, to take a few examples now to be
discussed, constantly recur in popular fiction as representatives of
various high and low stages on the scale.

Gilson, for instance, writing an exciting adventure tale about
Africa and Pygmies, feels obliged to give some of their history and
to decide their degree of progress. They are, he writes, the aboriginal
inhabitants of the Continent:

They were driven from the grasslands by the victorious Kaffirs
who spread across Africa from the Great Lakes to the West
Coast centuries ago. The dwarfs were, thus, split up into two
distinct families, namely the Bushmen of the Kalahari Desert
and the Pygmies of the Upper Congo. Both these races are of a
very primitive order of intelligence, in physical feature bearing a
greater resemblance to monkeys than to men (Gilson, 1919, p. 16).

Conjectural history is thus used yet again to claim that the most
primeval stage of human development is still to be found among some
tribes in Africa whose history has stood still for thousands of years
and who hence reveal man's proximity to the monkey.

By linking the pygmies with the bushmen of the Kalahari, Gilson
supports the claims made by other popular writers, such as Bertram
Mitford and John Buchan, and based on the then current ethnographic theory that the bushmen were the most primeval race in
Africa. But he asserts that one of the pygmy tribes with which his

book is concerned, the Batwa, 'are even lower in the scale of humanity than the bushmen' (ibid., p. 17). His evidence involves the inevitable value-judgments:

> They dispense altogether with clothing. Their features are hideous and their bodies so covered with hair that they have frequently been taken for a tribe of intelligent chimpanzees. . . . They are passionate, vindictive, jealous and without ties of affection. They have no religion and apparently no sense of honour. Only those who know the Batwa pygmies at their worst can realise that, sometimes, man is very little above the beasts (ibid., p. 18).

And their language, to introduce another criterion often used, is 'just about as comprehensible as the jabbering of apes' (ibid., p. 20).

The adventurers are guided by a pygmy who has been captured and brought to London to be measured, weighed and inspected by the Royal Academy. They take him through the jungle on the end of a rope since he is 'no more to be trusted than a fox' (ibid., p. 44). The true nature of the pygmy 'is that of the wild animal', cunning and alert (ibid., p. 49). Realising that the pygmy has all these characteristics because he is at such an early stage of evolution, the Englishmen appreciate the value of their civilisation: 'As Guy Kingston regarded this little creature who linked the Present with the world of ten thousand years ago, he could not but be moved at the great strides which civilisation has made' (ibid., p. 35). The criteria by which these strides are judged are, of course, those of Victorian England. Lack of clothing, honour, religion and language are all means of determining the 'advances' a society has made.

Gilson, like many popular writers, derived his 'facts' and many of the opinions behind them from the travellers' tales of the day, in this case from the books of Stanley.[2] Stanley, in fact, had not had good relations with the pygmies, and described them as 'malicious dwarfs' (Stanley, 1893, vol. 2, ch. 23). This attitude colours much of Gilson's account. A. B. Lloyd, on the other hand, a missionary whose exploits among the pygmies were recounted in *In Dwarf Land and Cannibal Country* (1899), got on very well with the pygmies and described them as friendly, intelligent and 'blessed' with certain basic religious ideas. This divergence demonstrates how far 'objective' accounts of primitive people were determined by the particular experience and the character of the observer.

Here, again, the general climate of scientific opinion had accustomed readers and writers of fiction to a framework of thought which served to justify their own ethnocentricism. It was a commonplace to see the Bushmen as missing links in the evolutionary chain and to place them low in the scale. By bringing in details of pygmy history, migrations and primeval origins and by mentioning a reputable traveller's account, Gilson hopes to add a thoughtful element to the tale of adventure. Kingston, 'though essentially a man of action, was by no means of a thoughtless disposition' (Gilson, 1919, p. 75). Likewise, Allan Quatermain condemns the normal run of hunters who take no trouble about the way of life of the people they meet, and praises those 'who collect traditions from the natives and try to make out a little piece of the history of this dark land' (Haggard, 1885, p. 19). Haggard attempts to make his stories more authentic by occasional footnotes which explain a native custom, citing actual travellers from whom he has borrowed the details of the ethnography.[3]

John Buchan, too, took a 'serious' interest in ethnography and wrote a book aimed at students of South Africa called *The African Colony* (1909). He describes the Bushman as 'one of the lowest of created types' still living in the Stone Age and prevented from advancing by the continual influx of 'superior' races. The Bushman was a kinsman of the pygmies of central Africa, a miserable fellow, 'troglodyte, small, emaciated, with protruding chest and spindle legs', who lived by primitive hunting, 'had no social organisation and whose only skill is following spoor and a rudimentary cave art.'[4]

Bertram Mitford echoes Buchan's sentiments in his novels of South Africa. The Bushman is 'no more than half ape', a 'descendant of the baboons' (Mitford, 1891, p. 199). When a Bushman kills a white man's wife, the English hero slowly burns him to death, cuts off his ears and revels in the torture. The white community are quite unperturbed at this 'rough justice'. They are concerned far more with an accusation of bigamy levelled against the Englishman. The cave in which he performs the torture is that of a Bushman and there are frescoes on the walls, 'repulsive, grotesque, obscene, the handiwork in bygone ages of the most primitive race in the world, now nearly extinct, the wild Bushman' (ibid., p. 204). The 'poverty' of their art and their physical resemblance to monkeys rank the Bushmen so low that the English need not regard them as human beings at all.

The Hottentot is little higher and Buchan believes that, as the Bushman died out, his blood mixed with the Hottentot. Since they had a tribal organisation and a certain domesticity, the Hottentots could even become 'house servants and herdsmen for the Dutch', whereas the Bushman had been entirely 'untameable' (Buchan, 1909, p. 12). But this criterion, the degree of domesticity, did not raise the Hottentot very high and he was 'bound to die out in the mixture of incoming races', 'fated to prepare the way for his successors' (ibid., p. 13). This application of the notion of 'survival of the fittest' to whole races justified the colonisers in taking over the lands of 'inferior', less 'fit' peoples. Similarly the white settlers in Australia defended their annihilation of the aboriginal by arguing that weaker races must inevitably give way to stronger.

This theme obviously provides scope for exciting battles in fiction in which the racial model is taken for granted. An imaginative exploitation is presented by Conan Doyle in *The Lost World*. He describes a group of twentieth-century adventurers going to the aid of men at an earlier stage of development as they struggle for survival. Once the battle against the apes has been won, then 'at last man was to be supreme and the man-beast to find forever his allotted place' (Doyle, 1912, p. 179). Professor Challenger comments on the significance of the struggle:

> We have been privileged to be present at one of the typical decisive battles of history, the battles which have determined the fate of the world. What, my friends, is the conquest of one nation by another? It is meaningless. Each produces the same result. But those fierce fights, when in the dawn of the ages the cave-dwellers held their own against the tiger-folk, or the elephants first found they had a master, those were the real conquests – the victories that count. . . . Now upon this plateau the future must ever be for man (ibid.).

The themes of the survival of the fittest and social evolution were made exciting by fictional personalities who displayed dramatically the superiority of the Englishman over primitive peoples. Likewise, Buchan's account of the failure of some races to win the struggle and the criteria used in popular fiction to 'prove' how low on the scale such races were helped to give popular currency to the theories of science. Edgar Rice Burroughs again presents his belief in progress in a 'set-piece' of jungle prose. Describing the dance of the apes, he suggests that it represents the origin of more sophisticated modern institutions:

> From this primitive function has arisen, unquestionably, all the forms and ceremonials of modern Church and State, for through all the countless ages, back beyond the last uttermost ramparts of dawning humanity, our fierce hairy forbears danced out the rites of the Dum-Dum to the sound of their earthen drums, beneath the bright light of a tropical moon in the depth of a mighty jungle which stands unchanged today as it stood on that long-forgotten night in the dim, unthinkable vistas of the long-dead past, when our first shaggy ancestor swung from a swaying bough and dropped lightly on the turf of the first meeting-place (Burroughs, 1917, p. 57).

Thus the possibility of progress is extended to the ape, and the details of evolution transformed from scientific theory to colourful fiction. Tarzan himself demonstrates the process of evolution in speeded-up form, advancing quickly as he grows up from the state of early ape to that of nineteenth-century European man. He finds a book and teaches himself to read: 'Tarzan of the apes, little primitive man, presented a picture filled at once with pathos and promise – an allegorical figure of the primordial groping through the black night of ignorance towards the first light of learning' (ibid., p. 53).

But if most Victorians accepted that the inferiority of the primitive was due to his representing an earlier stage of that progress so evident in English life, others held that the 'primitive' was inferior because he had degenerated from a previous higher state:

> The principal opponents of the philosophy of universal progress (for such it was, rather than a scientific theory) grounded their opinions partly in observation and partly in theological orthodoxy. Their most vocal representatives were Archbishop Whately of Dublin and the Duke of Argyll, who held that the original condition of man had been 'higher' than that of many living primitive peoples of the time, some of whom must, therefore, have degenerated when driven into harsh environments and now lacked the means or motive for independent self-improvement (Lienhardt, 1964, p. 9).

This theory was supported by accounts of primitive peoples living

on the site of some ruined city built by people with superior technology (and 'culture'):

> It was pointed out, for instance, that in Egypt, where masonry,
> goldsmith's work, weaving and other arts had once reached an
> extraordinary level of development, modern Egyptians were
> living in a condition of semi-barbarism, unable to reproduce
> the work of their forefathers (Hodgen, 1936, p. 19).

Such examples were used to disprove the theory of progress by
showing that some savages were in a condition inferior to that of
their ancestors and that 'high civilisation is as difficult to keep as
. . . to gain'. A vivid example was revealed by the ruins of Zimbabwe
in Rhodesia. This ancient stone city, it was supposed, required a
technology and artistic skill superior to that evident among the tribes
living there when it was discovered in the late nineteenth century.
So scholars argued whether a superior race, such as the Phoenicians,
had built it and then left the area, or whether the natives themselves
had constructed it but then degenerated to their present level.

In John Buchan's South African adventure story this conflict is
used to heighten the tension created by the possibility of a native
uprising. If natives had once been well enough organised to build
such a city, then they might be organised again, under a strong ruler,
and drive the British out. Such are the fears of Wardlaw, a school-
master in Buchan's novel:

> 'You know that the old ruins in Rhodesia, called Zimbabwe,
> were long believed to be Phoenician in origin. I have a book
> here which tells all about them. But now it is believed that
> they were built by natives. I maintain that the men who could
> erect piles like that', and he showed me a picture, 'were something
> more than petty chiefs' (Buchan, 1910, p. 57).

Whether the natives had degenerated or still had the potential of
their ancestors thus became an important political factor.

Rider Haggard, who left South Africa before the discovery of
Zimbabwe, but who had heard rumours of its existence, uses the
situation in a number of his novels. In *She* the Amahagger live just
across the plain from the ancient ruined city of Kor. The mounds of
masonry 'the wise said had once been houses wherein men dwelt
and it was suggested that the Amahagger were descended from these
men' (Haggard, 1887c, p. 77). Haggard uses the theme to create a

sense of mystery and awe around the city still inhabited by 'She-who-must-be-obeyed':

> I can only suppose that these cuttings and the vast caves that
> have been hollowed out of the rocks they pierced were the
> State undertakings of the people of Kor, who lived here in the
> dim, lost age of the world, and that, as in the case of the
> Egyptian monuments, they were executed by the labour of tens
> of thousands of captives, carried on through an indefinite
> number of centuries. But who were the people? (ibid., p. 107).

Since She herself was there when Kor was built, this description gives depth to accounts of her age and the nature of her life all those years, while the relation of these early builders to the present-day Amahagger lends an air of historical authenticity. She herself is concerned with scholarship, and tells the travellers of the greatness of the builders of Kor and how they were nearly destroyed in a pestilence. A few survived and they intermarried with Arabs and barbarians, so that 'the race of the Amahagger that is now is a bastard brood of the mighty sons of Kor and behold it dwelleth in the tombs with its fathers' bones' (ibid., p. 149).

This nostalgia for the glory of her earlier life and love, which has been the driving force of her immortality over 2,000 years and which gives the book the haunting quality that made it so popular, is rendered in terms of the contrast between the original inhabitants of Kor and their present-day descendants. The theme of degeneration is thus used to colour a romantic tale and to reinforce its claims to scholarship.

Charles Kingsley, a minister of religion as well as a popular writer, uses the theme with as much imagination but more moral purpose. If a society had degenerated it is because of their weak morality – likewise if a society has progressed, as nineteenth-century England so obviously had, it is because of a strong moral code. Thus Tom, the young sweep who degenerated into a water baby, has to seek regeneration through good deeds, learning much about other orders of life as he does so. He discovers, while in the river, that salmon don't like trout because 'a great many years ago they were just like us' but degenerated and

> grew lazy, cowardly and greedy. . . . No enemies are so bitter
> against each other as those who are of the same race. A salmon

> looks on a trout as some great folks look on some little folks,
> as something just too much like himself to be tolerated
> (Kingsley, 1863, p. 141).

In the same way, some Victorian men regarded the 'inferior' races of the world as having degenerated from a higher state like theirs.

In one of Tom's adventures the possibility of degeneration, hinted at by the trout, is linked to the Victorian moral code as a warning to those who break it. He is shown a book about the Doasyoulikes. As their name suggests, they are a lazy, incompetent people, whose decline is followed by turning the pages of the book in 500-year stages. At first they live a reasonably European existence until a volcano, whose warnings they have ignored, smothers many of them. Those who escape are too lazy to work the land and 'live miserably on roots and nuts and all the weakly little children had great stomachs and then died. "Why", said Tom, "They are no better than savages" ' (ibid., p. 269). Thus the pictures of 'savage' man brought back to England in exactly these terms are used to confirm him in his lowly position on the moral as well as the cultural scale.[5] The degeneration of the Doasyoulikes continues and only those most able to adapt themselves survive. Another 500 years finds them living in trees and growing large toes for the purpose. They forget how to use language and become like apes, 'all by doing only what they like'.

Man need not degenerate however – he may also progress, provided he adheres to Victorian ethics. Tom is told that, if water babies amend their thoughts, 'then they may grow back into land babies, with bigger brains and lose their tails and, after that, perhaps, into grown men' (ibid., p. 274). By the same criterion, savage tribes, however 'wicked' they may be, can improve if they make the effort, 'and some folks can't help hoping, with Bishop Butler, that they might have another chance to make things fair and even somewhere, somewhen, somehow' (ibid., p. 387). By following Christian ethics, we will progress 'up' the evolutionary scale, but if we are sinful and lazy, like the savages, then we will degenerate.

Most Victorian writers, however, believed in progress rather than degeneration. One of the main opponents of degeneration was Tylor, whose theory of 'Survivals' was largely formulated in order to undermine it. The discovery of the antiquity of man, together with the archaeological uncovering of more recent cultures in Egypt and Mesopotamia and the constant flow of information on contemporary tribes at various stages of 'development', led to a realisation that many links on the chain existed contemporaneously. Thus, examples of 'earlier' forms of social custom still existing today represented 'survivals' in the same way that fossils were 'survivals' of an earlier physical stage. This notion fitted in with the growing practice of looking to history to explain the present and, where no documentary proof existed, giving a documentary value to the findings of the comparative method. This suggested that the customs of other societies could be used to fill in the gaps in our knowledge of European history, since they represented examples of an earlier stage of European development.

Hodgen notes that 'To restore faith in progress, primitive people must be shown to take their appropriate position in the developmental series' (Hodgen, 1936, p. 9). For, once their position has been decided, they enable us to map out the history of man up to the present day. The Victorians' concern with the 'missing link' grew out of this search for 'links' at all levels of the chain, and many links can be discovered by collecting 'survivals' whose significance can only be ascertained in the light of comparative ethnography:

> Insignificant, moreover, as multitudes of the facts of survival are in themselves, their study is so effective for tracing the course of historical development through which alone it is possible to understand their meaning, that it becomes a vital point of ethnographic research to gain the clearest possible insight into their nature (Tylor, 1871, p. 17).

Thus Tylor attempts to encourage field workers to look out for 'survivals', those phenomena which 'remain as proofs and examples of an older condition of culture out of which a new has been evolved' (ibid., p. 16).

If single elements of culture can survive, so too can a whole culture. Whole primitive tribes may represent survivals of stages through which European man passed many centuries ago. Conan Doyle's 'Lost World' is a survival of the natural and cultural features of life long since. According to the advertisement in a recent edition, the book was the first of a wave of such accounts of survivals:

> On a high plateau in S. America a group of explorer-scientists led by the famous Professor Challenger, discover a huge

tropical marsh surviving from prehistoric times, inhabited by gigantic reptiles and the grotesque half-ape forerunners of man. . . . *The Lost World* was the first of the full-length novels of this kind (*The Lost World*, John Murray edn, 1964).

In their different ways, Haggard's lost cities and civilisations in Kor and the Heart of the World and D. H. Lawrence's Aztec descendants in Mexico made use of the same theme. But, if the doctrine of survivals was used to oppose the degenerationist school and to reaffirm faith in progress by putting primitive peoples in their 'appropriate position in the developmental series', it was starting from the same premises: that primitive man was inferior and that he could be classified according to ethnocentric criteria. It seemed hardly to matter why primitive man was inferior, since both sides accepted that he was. Johnson pointed out that, since criteria for perfectibility were variable, it was futile to oppose evolution and degeneration as Tylor and Whately had done (Johnson, 1927, p. 37). The same body of knowledge was being used by both sides of the argument to prove theories that were opposed in detail but based on the same terms of reference; and the information pouring in from the growing Empire was simply being incorporated into a European philosophic discussion based on European values. Likewise, the arguments of polygenists, and of whether races were species or varieties, started from the same fundamental assumptions about the inferiority of primitive man. Popular fiction, in presenting the different aspects of the arguments in dramatic form, gave this common framework general currency, so that the terminology of nineteenth-century science, with all its implications, became a familiar part of the Victorian language.

Racial theory in literature

Since popular literature used the classification and the hierarchy of nineteenth-century science as a framework for presenting fictional accounts of primitive peoples, the word 'race', the precise definition of which was a matter of central debate among scientists, came into general use for the units into which the peoples of the world were divided. The use of 'race' involves assumptions concerning the perpetuation of groups and their characteristics through inheritance which were not carried by such words as 'nation' or 'peoples':

When the Victorian epigoni of Condorcet and Adam Ferguson
used the adjectives 'savage' and 'barbarous' or 'uncivilised' the
connotations were no longer what they had been before 1800.
Along with 'primitive' and 'lower', these terms were now
applied to 'races' rather than 'nations' or 'peoples' and the
imputation of inferiority, although still in the first instance
cultural, was now, in most cases at least, implicitly organic as
well (Stocking, 1968, pp. 121–2).

The differences between peoples, emphasised by much of the
reporting, were made to seem even more extreme, fundamental and
permanent by being put down to race, to inheritance through fixed
groups.

Indeed, some writers believed that these groups were so fixed as
to be immutable. The different races were different species, they had
been created at different times, could not interbreed and were
permanently distinguished from each other. In 1774 Lord Kames, a
prominent 'polygenist' spokesman, published *Sketches of the History
of Man*, positing the tower of Babel as the origin of the differences
between races and thus claimed biblical authority for classifying
races as species. But perhaps the most influential exposition of the
doctrine came from Robert Knox, in a series of lectures in 1850
entitled *The Races of Man*. He believed that 'race or hereditary
descent is everything'. Literature, science and art are all expressions
of racial character and the course of history is determined by racial
antagonism and war. To support this contention he used the 'fact'
that a cross-breed could not survive in competition with 'pure' races.
If racial interbreeding did produce progeny, it might be fertile for
one or two generations, but would then revert to one or other of the
'pure' races.

Edward Long, a resident of Jamaica in the late eighteenth century,
was able to use such polygenist theory to support an intense ethnocentricism. He believed the Africans, imported to the island to work
the plantations, were 'brutish, ignorant, idle' and inferior in 'faculties
of mind' and that these qualities were the permanent mark of their
species. The criterion for a species was held to be that it cannot
produce fertile offspring when mating with another species, and Long
maintained that 'mulattoes', the offspring of white and black on the
island, were infertile. Having thus 'proved' that white and black were
different species, he divided 'genus homo' into three species –

Europeans and similar people, Negroes and 'orang-outangs'. Curtin claims that these ideas received wide support and he shows how they were still effective twenty years later when used by Charles White to emphasise the mental inferiority of the African and the striking differences between Negro and European races (Curtin, 1965, p. 44).

Nearly 100 years later, these views were being expounded, to popular acclaim, by the then President of the Anthropological Society of London, James Hunt. He had led a group of anthropologists away from the Ethnological Society because he believed scientists should be more deeply committed to current politics and less to humanitarian pursuits, and because, as a polygenist, he disagreed with the predominantly monogenist ethnologists. He gave a paper in August 1863 to the British Academy entitled 'On the Negro's Place in Nature'. In it he claimed that the Negro was intermediate between the highest and the lowest races, there being six below him and six above; that differences between races were not only external but also internal (mental and moral); that the Negro was nearer to the ape and had a smaller brain than the European. History, he asserted, showed that the Negro cannot be improved: Negro children advance until puberty, then stop and remain mentally like children (any Negroes who had been famous and successful could be proved to have European blood); the Negro race had been what it was then from remote antiquity; there was no evidence that the Negro had degenerated from a higher civilisation; there was as good a reason for classifying the Negroes as a distinct species as for distinguishing the ass from the zebra; the Negro was inferior intellectually to the European and better off under his guidance; and the analogies were more frequent between the Negro and the ape than between the European and the ape.

This interpretation of the scientific framework of racial studies provided a basis for many who still defended slavery and later for colonialism and the 'white man's burden'. Some speakers at the meeting disagreed with Hunt, some thought the Negro at least had the potential to 'improve', some quoted Negroes who had 'succeeded'. Most agreed with him and, like Winwood Reade, argued the economic benefits of slavery to the white man and the moral benefits to the Negro. It was in their own interests to keep them in chains. But everyone accepted Hunt's terms of reference: that the racial model was the most valuable for understanding society.

Most of the leading naturalists, however, had been monogenists, believing in only one Creation and in the mutability of species. Races could interbreed and had not been created separately. Prichard based his monogenism on the Mosaic theory of creation. Since the world was only about 7,000 years old,[6] cultural changes had to affect physique very quickly for there to be such variations as were evident in the world. 'Physical structure was, thus, highly malleable' (Banton, 1967, p. 28). The undermining of the authority of the Bible and, in particular, the discoveries of archaeologists who claimed a much longer history for the world, damaged this part of Prichard's argument. As Curtin observes: 'While it [the 'Darwinian revolution'] neither confirmed nor denied the pre-Darwinian racial theories, its consequences were to be far more disastrous to the supporters of Christian and anti-racist monogenists than to their opponents' (Curtin, 1965, pp. 363–4).

But the monogenists too had leant support to the racist elements of polygenist thought – Linnaeus, Blumenbach, Buffon, Kant, Cuvier and Camper were all monogenists, but they tended to draw such strong distinctions between races that the races might just as well have been created separately. These monogenists classified races in a hierarchy, confused external and internal criteria and were divided as to whether races were species or varieties. The monogeny versus polygeny debate, which aroused such emotions at the time, merely gave publicity to assumptions shared by both sides with regard to 'primitive' peoples.

Darwin's *Origin of Species*, while undermining monogenist faith in the Bible on the one hand and polygenist belief in separate creations on the other, afforded support primarily to the racist ideas of the polygenists. His theory pushed the formation of different races back into such a remote epoch that, to all intents and purposes, the differences between races were 'primordial'. He himself included the unit of 'race' in his evolutionary scheme and lent authoritative support to contemporary scorn for the 'lower' races:

> For my own part, I would as soon be descended from that heroic little monkey, who braved his dreaded enemy in order to save the life of his keeper, or from that old baboon who, descending from the mountains, carried away in triumph his young comrade from a crowd of astonished dogs – as from a savage who delights to torture his enemies, offers up bloody sacrifices, practises infanticide without remorse, treats his

wives like slaves, knows no decency and is haunted by the grossest superstitions (Darwin, 1871, p. 619).

Thus when Stocking writes of four major polygenist themes still to be found in post-Darwinian anthropology, we can hardly be surprised; for the attitude to 'primitive' man common to that school of thought seems to have been shared by Darwin himself. Stocking cites as surviving polygenist tenets that the cultural differences of man are a direct product of physical, racial differences; that the distinguishing physical differences between the races are virtually primordial; that the most important differences were to be found by comparing the skull and the brain; and that out of the heterogeneity of modern populations can be reconstructed 'types' which are representative of 'pure' races from whose mixture modern populations are derived (Stocking, 1968, p. 56).

These arguments underlay nearly all descriptions of alien peoples in the late nineteenth century. Nor was it merely a 'bookish' argument – the theories were hotly debated by academics and laymen alike, as the minutes of the Anthropological Society of London reveal. These minutes demonstrate how the abstractions of the scientists are expressed when they become part of the rhetoric of public debate. They are focused, at one level, on a central theme, such as slavery or the Jamaica Revolt[7] and, at a more detailed level, are reduced to concrete examples. Thus the argument about the effect of environment on character and race, which required many tomes of detailed polemics when presented as doctoral theses, could be reduced in the debating hall of the Anthropology Society of London to an individual's passing observations. Dr B. Seemann,[8] in order to show that climate influences racial characteristics, cites a concrete example: 'Cattle taken to America become so stupid that they lose the instinct of self-preservation and the trains on the American railways are obliged to be provided with cattle catchers, as the animals will not get out of the way' (*Anthropology Review*, I, vol. 1, p. xxiii). If animals deteriorate because of the American climate, so too do human beings. Bendyshe, for instance, regretted that Europeans in America were degenerating because of the climate and would soon become as low as the Red Man (*Anthropology Review*, VII, p. xxxiv).

These comments are not just *ad hoc* theories invented by travellers to account for strange phenomena, they are the considered opinions of members of a learned society, using these particular examples to reinforce commonly accepted theory. The theory precedes the 'facts'. And this process was the means by which the theories of academics were presented to a wider public. The *Popular Magazine of Anthropology*[9] which set itself up as an intermediary between science and the 'people', and the Anthropological Society of London, with its open meetings and political debates, were passing on the ideas we have been considering to a large and very interested audience.

If academics themselves resort to the technique of rhetoric, it is no surprise to find popular writers similarly reducing their ideas to exciting characterisations which simplify the ideas and render them more memorable. The writers are not necessarily consciously translating the learned into the popular (although Rider Haggard, at least, certainly had some such pretensions). They are merely dealing with their particular material in terms of a framework of thought that owed much to current scientific discussion. Academic studies are not always closely in touch with the general public (in terms of anthropology, present-day literature is often about fifty years behind), so it is of particular interest to see how much the popular writers of the turn of the century refer back, consciously or unconsciously, to the academic theories of their time. Occasionally, specific references to scientific studies can be found in the fiction. The object here is less to point these out than to demonstrate the use of general themes, to show what happens to them in the literature, and to show the subservience of empirical phenomena to the framework of thought of the observer; also, to suggest how a rigid framework could so be altered by individual writers working within it, that each work of fiction (to different degrees) not only perpetuates but also helps to change the image of 'primitive' peoples presented by the scientists.

Many of the preconceptions of nineteenth-century science may, in turn, have been influenced by contemporary politics and the mass media; but the popular fiction with which this work is considered became wide-spread only in the 1880s, after the basis of the racial model had been laid down by Blumenbach, de Gobineau and the anthropologists. So the influence of scientific ideas on this literature may more clearly be observed than the influence of the literature on science. Thus the arguments between polygenists and monogenists, whether races were species or varieties, or whether different races could successfully interbreed, and the use of the word 'race' with its scientific implications of heredity and permanence, constantly recurred in popular fiction, where they provided the theoretical background to 'descriptions' of other cultures.

The work of Charles Kingsley, for instance, attempts to answer the polygenist position by showing that Darwin's theory of evolution need not undermine faith in God, or in the basic tenets of monogeny:

> I have gradually learnt to see that it is just as noble a conception of Deity to believe that He created primal forms capable of self-development into all forms needful pro tempore and pro loco, as to believe that He required a fresh act of intervention to supply the lacuna which He Himself had made. I question whether the former be not the loftier view (Kingsley, 1857, vol. 2, p. 287).

Kingsley's opinions reached a wider audience; for he incorporated them into a work of fiction that took a long and humorous look at the implications of the discussion about Darwin, progress and race. *The Water Babies* was one of the most popular of a large number of creative works attempting to add some element of imagination to the debate, as Henkin has shown in *Darwinism in the English Novel*.

Darwin had proved that species were not fixed but could transform into each other, given the lengths of time that archaeologists and palaeontologists had discovered to be man's heritage. Kingsley takes this to its logical conclusion and proposes transformations which seem quite incredible, but which he is able to support by the same criteria:

> If there are land babies, then there may be water babies, if all else in creation can change, may not man, the crown and flower of all things, undergo some change as much more wonderful than all the rest as the Great Exhibition is more wonderful than a rabbit burrow (Kingsley, 1863, p. 18).

To many, however, the human species was not so flexible. The different races of man had been distinct for so long that it was better they should remain distinct, since the changes caused by interbreeding were detrimental. De Gobineau, envisaging the white race as a natural aristocracy, argued against its 'blood' being debased by interbreeding:

> The white race originally possessed the monopoly of beauty, intelligence and strength. By its union with other varieties,

hybrids were created, which were beautiful without strength, strong without intelligence, or, if intelligent, both weak and ugly (Gobineau, 1915 edn, p. 209).

Such theories affected the actual relations of white and black when they conflicted with the feelings of individuals 'in love' with a member of another race. And, in literature, there arises a conflict for the writer between his romantic sympathy with a pair of lovers and the racial doctrines of his society. In Rider Haggard's work, this conflict is often expressed by the arguments of the two white heroes in the adventure, the one in love with a coloured girl, the other watching from outside and seeing the problems his companion is blind to. In *King Solomon's Mines*, Good becomes involved with an attractive Zulu girl and thinks of taking her back to England with him. Haggard remarks, 'women are women the world over', as if in defence of their liaison, but Quatermain refuses to consider any marriage, since he does not believe that two races can successfully combine. He expounds the problems of taking the girl back to England and she herself acknowledges her natural inferiority and accepts that 'white can never meet black'. The problem is solved, rather facilely, by her death in an attempt to save the Englishman and, in dying, she recognises that this has saved considerable difficulty. The Zulu king agrees: 'That which flies in the air loves not to run along the ground.' One cannot expect white people to live with black (Haggard, 1885, p. 239).

In *Heart of the World*, again, the matter is treated in considerable detail and, again, the natives themselves support the racialism of the Europeans. Maya, an Indian princess, is concerned that Strickland will consider it beneath him to marry her: 'Remember, I am but an Indian girl and you are one of the white lords of the earth. Is it well that you should love me?' Strickland is prepared to love her because she is of high blood: 'You are the noblest woman that I have known and you saved my life' (Haggard, 1896, p. 176). But Ignatio, an Indian himself, thinks it would be better if Strickland separated from 'this girl who is not of his blood and colour and whose love soon or late would be his undoing' (ibid., p. 263). In this case also, the problem is solved by her death. That she could have been considered at all was due to her nobility and to the fact that she is nearly white, whereas the poor native girls who love white men in *She* and *King Solomon's Mines* have to be abandoned.

In *Allan Quatermain* the white hero does marry a native girl. But he does not bring her back to his own country. She is partly white and she is queen of a people who are not entirely 'savage' and whose potential for improvement he can exploit. She has a magnificent palace, as well built as any western work, and she is as intelligent and emancipated as many white women. There are so many such qualifications to this event as a representation of inter-racial marriage that it can be seen less as a concession to the idea of equality or a compromising of Haggard's racial views than as merely an extension of his belief in the benevolence of white rule in Africa.

Although many of Haggard's objections to inter-racial marriage are based on assumed social incompatibility between races, his treatment of cross-breeds throughout his work suggests that the 'scientific' arguments about hybrids also lie behind his objections. The villains in his stories are often the product of such a marriage, and the failure of cross-breeding can be seen in their characters. In *Heart of the World*, Jones gives up his attempt to make friends with his neighbours, 'for these men proved to be half-breeds of the lowest class, living in an atmosphere of monotonous vice' (Haggard, 1896, p. 30). Instead, he turns to Don Ignatio, a pure-blooded Indian, who considers that the purity of his blood raises him above them. When a group of half-breeds on a boat refuse to share a cabin with him, he retorts indignantly: 'As an Indian of pure blood, I was not thought fit for the company of these cross-breed curs' (ibid., p. 105). Don Pedro, the leader of the 'curs', is cast in the mould of the romantic villain. He has a room set aside in which guests can be bloodily murdered for their money as they sleep and he suffers poetic justice through the courage of an Indian servant (who is himself killed) making a temple collapse on him. Thus, the ancestral shrines of the Indian race exact their toll of this cross-breed who has attacked the descendants of the pure-blood race which built them. It is continually suggested that cross-breeds are inherently villainous and evil.

This literary expression of the scientific theories of hybrids, even those of European origins, is made explicit in *Jess*. The villain, Muller, is half English and half Boer and has inherited the worst qualities of both. Very early in the story, Silas Croft warns: 'You can deal with an Englishman and you can deal with a Boer but cross-breed dogs are bad to handle' (Haggard, 1887b, p. 38). Muller himself believes that he gets his intelligence from his English heritage and proudly asserts 'English blood is the best in the world'; but he is unable to capitalise on it because, like de Gobineau's hybrids, the blood of other races weakens the English qualities in him. His intelligence is offset by a bestial quality due to his Boer blood and to the fact that two bloods were mixed in him. Haggard analyses Muller's character against this scientific background:

> Such a character, in its developed form, is fortunately practically impossible in a highly civilised country. The dead weight of law would crush it back to the level of the human mass around it. But those who have lived in the wild places of the earth will be acquainted with its prototypes, more especially in those places where a handful of a superior race rule over the dense thousands of an inferior (ibid., p. 243).

Haggard had a strong dislike of the Boers and characterises them as 'barbarous', in contrast with the 'civilisation' of Englishmen. Muller, by combining both, is thus

> at the junction of the waters of civilisation and barbarism, too civilised to possess those savage virtues which, such as they are, represent the quantum of innate good Nature has thought fit to allow in the mixture Man, and too barbarous to be subject to the tender restraints of cultivated society, he is at once strong in the strength of both and weak in their weaknesses (ibid., p. 244).

Here the conflict between primitivism and progress becomes more intense because it is within a single character. The 'quantum of innate good', seen most clearly nearer to Nature, is the element of the noble savage that Haggard perpetuates in his novels, but it is put into perspective by the comparison with the 'tenderer restraints of civilised society', and both qualities are assumed to be part of one's racial heritage. Thus Muller, being the product of both backward and civilised races, has the qualities of both: 'Animated by the spirit of Barbarism, Superstition, and almost entirely destitute of the spirit of Civilisation, Mercy, he stands at the edge of both as a terrific moral spectacle as the world can afford' (ibid.). But, when the two are mixed, they do not produce a middle stage. Muller is nearer to barbarism than to civilisation, cross-fertilisation leads to decline. This, according to Haggard, is just as well, since, if Muller had leant a little more in either direction, he would have been really dangerous:

Had he been a little more civilised, with his power of evil
trained by education and cynical reflection to defy the attacks
of those spasms of unreasoning, spiritual terror and
unrestrainable passion that have their natural dwelling place in
in the raw strong mind of uncultivated man, Frank Muller
might have broken upon the world as a Napoleon. Had he
been a little more savage, a little more removed from the
unconscious but present influence of a progressive race, he
might have ground his fellows down and ruthlessly destroyed
them, like an Attila or a Chaka. As it was, he was buffeted
between two forces he did not realise even when they swayed
him and, thus, at every step in his path to a supremacy of evil,
an unseen power made stumbling blocks of weakness, which,
if that path had been along a little lower or a little higher level
in the scale of circumstance, would surely have been deadly
weapons of overmastering forces (ibid.).

That Haggard should analyse a character in such theoretical terms
is due to the influence of scientific theory on the general public at
the turn of the century. Like the writers to the *Popular Magazine
of Anthropology* he was trying to help the public 'keep pace with the
rapid advance of science' and, by representing theory in terms of a
character whose actions affect the course of an exciting adventure,
he shows the significance of that science on the ground.

Most of the preconceptions of contemporary science are to be
found in this character-study. Different races are characterised by
different qualities – the Boer is 'barbarous' and thus 'subject to
spasms of unreasoning spiritual terror and unrestrainable passion'
and has a 'raw, strong . . . uncultivated mind', whereas the Englishman is 'civilised' and thus 'trained by education and cynical reflection' and subject to 'tenderer restraints'. And these qualities are the
direct product of inheritance, passed on by races through the blood.
It is not always clear whether Haggard is suggesting that the presence
of English society in South Africa has influenced Boer society, which
is a reasonable analysis. He certainly does not put down the conflict
in Muller's character merely to such a social conflict – otherwise
all Boers would be equally subject to it. His main concern is to point
out the influence of Muller's racial inheritance in causing the conflict
in him, and he thus accepts current scientific belief that such 'internal'
qualities as 'passion' and 'tenderness' can be passed on 'in the blood'

through the members of a race. So, despite many signs of 'liberalism' elsewhere in his works, he perpetuates the myth of 'racial purity' adopted by Hunt and the members of the Anthropological Society of London. Haggard is not a 'racist' in the modern sense, but his novels reproduce the racial theory of his age.

John Buchan, too, dislikes the half-breed even more than he does the 'pure' native of South Africa. Recalling a tale in which Sir Percival met a lion fighting a serpent, he uses these two creatures as symbols of the 'pure' native and the hybrid: 'He [Sir Percival] drew his sword and helped the lion, for he thought it was the most natural beast of the two' (Buchan, 1910, p. 123). Likewise, Buchan's hero thinks the pure native more natural than Henriques, so determines to 'spoil the serpent's game'. And the continual characterisation of half-breeds as villains suggests that current scientific theory is being used to reinforce a common fear of anomalies. De Gobineau and Hunt, by scorning the hybrid as biologically unsound, lent support to the general distrust in an ethnocentric age of any bridging of the rigid categories into which mankind was put.

In popular fiction the 'cultural hybrid' is scorned as much as the racial. Kipling, for instance, is distrustful of the Russian who tries to transcend the categories in which Europeans have placed him:

> Let it be clearly understood that the Russian is a delightful person till he tucks in his shirt. As an Oriental, he is charming. It is only when he insists upon being treated as the most easterly of western peoples instead of the most westerly of easterns that he becomes a racial anomaly extremely difficult to handle. The host never knows which side of his nature is going to turn up next (in Maugham (ed.), 1952, p. 18).

Kipling here suggests that one is born with certain racial traits, and that one should not reject these and adopt the character of another race. He thus adds to the scientific distrust of the biological hybrid the cultural xenophobia of the nineteenth-century Englishman towards the character who chooses to be a 'racial anomaly'. It is bad enough to be born between racial groups. The Borderline tribes of India, for instance, inherit pride of race from their white ancestors and humility and impulses to crime from their black, and this makes them very difficult to deal with (Kipling, 1888, p. 77); but actually to choose to reject one's background and adopt another is more disastrous. He has nothing but scorn for the Indian who tries to imitate the white man, while he retains a patronising regard for those who keep their place and follow the customs of their own society. The educated native Member of Parliament, for instance, is of no use at all in giving information about the country, whereas 'the real native – not the hybrid university-trained mule – is as timid as a colt and needs coaxing to give information' (ibid., p. 203). Like Buchan's use of the lion and serpent, Kipling's comparison of 'real' natives with colts and educated ones with 'mules' vividly symbolises the concern of a racially conscious age with 'purity'.

The concern with categorisation, classification and hierarchy both in the English class system and in the study of the races of mankind; the belief that English economic and political success was due to English racial heritage; and the replacement of faith in the Bible by faith in the precise, rigid and laboratory-oriented principles of science – all these factors contributed to an inflexibility in Victorian representations of other peoples. A distrust of anomalies, caused partly by the continual attempt to define precisely the different groups of mankind, was reinforced by specific scientific pronouncements about the nature of 'hybrids', so that the Englishman was wary of anyone who seemed to be crossing racial boundaries, just as he was scornful of anyone who tried to cross Victorian class barriers. Muller, Henriques and the Borderline tribes, like the mule and the zebra so often referred to in scientific journals, are symbols of Victorian class and race consciousness and they represent that combination of scientific theory, ethnocentricism and imaginative writing which lay behind Victorian collective representations of mankind.

Chapter 5

Heredity and environment

The widespread acceptance of the theory that 'cultural characteristics' can be inherited genetically is an important source of many nineteenth-century representations of other peoples. For some, 'culture', 'race', 'nation', etc. were interchangeable terms. In *Philosophie zoologique* (1809), Lamarck departed from the traditional belief in fixity of species and 'bound all animated nature together by the evolutionary doctrine of transformism. External circumstances modify the way of living and create new habits and necessities which bring about a change in the structure of organs' (Penniman, 1935, p. 58). Thus, transitions were effected from one species to another and there was an inward urge in organisms to realise their utmost wants and to express this urge in change of habits and structure (Stocking, 1968, p. 234). Lamarck maintained that these changes were 'acquired' habits adopted as a response to environment and passed on as 'instincts' to the next generation. The implications for racial studies were that, over a period of time, the members of a particular social community, by adopting similar habits and customs, would pass on similar 'instincts', hereditary characteristics relating to that social environment. The community became a 'race', so that the English, for instance, were in the process of becoming a 'true race' under the conditioning of their common social environment.

Stocking demonstrates the influence of this idea on racial thought in America at the turn of the century. Paul Reinsch, for example, assumed that 'the cranial structure of the negro may be affected by a change in its social, political and economic conditions' (ibid., p. 244); and Ellwood held that a Negro child in a white family would have a different attitude to society, religion and life because its 'natural instincts' and 'race habit' were inherited from parents with different social ideas (ibid., p. 246). According to this theory, over a long period of time environmental influence become incorporated in Man's total constitution. Consequently, it will be an equally long time before a different environment has a similar effect.

Prichard, in England, after first denying that acquired characteristics could be inherited,[1] later gave support to Lamarck's contentions:

> Varieties of form or colour, as they spring up in any race, are
> commonly called accidental, a term only expressive of our
> ignorance as to the causes which give rise to them (Penniman,
> 1935, p. 81).

In fact, these variations are selected, just as domestic breeders select the best of their stock. One cause of variation, and thus of physical change, was culture. If a person's culture determined his physical characteristics, then his physique could be used as an index of his culture – head shape and colour were significant for suggesting what a person's culture was likely to be.

Against Lamarck, Darwin, in the *Origin of Species* (1858), claimed that the variations selected were random. But, like Prichard, his view changed and, in *Descent of Man* (1871), he tries to account for the appearance of particular variations by sexual selection. The following year, in *Expressions of the Emotions in Man and Animals*, he adopts a more Lamarckian position:

> Inherited movements of expression may have had a 'natural'
> and 'independent' origin but, when once acquired such
> movements may be voluntarily and consciously employed as
> a means of communication. . . . The tendency to such movements
> will be strengthened or increased by their thus being voluntarily
> and repeatedly performed and their effects may be inherited. . . .
> As most of the movements of expression must have been
> *gradually acquired, afterwards becoming instinctive*, there seems
> to be some degree of a priori probability that their recognition
> would likewise become instinctive (Darwin, 1872, pp. 256, 358).

Thus Darwin did not finally refute Lamarck. Indeed he himself seems here to be actually lending support to the idea that acquired characteristics could be inherited.

The older problem, whether character was most influenced by environment or heredity, was given new force and significance by the discoveries of nineteenth-century science. Again, therefore, when popular writers took up this debate, they were able to refer to contemporary science for support and authority. Aristocratic babies brought up in a humble rural setting had been a popular European literary theme from Greek myths to Spenser and Shakespeare. An obvious example is Perdita in *The Winter's Tale*, child of a prince but reared in the countryside. A conflict arises between the values of court life inherited from parents she has never known and the values of rural life taught by the rustic couple who adopted her. Like most such figures, she is eventually found by 'her own kind' and returns to the court, improved by her sojourn with nature.

In the nineteenth century, this theme was given new life in fiction by the theories of Lamarck. Many babies reared entirely in a primitive setting retain, in fiction, the social values of nineteenth-century England, inherited from their superior parents. A well-known example is Tarzan. The son of Lord Greystoke, he is left alone in the West African jungle while only a few months old, his parents having been killed by a tribe of apes (Burroughs, 1917). A motherly ape adopts him and brings him up, but his heritage soon shows his superiority to her kind and ape company bores him. Still more does he feel superior to the 'primitive' men, who also inhabit the jungle, even though his upbringing and environment have been entirely among apes. For he inherits the qualities of his aristocratic father. When he instinctively makes a bow to the first European woman he meets, 'it is the natural outcropping of many generations of fine breeding, a hereditary instinct of graciousness which a life-time of uncouth savage training and environment could not eradicate' (ibid., p. 177). He delights in cold baths, which his companions scorn, he longs for houses, books and hard work and 'at the bottom of his little English heart beat the great desire to cover his nakedness with clothes' (ibid., p. 64). The morals of Victorian life have been passed on to him, even though he has spent all his life in the jungle. One generation of social conditioning (and Lamarck would have agreed) is not enough to erase generations of hereditary good breeding. Thus it is not Tarzan's humanity which makes him so superior to the apes, and still more to the human savages whom the apes see as their enemies, but rather his British heritage.

But another, derivative, Tarzan figure achieves his superiority through training as much as through heredity. *Tabu Dick* was written for Patrick Greene's nephews who had wanted 'a jungle character who could give . . . Tarzan a good fight and that he should be white, unhampered by love affairs and have adventures with elephants, leopards, crocodiles and savage warriors' (Greene, L. P., 1935a, Dedication). Tabu Dick was left alone in the jungle as a young boy, when his mother was killed by the natives and his father later died. But before dying, his father had anticipated the problems of a white child alone in the jungle and set a taboo that Dick was not to be touched by anybody. This made Dick develop remarkable reactions and extreme physical fitness and co-ordination, to practise which he encourages natives to throw spears at him so that he can dodge them. According to his father, Dick is going to 'the finest school in the world – the school of experience' (ibid., p. 15), and from childhood he develops a fine physique both through training and environment; for 'Africa's sun speeds on a boy's development' (ibid., p. 16).

As he developed this physical side of his nature, he outstripped even the natives in knowledge of the jungle and acuteness of senses (thus joining the growing list of white noble savages in popular literature).[2] But while this had come about by training and environment, by his heritage he 'retained the white man's ability to take mental short cuts and to make direct logical conclusions', which the native was assumed to lack (ibid., p. 21). Here Greene, like Burroughs, emphasises the importance of inherited 'culture' in human development. But he does not go as far as Burroughs, since he does not show Tabu Dick as having inherited any more cultural idiosyncrasies than his deceased father could have passed to him directly. Dick is already a well-developed youth when his father dies. The original Tarzan, entirely devoid of European contact, inherits as many European cultural values as Burroughs could call to mind. Dick's skills on the other hand, are a combination of immediate heredity and of training. They are 'simply a demonstration of the perfection to which the human body can attain given good breeding, intelligence and well-ordered training' (ibid., p. 67):

From his father's people – they had always been accounted giants among men, even in those rock-girt glens of Scotland

which breed big men – he had inherited his powerful frame,
big-boned and well-muscled. From his father, too, he had
inherited courage and singleness of purpose, united to wise
caution.

To his mother's people – the blood of kings of old Ireland
flowed in their veins – he owed his quick brain, his
supersensitiveness, his love of fun and his indomitable courage.

And, wedded to this ancestry, Tabu Dick's early training had
developed him to a state of human perfection (ibid., pp. 67–8).

The English aristocracy are not represented in this genealogy as they
are in Tarzan's. Moreover Greene constantly stresses the importance
of training as well as of ancestry. By training, latent abilities can be
brought into use again: 'Tabu Dick's training had developed in him
a power which we are all heirs to but which has withered for lack of
use. It is Nature's law. Mistreat one of her gifts, and the gift is lost'
(ibid., p. 109). And:

There are occasions when a man will act in a way for which
there seems to be no reason. He will explain that he was led
by 'instinct' or that he had a hunch. Actually, that 'instinct',
that occasional 'hunch' is the last feeble stirring of a long-
disused natural ability.

It takes only a few generations of wrongly directed training
to turn a hunting dog into a house pet. A few years of civilisation
destroys a native's ability to follow spoor (ibid.).

And Tabu Dick represents what happens when such training is
directed towards latent instincts: 'All his senses were fully developed.'

Tarzan, on the other hand, was trained by apes but inherited
Victorian gentility. Tabu Dick was an 'ideal savage' physically but
his senses and his knowledge of the bush were 'directed by a civilised
brain' (ibid., p. 109), a brain he had inherited, different in quality
and reasoning power from that of the natives. Even his success,
therefore, cannot be entirely put down to nurture and environment,
both of which he shares with the natives. Here, ultimately, as in the
Tarzan stories, the white man in the jungle excels because of his
superior brain, which enables him to learn the skills such as tracking,
for which the natives are renowned, more easily than they can learn
'civilised' abilities, such as reasoning.

The qualities the natives have developed, those needed to overcome their environment and always emphasised in the noble savage tradition, are tracking and skill in bushcraft. The theme of the Indian tracker is central to the American tradition of romance, and Fenimore Cooper's Natty Bumppo must have provided a model for many English writers in their descriptions of 'primitive' life. Umslopogaas is a fine tracker; Buchan's natives have an acute sense of smell which aids their bushcraft; and Gilson's pygmies are 'masters of the wild'. But, if the environment brings out these commendable qualities, it also imposes limitations. Gilson puts considerable stress on the effect of the Congo forest on its inhabitants:

> There is no doubt that sunlight is very necessary to human life. Man was not meant to live in an interminable semi-darkness, as witness the stunted growth of the pygmies and the intellectual backwardness of the cannibal tribes of the Congo (Gilson, 1919, p. 46).

If some could argue that Negroes were black because they lived in the sun, Gilson could equally well claim that pygmies were short because they lived in forests, though he fails however, to account for the 'gigantic cannibals of the Aruwimi' (ibid., p. 17), who also live in the forest.

Thus environmentalists were suggesting, though on different grounds, that the differences between races were in practice as permanent and distinctive as if they were the result of heredity. The boundaries between races were just as difficult to cross, whether represented as environmental or genetic in origin. Gilson claims that the white man could not survive long in the forests and the pygmy 'can't live in England. Think what the climate must mean to him' (ibid., p. 24).

But white men did live in the jungle and natives did come to England and learn English habits. Characters who crossed the racial, national and environmental boundaries were important to the Victorians because they helped define those boundaries, as we have seen earlier in considering the 'hybrid'. Victorians were suspicious, not only of biological hybrids but of those 'cultural hybrids' who had inherited one background but tried to adopt another. These characters, the white man in Africa and the black man in European clothes, present a dilemma which is central to Victorian conceptions of race and culture and popular writers devote a considerable amount of space to them.

Interest in education in Victorian England contributed to the heredity versus environment debate. If the child's mind was a *tabula rasa*, as Locke had maintained, then cultural characteristics must have been acquired by training. But in that case, logically, the savage should have been able to learn 'civilised' behaviour. On the other hand, if cultural characteristics were inherited, then those inherited by white men were superior to those inherited by black. And if they were learnt, then those taught in white schools were superior to those taught in black. It was easier for the white man to learn the few skills of savage life than it was for the savage to learn the many skills of civilised life. Thus, whether the writer of fiction thinks heredity or environment more significant, in the very nature of the argument the stereotypes of 'primitive' peoples are preserved as they are in the scientists' debates.

When the travellers in *Allan Quatermain* meet a young girl who has been brought up all her life on a mission station in the African jungle, they are adding to a theme familiar to writers and scientists alike. Quatermain, seeing the young Flossie, compares her with 'civilised' girls:

> This child of the wilderness had more courage, discretion and
> power of mind than many a woman of mature age nurtured
> in idleness and luxury, with minds carefully drilled and educated
> out of any originality or self-resource that nature may have
> endowed them with (Haggard, 1887a, p. 89).

It is assumed that environment is the chief force shaping her character, irrespective of her heredity. But Haggard, having expounded the traditional primitivist theme that nature educated better than civilisation, finds himself in conflict with the nineteenth-century philosophy of progress, which placed Victorian man, and thus his educational system, at the top of the evolutionary tree. So Flossie is eventually sent back to England, 'lest she grow up wild and shunning her race' (ibid., p. 93). If nurture is best then it must be civilised European nurture, not primitive African.

The problem is inverted in A. E. W. Mason's *The Broken Road*. A young Indian prince is brought to England to be educated, against the advice of a wise British officer, who feared that, to be suspended between two cultures, with a heredity opposed by education, will deeply disturb the boy when he returns home. This is exactly what happens to him. He returns to India suffering from the conflict

between his Indian heritage and his British education. He attempts
to assimilate one to the other. That he fails and must eventually be
deposed by the British to eke out a bare existence among the riff-raff
of Rangoon emphasises the overwhelming influence of heredity
which dominates the veneer of education and which Ali finally turns
to as the most 'meaningful alternative of action'.

Some further detail is of interest. The prince's life at an English
public school is an example of a common literary device of placing
'primitive' people in a 'civilised' setting.[3] He is assimilated in a number of ways. His name is corrupted from Shere Ali to 'Sherry Face'
(Mason, 1907, p. 56). He finds difficulty, 'as the child of a grasping
treacherous race', in accepting that 'honour was always good, even
if unprofitable', but playing games, making friends and going to
parties soon 'overlaid his character' (ibid., p. 54). And so, when he
has to return to Chiltistan, he feels he is leaving home, not going
to it. He falls in love with an English woman who only wants him
for his jewels and social interest; the thought of leaving her and the
ballroom world in which he says farewell makes him wonder if he
really wants to go to India:

> 'Do I belong here', he asked, 'or do I belong to Chiltistan?'
> On the one side was all that, during ten years, he had
> gradually learned to love and enjoy; on the other side was his
> race and the land of his birth (ibid., p. 91).

In India he is told by a District Commissioner to rule like a native
prince and marry a native girl and his background makes him
revolt:

> He was aflame with indignation. So he was to be nothing, to do
> nothing, except to practise economy and marry – a nigger.
> The contemptuous word rose to his mind. Long ago it had
> been applied to him more than once during his early schooldays,
> until desperate battles and black eyes had won him immunity.
> Now he used it savagely himself to stigmatize his own people.
> He was of the White people, he declared. . . . I am one of the
> Sahibs. This fool of a Commissioner does not understand
> (ibid., p. 95).

The Commissioner, in fact, had been testing him because he was
afraid the prince's education might have had just this effect. Shere
Ali's values are those of England; the face which springs to mind

when he thinks of marriage is that of the English woman he loves: 'Not in Chiltistan would he find a woman to drive that image from his mind' (ibid.).

He soon discovers, however, that the white people with whom he identifies, who fêted him and treated him as an equal in England, now regard him as an inferior in India. He is told a story of native bravery in battle and that it cannot be rewarded with the VC as white bravery is; promotion in the army is reserved for the white race. Finally, the white woman he loves rejects him because he is a 'nigger'. He still tries to prove that he is one of the Sahibs by wearing white men's clothes and scorning the garb of native princes: 'They are content, but I was brought up in England and am not' (ibid., p. 121). But the whites see all natives as the same and fail to distinguish Shere Ali from his countrymen.

Repeated rejections by the white community and animosity from the Indians for his desertion unsettle him and he begins to wonder which is his home: 'It is neither in England nor in Chiltistan. I am a citizen of no country. I have no place anywhere at all' (ibid., p. 127). He is in a classic state of 'anomie', of dissociation from both sets of values; neither upbringing on the one hand nor heredity on the other can be entirely overcome: 'He had been made and moulded and fashioned and, though he knew he had been fashioned awry, he could no more change and rebuild himself than the hunchback can will away his hump' (ibid., p. 132). But gradually heredity begins to dominate. He is told by an English colonel that the purpose of his English education was to make him aware of the strength of the British army and the futility of revolt so that he would be a docile and obedient ruler. The prince begins to realise the falsity of clinging to the white people when they merely make use of him like this.

So he rejects the symbols, the silk hat and the Western expression of face: 'It was as if a European suddenly changed before your eyes into an Oriental' (ibid., p. 142). The English Commissioner realises that the only hope for the prince, the only way he can reassert his identity, is to return to the spirit of his own race:

> I don't know how many of the old instincts and traditions of his race and his faith are still alive in him, underneath all the Western feelings and Western ideas to which he has been trained. But if they are dead there is no chance for him (ibid., p. 147).

A boxing match between a coloured man and a white man becomes the symbol of this re-alignment, as he cheers the black man to victory. A conversation he overhears between Englishmen objecting to white women losing native respect provides the opportunity to express this new feeling. He interrupts them savagely: 'And, indeed, there was very little of the civilised man in Shere Ali's look at this moment. His own people were claiming him. It was one of the grim, keen tribesmen of the hills who challenged the young Englishmen' (ibid., p. 184).

His training is still sufficiently strong to prevent him 'making a scene' but he is now in a frame of mind which his revolutionary countrymen are easily able to play upon. They do him homage as a prince and show him the hardships and ill treatment of native life under the Raj and he succumbs: 'The longing at his heart was for his own country, for his own people . . . He had his place in the world' (ibid., p. 195). There is a brief relapse when he sees a church and meadow set out like Eton and feels nostalgia for this early life, but the blood of his fathers is too strong for these superficialities of education. The Commissioner comments on the process:

> England overlaid the real man with a pretty varnish. And the varnish peels off easily, when a man comes back to the Indian sun. There's not one of these people from the hills but has in him the makings of a fanatic. Given the circumstances, neither Eton nor Oxford, nor all the schools and universities rolled into one, would hinder the relapse (ibid., p. 218).

Thus heredity overcomes the effects of environment. The theories of Darwin and of racist anthropologists have superseded the educational theories of Locke and Hartley. It merely remains for the writers and travellers to show which characteristics are passed on by which peoples.

Thus, when an Englishman educated at Eton and Oxford finds himself in a primitive land, he can rise above his savage environment by calling on his superior heritage. Tarzan remains English as Shere Ali remains Indian, though, in the latter case, the effects of environment take longer to be overcome. In *The Coral Island* again, when three young boys are shipwrecked, they soon dominate the environment due to their Victorian skills. Jack comments, 'we have no lack of material here to make us comfortable, if we are only clever enough to use it' (Ballantyne, 1858, p. 38). So they make weapons, a bower and a boat, work hard, take a cold bath every morning and construct an aquarium, in which the scientifically minded narrator can observe the habits of marine life in minute detail. However, after being horrified by numerous scenes of bloody native life, Peterkin wonders whether this heritage may succumb to the effects of environment: 'I begun to find that such constant exposure to scenes of blood was having a slight effect on myself, and I shuddered when I came to think I, too, was becoming callous' (ibid., p. 171). It was, indeed, a constant fear of sojourners in savage lands, including missionaries, that they would succumb to their savage environment, but they finally had the support of Darwin and the scientists for their emotional dependence on the superiority of their inheritance.

But if a white man's heritage is what enables him to succeed in a primitive setting, the primitive man is less fortunate. His heritage is what prevents him from succeeding in a Western setting. And this fact is symbolised in literature by the incongruity of native characters wearing European clothes. When Shere Ali returned to India, much importance was placed on the clothes he wore and, when he rejected the silk hat for Indian dress, his conversion was complete. He had recognised that, though he wore Western clothes in the same way that he cultivated a veneer of Western culture, beneath the surface he remained what he was born, an Indian, and the clothes had been a false attempt to deny this. For other popular writers, too, clothing serves as a major symbol of the differences between cultures. When the clothes of one race are adopted by the members of another, the internal conflicts between the races are rendered in concrete and often picturesque terms. Tarzan, Quatermain and Tabu Dick, by wearing animal skins, represent the adoption by a white man of the qualities of the noble savage. And when the process is reversed and the native wears Western clothing, he is likewise adopting Western values. But, whereas the white man can successfully acquire the worthwhile characteristics of the native, while retaining the character he has inherited, the native in literature has more difficulty in acquiring the characteristics of Western culture and his hereditary qualities remain stronger. Tabu Dick combines his civilised brain with savage bushcraft, but Shere Ali cannot combine the nature of the Indian hill people with the refinements of European education. For the popular writer, the debate between heredity and environment is more important for reaffirming the superiority of the white man than for resolving an ancient problem.

Thus when the natives are shown in Western dress, it is often to prove how badly it fits. This is sometimes merely another excuse for light relief at his expense. Gilson's travellers find a pygmy wearing Crouch's cast-off tattered garments and are much amused:

Though Crouch was a small man, the pygmy thus adorned wore his knickerbocker breeches buttoned at the ankle instead of below the knee. Even then, they were so voluminous and baggy that they resembled a skirt. The proud possessor of this exceedingly ragged and disreputable pair of nether garments strutted about with pride, holding the breeches up with both hands. His appearance was all the more ridiculous since he had the coat on the wrong way round, having thrust the left arm into the right sleeve. The coat, it may be added, reached to his knees (Gilson, 1919, p. 218).

But sometimes the significance of the native wearing Western dress is made more explicit than in such mockery as this, which merely serves to devalue the dignity of the native and to re-emphasise the difference between him and the white man. John Buchan uses the situation to 'prove' that, even when the native seems to have been educated into Western habits, his new-found culture is only a veneer. When the clothes come off, so, too, will the culture.[4] John Laputa is a South African native who has been converted to Christianity and has come to Scotland to preach as a missionary. But Davie, the schoolboy hero, sees him on the beach near the kirk where he has preached, stripped naked and practising some primitive rite. This puts him back in the category of a noble savage: 'In his minister's dress, he had looked only a heavily-built native, but now in this savage dress I saw how noble a figure he made' (Buchan, 1910, p. 90).

Laputa, in fact, is the leader of a native politico-religious uprising and he has adopted Western clothes merely to obtain information necessary for his plans. Davie follows his progress and takes great interest in his different roles, each symbolised by a change of clothing. In a hidden cave in South Africa, where he is inciting rebellion, he adopts a political role and so puts on a leopard skin cloak and kilt, taking up a spear and shield. Davie comments: 'Now he was more king than priest, more barbarian than Christian' (ibid., p. 109). He summarises these changes later:

I had seen Laputa as a Christian minister, as the priest and king in the cave, as the leader of an army at Dupree's drift

SIL—I

and at the kraal we had left as the savage with all self-control
thrown to the winds. I was to see this amazing man in another
role, for now he became a friendly and rational companion
(ibid., p. 164).

Their level of conversation leads Davie to ask why such an educated and intelligent man is 'trying to put the clock back. You want
to wipe out the civilisation of a thousand years and turn us all into
savages. It's the more shame to you when you know better.' Laputa's
reply places him firmly in the noble savage tradition:

You misunderstood me. It is because I have sucked civilisation
dry that I know the bitterness of the fruit. I want a simple and
better world and I want that world for my people. I am a
Christian and will you tell me that your civilisation pays
much attention to Christ? (ibid.).

Laputa's rejection of Western civilisation, then, is partly intellectual, and his changes of clothing are conscious and political. But he
is not entirely a noble savage; he also belongs to the ignoble savage
tradition of nineteenth-century positivism, and his rejection of
Western dress is also a return to his savage heritage.

Kipling takes this for granted and creates situations for his tales
out of it. An Indian who had a white ancestor finds that this stands
him in good stead in a crisis: 'the old race instinct of courage' overcomes years of training as a native and he is able to face an enraged
mob and shoot at them, killing some fellow Indians, in order to
prevent a riot (Kipling, 1888, p. 81). But he feels remorse at this act
which Kipling, partly perhaps to keep faith with his Anglo-Indian
audience, had characterised as 'good work' and a sign of 'strength'.
And this remorse is represented as due to the fact that the Indian is
finally losing the last drops of his English blood, the loss of his
white heritage. Had his English blood been dominant, he would
have felt no remorse. Kipling thus manipulates current racial theory
to make a good story. The loss of one's heritage in these circumstances is hardly 'scientific'.

Michele, as he is called, could do a white man's job because he had
traces of white blood but, when full-blooded natives try to do such
jobs and adopt a veneer of civilisation, they are attempting something
for which they are racially unsuited. Such people are the 'hybrid,
university-trained mules' of whom Kipling is so scornful, and he

appeals to his readers not to be fooled by the educated Indian: 'In India nothing changes in spite of the shiny, topascum stuff that people call "civilisation"' (Kipling, 1888, p. 262). John Chinn discovers this when he goes with his native servant, a sergeant in the British army, to the man's own tribe. As the leader of the Bhils 'yells and capers with his naked fellow-dancers of the scrub', Chinn exclaims 'Good Heavens, and this blinking pagan is a first-class officer!' (in Maugham (ed.), 1952, p. 58).

The way Kipling can use these popular preconceptions is demonstrated in 'The Miracle of Purum Bhagat'. A brilliant native administrator, decorated by the British, gives up everything at the height of his fame and becomes a Sannayasi beggar, fulfilling a long-held romantic dream. Since his ancestors come from the Himalayas, he directs his pilgrimage there: 'The least touch of hill blood draws a man back to where he belongs' (ibid., p. 277). But this story, though given force by the myth of racial heritage, is basically in the romantic pastoral tradition and Purum Bhagat's life alone with nature, communing with the wild animals, is told sympathetically and powerfully. His eventual race to save the village from an avalanche brings out, momentarily, the old powers of organisation that he learned from the British. But, when the village build a temple in his honour, it is to acknowledge the Indian heritage which brought him to the village in the first place and enabled him to live as a Sannayasi, even after a 'civilised' training. Heritage and training combine successfully in a native for one of the few times in popular literature, and Kipling creates out of the scientific ideas of his day and the literary tradition of his culture an imaginative and evocative tale.

The terrestrial paradise – primitivism versus progress

Kipling's hero is a 'cultural hybrid', not only in that he was born in one culture and brought up in another, but also in that, having spent much of his life within one culture, the Anglo-Indian civil service, he then moves to another environment, an isolated Tibetan village. Likewise Flossie, having been brought up in Africa, is sent back to England, and Shere Ali, after an English education, goes back to India. The contrast is not only between heredity and environment, but also between one environment and another. Even those who believe that heredity is the strongest influence still acknowledge the importance of environment. Thus another conflict can be discerned in nineteenth-century attitudes to 'primitive' man, that between the environment of the natural world and the cultural, urban environment of Europe. The heirs of Rousseau and the romantic poets celebrate the natural setting which, they claim, affects the nature of its inhabitants favourably, while the advocates of progress believe the cultural environment of nineteenth-century England provides the best education.

This argument was mostly carried on by those who subscribed in the first place to the theory that environment affected character. But even Edgar Rice Burroughs admits that environment is important and so takes part in the general debate as to which environment is superior. To some, the primitive environment is a terrestrial paradise, to others it is a dangerous jungle. In both cases, it affects the nature of the traditional inhabitants, the natives, and the nature of those who have just arrived, the white colonists. There is a long tradition in European literature, from Greek myths of the Seven Isles through the Bermuda pamphlets and Shakespeare's *The Tempest*, to Wordsworth's pastoralism, that life nearer to nature is more virtuous and 'real' than in the superficial urban environment that man creates for himself. But in the nineteenth century this tradition came into conflict with the belief in progress and in the superiority of European civilisation, and this presented the popular writer, particularly, with a dilemma that led to inconsistencies within his novels. His literary heritage and romantic bent inclined him to extol the virtues of the natural setting, but his cultural heritage and rational belief in progress inclined him to extol the 'civilised' setting.

Tennyson's resolution of the problem is typical for many romantic writers at the time. He places the natural setting in a dream, so that, when he awakes, he can put it in perspective in terms of his ultimate belief in progress, in the superiority of European people and the European setting. The terrestrial paradise and the noble savage can excite the imagination and can be used to point out some of the faults of European life; but they are, ultimately, trivial and fanciful compared with the European achievement:

> Fool, again the dream, the fancy! But I *know* my words are wild,
> But I count the gray barbarian lower than the Christian child.
>
> (*Locksley Hall*)

In this he is supported by most of his contemporaries and by the new romance writers. But they, like him, cannot entirely avoid the dream; and his own description of primitive goodness and simplicity, derived from the long tradition of English romantic and pastoral writing, sets the tone for many such descriptions in the novels:

> . . . Ah for some retreat
> Deep in yonder shining Orient, where my life began to beat;
> . . . Never comes the trader, never floats an European flag.
> Slides the bird o'er lustrous woodland, swings the trailer from the
>   crag;
> Droops the heavy-blossomed bower, hangs the heavy-fruited tree –
> Summer isles of Eden lying in dark-purple spheres of sea.
> There methinks would be enjoyment more than in this march of
>   mind,
> In the steamship, in the railway, the thoughts that shake mankind.
>   (*Locksley Hall*)

This dream is shared by many travellers to exotic lands in the late nineteenth century. W. M. Kerr writes of 'Isles of Eden' from personal experience:

> The civilised poor man is not half so happy as the untutored
> savage, although the latter lives far beyond the sound of
> church bells. Can it be that heathen freedom and plenty in the
> wind-swept wilderness are preferable to civilised starvation in
> the polluted atmosphere of a rotten hovel? The subject is
> worthy of consideration (Kerr, 1886, p. 253).

Although most writers return ultimately to the 'march of mind' (and tend to forget about the 'rotten hovel') and the dream fades for them as it did for Tennyson, nevertheless it plays an important part in the romance fiction of the day.

While we can trace the use of the theme of the terrestrial paradise through the particular events of colonial life and the particular experience of the authors who write about it, ultimately they are set within the framework evident in Tennyson. However pleasant this side of primitive life may appear, it is inferior to the quality of life in the writer's own society. The discoveries of travellers in Britain's expanding Empire brought the theme home to the general public in geographical terms, and the theories of anthropologists brought it into general philosophic discussion. With attempts to settle on the coast of Africa, the high mortality rate of Europeans had led to fears of the African climate, expressed in the title of

Rankin's book *The White Man's Grave* in 1836. But it also tended
to increase hopes of a more hospitable interior and these hopes, with
occasional travellers' reports and a growing mystique about such
inland towns as Timbuctu, gave rise to strong belief that the interior
would live up to those expectations of 'tropical exuberance' which
the coast had failed to fulfil. It was expected that nature would
provide, with little help from man, and the assumption of extreme
fertility of the soil led to idealistic settlements and to theories of the
inherent goodness of natives whose lives were spent amidst such
luxuries of vegetation. Since the coastal areas did not match up to
these ideals, new attempts at a 'medical topography', at finding
places where the climate was less malevolent, focused on inland
regions, and such well-publicised expeditions as those up the Niger
kept public interest alive (Curtin, 1965, part iii).

Besides these medical and geographical encouragements, the myth
was given a religious context by the Swedenborgian philosophy of a
new purer religion arising from within Africa as Christianity began
its inevitable decline. Particular writers who used the theme were
influenced by their personal experience of beautiful hidden valleys
or of myths about them among native peoples themselves. This was
the case with Rider Haggard, whose romances inspired a genre of
literature which were set in exotic lands and which used the theme of
the lost paradise as a focal point.

His own stay in Africa and the rumours about Zimbabwe added
a specific colouring to these general ideas. Haggard used the
mechanics of noble savage literature as a framework for his stories.
The approach to his inland 'paradises' is always along devious,
hidden routes, which ensure that the hero is one of the few white
men ever to reach that land. An opportunity is thus provided to
see the 'savage' in his natural condition and also to hear comments
on Western society from those to whom it is unfamiliar.

The entry to Kukuanaland in *King Solomon's Mines* is across a
difficult range of mountains and a desert, and one of the party dies
of the hardships on which the author dwells in some detail. The
excitement is enhanced by this kind of description but it also serves
to emphasise that the people of Kukuanaland are unlikely to have
met any travellers before. The land with its luxuriant vegetation is
referred to as an 'earthly paradise' and that the natives themselves
are aware of this is suggested by the Zulu tale of men going out into
the wilderness and finding a beautiful place there. But the tradi-

tional theme of nature alone providing such beauty is modified somewhat by Quatermain's comments on the view from Sheba's Breasts: however beautiful the view, it needs man to make it complete; his experience of living so long in the wilds has taught him the value of civilisation. Thus there is already some suggestion of the way Haggard intends to use the theme. The book ends with the white men leaving and Umbopa, the king, assuming his rightful position as head of the country. While thanking Quatermain and his friends for their help, Umbopa gives a tirade on the evil influence of the white races on the black. In future, no visitors will be allowed into his country to destroy it as he has seen the natives ruined in other parts of Africa. He cites tales of white traders with guns and gin causing an indigenous people to decline, and the references must have rung true to a reading public accustomed to hearing accounts of whole races being wiped out on contact with the whites through drink, disease and warfare.[5]

Passages such as this would seem to support the romantic ideal of leaving the native to lead his own 'noble' life, free from the harmful influences of 'civilisation', and the conclusion of *King Solomon's Mines* seems, at first sight, to endorse this. But Haggard is no primitivist, he believes firmly in progress and in the superiority of European and particularly English culture. He acknowledges the harmful aspects of contact but he believes that, eventually, the inferior races will be improved by it. Thus, whenever his characters leave an inland 'paradise', it is always under the improving influences of someone with Western ideals. In this case, Umbopa has spent all his life among white men and measures up to Haggard's highest ideal, that of an English gentleman. Although adhering to some of the 'inferior' native ideas, such as the necessity for killing, he has something of the proselytising zeal of the white colonist. He intends to improve his country, to run it by the standards of his white masters, and the moment he is king he turns to Quatermain for advice. In fact, he represents the colonist's ideal of the Europeanised native looking to Europeans for a model. He agrees to Quatermain's requests that he give up uncivilised customs. This in fact is the bargain the travellers require to help him, and we are assured when they leave that Kukuanaland has become in spirit, if not in fact, a colony of the British Empire.

Similarly, in *Allan Quatermain*, the evils of uncontrolled Western influence are expounded and the country of the Zu-Vendi is to be kept free from them, yet in the end the country has come under enlightened Western influence and the suggestion is less that all white influence is bad than that only genteel English influence is good. Sir Henry Curtis becomes king of the land and believes it his 'sacred duty' to 'preserve the blessings of comparative barbarism'. Modern life has brought many evils and is no happier than that of the Zu-Vendi, and he does not intend to ruin their happiness by bringing in tourists, politicians and teachers, who inevitably degrade the unsophisticated native peoples through disease, drunkenness, gunpowder and general demoralisation. All the elements of primitivism are contained here, but the conflict with progress is seen in the fact that an Englishman is left to rule the country. English notions of benevolent imperialism were based on the inferiority of the native and his need for protection from both 'barbarism' and the 'worst' aspects of civilisation. Sir Henry Curtis has really been appointed Governor General of yet another colony, with certain idealistic restrictions.

This solution to the problem of reconciling primitivism and progress by a parochialism that allows both, represents a new approach to the traditional paradise theme, based on Victorian morality and influenced by political expediency, scientific discoveries, travellers' reports and anthropological theory. The 'nature versus nurture' argument has been adapted to allow for European man's newly-extended control of his environment. The grafting of shoots on trees, the ability to adapt and control nature which Perdita so abhorred, is the basis of the white man's superiority. This control was seen as one of the criteria for European man's high place in the moral scale. Livingstone, observing the limited effect the African had on his environment ('the very rocks are illiterate'), saw a useful moral. He wondered whether 'the stagnation of mind in certain nations might not have been designed by God so that the fruits of science and invention might be associated with Christianity' (quoted in Cairns, 1965, p. 79).

The fruits of cultivation are brought to Africa by a missionary family in one typical scene from *Allan Quatermain*. The travellers come across a mission station which has all the features of the natural paradise, but it turns out to be a cultivated one. It has a magnificent garden with numerous fruits and it takes very little effort to grow anything: 'A rose cutting will bloom in a year' (Haggard, 1887a, p. 33). However, it is man's modification of the natural order, as well as the beautiful and productive climate, which has provided this display. The fruit trees are grafted and the contrast is pointed with the land around, which has as much potential but is not cultivated by the natives. The implication is that, just as the people have potential but need European aid to realise it, so the land of Africa could become a paradise under European influence. This justifies trusteeship, perpetuates the myth of tropical exuberance, and puts nature in her place as European man's servant.

Many intrepid adventurers set out in Victorian literature to find lost lands and most, like Quatermain, discovered inhabitants very different from those of the surrounding country, because the difficulty of access had prevented contact. Conan Doyle takes this to a logical conclusion in terms of the science and ideas of his age when his travellers in *The Lost World* discover a plateau in South America that is a survival of the Stone Age. This survival had been possible because the plateau is cut off from the land around. It stands many hundreds of feet above the plain, with sheer rock faces forbidding entry. But the travellers climb a near-by pinnacle and fell a tree from it across the gorge to the top of the plateau, thus arriving by a route as devious as those of Allan Quatermain and the knights of fairyland to their respective gardens of Eden.

As they search the plateau, traces of the tropical paradise theme recur: 'Both in its temperature and its vegetation it was almost temperate'. But contained within this modern Eden is the traditional serpent, and the travellers endure many hardships in exciting battles with pterodactyls, dinosaurs and ape tribes. The theme of danger lurking beneath the beauty of the tropics, which Conrad presented in terms of the jungles of the Malay Archipelago, is here made directly relevant to the contemporary discoveries of palaeontology and archaeology. Science is literally 'brought to life'.

Other lost worlds provided different perspectives, but in all of them the scientific theories of nineteenth-century England have taken over the old literary device of the terrestrial paradise and made it relevant to contemporary thought. Whereas in Conan Doyle the lost world is a haven of prehistoric monsters and in Haggard a potential paradise, once British trusteeship and 'nurture' can be established, in John Buchan's *Prester John* it represents the threat of a religiously oriented nationalism that would sweep the white man back into the sea.

At the beginning of the century religious interest in Africa was coloured by the theories of Emmanuel Swedenborg, who believed that God created a series of 'true' churches, each in whatever part of the world there was the most perfect knowledge of God, and that each declined to be replaced in turn by a new church. As far back as 1857 he claimed that the European church of Christianity was declining and would be replaced by a new church arising, as mentioned (p. 122 above), from the centre of Africa, where people thought more 'internally'. He produced a map of Africa and suggested that the 'celestial' region was in the centre and from it would radiate a new religion (Curtin, 1965, p. 26). He was interpreted by contemporaries as dividing the black and white races. The black races, cultivating the will and affections, would establish the celestial kingdom of God in Africa, to replace the ancient Christian spiritual kingdom based on white cultivation of understanding (Swedenborg, 1890). The idea that African religions were racialist and nationalist was fostered by stories of native leaders who had used much force to combine different tribes against the white man, as the Mahdi had done in the Sudan. Such leaders are a commonplace of anthropology, as of modern African politics.

Thus in *Prester John*, European fears of a native uprising in South Africa are supported by accounts of a Swedenborg-like religion called Ethiopianism, arising from within Africa. (This is an early hint in fiction of awareness of black nationalism, then politically embryonic.) The story of Prester John, King of Abyssinia in the fifteenth century, demonstrates how Christian and African beliefs are combined into a new religion with a nationalistic force (Buchan, 1910, p. 57). Buchan suggests that the influence had moved south, symbolised in a native fetish, and had helped Chaka, the Zulu king, to create his powerful empire at the beginning of the century. And now, he conjectures, another leader may arise to adopt the symbol, the name and the religion, and to combine the disparate peoples of South Africa against the white man (ibid., p. 76).

This religion is dramatised by Buchan in terms of the paradise theme. The place in which it is practised is a large plateau, which the hero discovers by accident since it is hidden behind deep vegetation, in the tradition of all such places. From the plateau there is a 'wonderful prospect', the land is fertile, 'a haven of green'. Davie, looking around South Africa for the first time, had remarked on its beauty: 'Whatever serpent might lurk in it, it was a veritable Eden I had come to.' Now he has found the serpent whose implications for the Englishmen in South Africa are as disturbing as they were for the mythical inhabitants of the first garden.

Thus the theme of a terrestrial paradise, and the literary machinery that traditionally accompanies it, provide a focal point for many diverse opinions on the nature of man in general and 'primitive' man in particular. In Africa a few fortunate travellers did discover peaceful inland states whose bucolic simplicity seemed to be that of a real Arcadia. Thomson, visiting the 'Wankonde' on the northern shore of Lake Nyasa, was deeply impressed by their happy state – 'a perfect Arcadia, about which idyllic poets have sung, though few have seen it realised' (Thomson, 1878, p. 226). And from the time of the Bermuda pamphlets and *The Tempest*, the West Indies had been famed for its abundance of vegetation and its vernal airs.

But for the most part, travellers' reports of the newly discovered lands in the late nineteenth century told of savagery and barbarism, of continual wars and bloody customs which all but destroyed the image of the 'noble savage' for some time. However, the old framework remained. We thus find descriptions which commence in the traditional way. Travellers overcome the usual problems of entering the hidden land to find a 'veritable Eden' untouched by the debilitating influence of modern civilisation. But then the knowledge of European man's place at the top of the evolutionary tree and his inherited superiority over these earlier forms of life forces the author to place in this paradise a race of men as savage and bloodthirsty as the travellers' tales had led people to expect. These lowly creatures have failed to take full advantage of their environment; so they require the benevolent trusteeship of their superior white brothers to put them on the right path. The terrestrial paradise now harbours an ignoble savage. Every nineteenth-century Eden has its serpent.

This is the conflict in Haggard's works. The setting brings out the problem of primitivism versus progress, and the writer finds the literary tradition at variance with his scientific knowledge or philosophical conviction. Elements of each exist side by side in his work, reflecting in microcosm the conflicts of the day. Meanwhile, other writers incorporate new themes into the tradition. Conan Doyle's lost land, with its traces of luxuriance, has become an ethnological museum, while Buchan's is the centre for a nationalistic religious revolt by the Africans. Thus by the time the reader meets the native himself, a number of preconceptions have been built up, drawing upon diverse themes such as the English pastoral tradition, the implications of palaeontological discoveries, Swedenborg's theory of religion and Darwin's *Origin of Species* and other scientific enquiries. A framework of this sort, while reflecting the discussions of the day at all levels, made it difficult to study a people's way of life, their customs and institutions, with the detachment that modern anthropology requires. On the other hand, it did bring before the general public the ideas of the leading scientists; so that, through such literature, the two were probably closer together than they are today. If the presuppositions of this literature seem somewhat distorted to modern readers, it is because they derive directly from the equally dubious ideas of many nineteenth-century scientists. What this represented as far as assessments of savage character and psychology are concerned we have now considered. In the following chapters we turn to representations of primitive social institutions.

Chapter 6

'Primitive' politics in popular literature

Just as the attitude of the Victorians to the customs and 'character' of 'primitive' people was conditioned by evolutionary theories, so were their conceptions of 'primitive' institutions. The political institutions of 'savages' were assumed to lack the subtlety and intelligence of European democracy, since 'savages' themselves lacked both subtlety and intelligence. Since 'primitive' societies represented earlier stages of human development, their political institutions were also immature, even if they did display features of a much earlier period in Europe. The virtues of democracy, however, belonged not only to European social history but also to racial history – it was an inherent characteristic of the Anglo-Saxon race:

> 'Such specifically Anglo-Saxon attributes as reason, restraint, self-control, love of freedom and hatred of anarchy, respect for law and distrust of enthusiasm were actually transmissible from one generation of Anglo-Saxons to the next in a kind of biologically determined inheritance' (Curtis, 1968, p. 8).

Conversely, the lack of these qualities in 'primitive' peoples was the result of their racial heritage. Savages inherited a tendency to anarchy, or despotism, lack of restraint and inability to adhere to democratic principles.

Rousseau, Hobbes and Locke had accustomed Europeans to talk

of a 'pre-social' state, and the writings of anthropologists supported the idea that examples of such a state were to be found in the jungles of Africa, South America and Malaysia where 'primitive' peoples lived, so that their political institutions were not only racially inferior but historically prior to those of Europe. Once the idea of a 'pre-social' state was accepted, different writers could attribute to it different characteristics – to some it was an idyllic state with none of the cares of European life and no need for rules and regulations; to others it was a state of continual anarchy, while to others it was ruled by harsh tyrants.

Many of these notions of political evolution were developed before Darwin made the idea of evolution popular, and Burrow (1966) shows how many of the preconceptions about primitive peoples derived from the political historians and philosophers. John Stuart Mill rejected the deductive framework of Bentham and the utilitarians, who assumed that ethical principles of universal validity could be deduced from introspection on their own nature. He called the essential unity of man into question; and the evidence being brought back of other social orders reinforced these doubts. Evolutionary social theory, claims Burrow, helped to reformulate the essential unity of mankind on the basis that the different societies were all stages on the same progressive scale, so that an uncomfortable relativism was avoided. He traces anthropological interest in evolution and 'survivals' to the philosophy and political theory of the age rather than to biological studies. The problem of the apparently vast differences between the political institutions of Europe and the way of life of 'savages' was thus solved by using the framework of evolution, which helped to reinforce European superiority and to justify 'political trusteeship'.

That this philosophical framework influenced attitudes at all levels of Victorian society is suggested by Godfrey Lienhardt: 'Sociological investigators as well as men of affairs may be influenced more than they recognise by philosophical and psychological theories of the nature of men and the state' (Lienhardt, 1964, p. 63). That popular fiction was influenced by, and in turn helped to spread and influence, the ideas of political theorists is evident from the interest shown in the novels of the time in demonstrating the 'pre-social' condition of 'primitive' man, whether it be anarchy or despotism. Hobbes had declared that the 'pre-social' state was one of continual war and anarchy. The State is an artifice invented to prevent the natural tendencies of man towards strife and apathy; the way in which order is achieved is by a 'social contract' which is only found in 'higher' societies. Contemporary 'primitive' societies were examples of an earlier condition; and, going out expecting the anarchy or despotism of 'natural' man, travellers easily fitted examples of warfare, particularly in Africa, into this preconceived framework.

Ballantyne's 'classic' *The Coral Island* exactly reproduces the popular image of native life as anarchical, beset by continual warfare and dominated by corrupt, power-crazy chiefs whose power rests on the principle of the survival of the fittest and that 'might is right'. This caricature of the lack of order in 'primitive' society is given vivid expression in the battle scenes. Three English boys, like the modern television camera, peep from behind the bushes as opposing armies line up. The initial order of battle is soon abandoned, however, and the natives entirely lose control of themselves. The boys become commentators as well as cameras:

> Soon after we arrived the attack was made with great fury.
> There was no science displayed. The two bodies of savages
> rushed headlong upon each other and engaged in a general
> melee . . . and as they brandished their massive clubs, leaped,
> shouted, yelled and dashed each other to the ground, I thought
> I had never seen men look so like demons before (Ballantyne,
> 1858, p. 210).

To Europeans, used to an ostensibly conventional form of warfare, the apparent lack of rules in 'primitive' battles was disturbing. Later commentators (such as Fortune, 1947) have demonstrated that many small-scale societies have highly ritualised warfare, and European history in the last hundred years has dispelled the self-image of chivalry and honour; but in the late nineteenth century, accounts like Ballantyne's were accepted as self-evident.

That such bloodthirsty scenes are an everyday event in 'savage' society is a central theme of the novel. When the boys first arrive at the island, Ralph tells them 'the heathen savages are at war among themselves', which comes as no surprise to them after their childhood reading. They explicitly relate their expectations (for example, that natives are 'a bloody and deceitful tribe') to what they find on the island.

If the natural state of man was so wild and anarchical, the only possible method of social control was the exercise of force by a tyrant; in the primitive struggle for survival, the strongest would win. While the idea of 'primitive' political life as despotism depends to some extent on the framework of thought that sees 'primitive' life as 'pre-social', and 'pre-social' life as naturally anarchical, the image was also affected by less philosophical interests. The beginning of the century saw the exaltation of self-reliance and the theme of the self-made man as industrial output expanded. If the poor were poor it was their own fault, and if some men were successful it was because they deserved to be. Thus certain men were natural leaders and would inevitably get to the top. Carlyle, for instance, saw heroes and individual great men as the focus of social order and believed a people deserved the leaders they got. If European social control was in the hands of a few powerful leaders, then 'primitive' peoples, with their tendency to chaos, likewise needed strong individual leaders though, being savages, they would lack the constraints on their power evident in European politics. There was hence a natural inclination to despotism in the 'primitive' state.

From the point of view of British governors in the colonies, a single powerful king was easier to deal with than a lot of local chiefs. There was a tendency to assume that strong government was better for the natives because it was more convenient for the colonisers. Likewise travellers found it easier to travel in those areas with strong kings, and hence assumed this was the only way the native could be controlled. Elmslie wrote: 'Despotic rule is often the only kind suitable among the uncivilised people. Until the people are governed by higher principles than those common among "nature-peoples", a despotic ruler is a Divine institution to keep in check greater evils' (Elmslie, 1899, p. 118).

Among the savage and bloody tribes whom the boys in Ballantyne's novel meet, the man who becomes chief is 'the biggest and most bloodthirsty of the lot' (Ballantyne, 1858, p. 199). The scorn directed at him indicates European scorn for any native institution. When he has to be fed by his wife, or kills off his subjects at will in a drunken rage, or receives gifts with 'kingly indifference', the debauchery of his character is intended as a measure of the weakness of his subjects. That they are prepared to be killed rather than strike back when he is drunk and that they take his word as law, is intended to reveal the mockery of 'primitive law' and to be an indictment of the passivity of 'primitive' man – they deserve what they get. In an era when Smiles's *Self-Help* was still popular and the principle of *laissez-faire* had exalted the virtues of independence and self-reliance, anyone who put up with such a despot had only himself to blame.

The theory of self-help was given a new lease of life by the Darwinian representation of the natural world as engaged in a perpetual struggle for survival in which the 'fittest' won, this being mistakenly believed by many to mean the 'strongest'. 'Primitive' peoples were supposed to live nearer to nature anyway, and were therefore assumed to be more subject to this law than civilised man. They could thus be looked down upon for being so weak as to give in to despots on the one hand, and on the other for not having advanced beyond the animal struggle. The phrase 'the law of the jungle', intrinsically contradictory in its assumption that the animal kingdom was not regulated or ordered, was applied to human societies whose only form of political control seemed to be force. The hero of *The Coral Island* sums it up: 'Now I understand . . . that the island is inhabited by thorough-going, out-and-out cannibals whose principal law is "Might is Right and the weakest goes to the wall" ' (ibid., p. 199).

Ballantyne's technique of denigrating 'primitive' institutions by denigrating the character of those who operate them is common in the fiction of the day, and despotic chiefs are a continual source of sneering light relief. Wallace's account of the 'big king' in his West Africa stories depicts native rule as despotic and native rulers as eye-blinking buffoons. The 'big king' is 'a vicious old man, if Sanders was any judge of character' (Wallace, 1911, p. 175), and his strength lies in confining his 'injustices, his cruelties and his little wars within the boundaries of his state', while in *The People of the River* one chief gambles his state away and another sells it to the highest bidder. Such activities debase the office of chiefship, and Wallace adds to this by his descriptions of the physical appearance of the chiefs themselves; one he describes as 'an old man squatting on a heap of skins and blinking like an ape in the sunlight' (Wallace, 1912, p. 83), while another, who is a mere boy, is firmly put in his place by the use of the mock heroic technique; ' "You are a great king" he said to the sleepy-eyed boy who sat on a stool of state, regarding him with open-mouthed interest. "When you talk the earth shakes at your tread" . . . "Oh, ko, ko" giggled the king, pleasantly tickled' (ibid., p. 15).

Thus Sanders, the district commissioner, is justified in not taking native leaders seriously, a practice noted by Cairns in missionary propaganda: 'There was also a tendency to use comments on cultural differences to provide comic relief to the reader and simultaneously to re-affirm white racial and cultural superiority' (Cairns, 1965, p. 98). By devaluing the institutions of 'primitive' society, Sanders justifies the British presence and emphasises the image of 'savage' life before colonisation as continual intertribal warfare and rule by petty tyrants unworthy of their role.

Henty and others, whose stories concern the activities of British troops in 'savage' lands, inevitably emphasise the war-like character of 'primitive' peoples, since the main reason their heroes meet them is to fight with or against them. In Henty's story of the Mahdist wars, the Dervishes are seen as crazed savages whose only political control stems from the religious obeisance they pay their fanatical leader. Compared with the ordered British troops they are disorganised and ill-disciplined, and the British have a moral obligation to free the towns and the hard-working peasants from such tyranny. There is a hint that some organisation exists in their political life; Henty remarks that the Mahdi's son, Mahmud, is limited in his control over the troops by the power of the Emirs, who have some say in his actions (Henty, 1902, p. 103). But the Madhi remains the ultimate power, and Henty does not elaborate on the social organisation and inbuilt checks on power, preferring to leave an impression of wild, fanatical despotism which justifies the British presence.

This argument is also used by A. E. W. Mason to demonstrate the good work being done in India by British administrators who introduce justice and order to a lawless people. In *The Drum* he describes native societies as 'little treacherous savage kingdoms between the borders of India and the Hindu Khush' (1937, p. 9) and 'every one of these sixpenny thrones is built up on blood and treachery' (ibid., p. 19). The British attempt to stop such 'bad customs as raiding and selling into slavery' and they adopt the role of king-makers, forcing local nobles to kneel to the prince the colonists support (ibid., p. 120).

Kipling's India similarly consists of petty potentates who require the British presence to observe law and justice. These native states are 'the dark places of the earth, full of unimaginable cruelty, touching the railway and the Telegraph on one side, and on the other, the days of Harun-al-Raschid' (in Maugham (ed.), 1952, p. 174). The British administrators discuss their relations with local leaders in the same patronising terms as colonists in Africa and the South Seas,

complaining in one instance of the 'miserable intrigues of an impover-
ished native state whose king alternatively fawned and blustered for
more money from pitiful revenues contributed by hard-wrung
peasants and camel-breeders' (ibid.). Kipling's tales tell more of the
problems of the British administrator and of Indian life through his
eyes than of the detail of the political institutions of Indian states;
hence they perpetuate the image provided by those travellers in
Africa who are in favour of those who keep order at whatever cost.
Describing an administrator's report on a native kingdom, Kipling
notes that he is obliged to 'pretend they are as well administered as
those under direct British rule' and thus to hide rebukes against
local leaders for 'filling offenders with pounded red pepper and
eccentricities of that kind' (Kipling, 1888, p. 102). The flippant tone
with which such exotic examples of native political activity are
described implies they are commonplace and suggests, in a patronising way, the need for British control and the superiority of the British
political system.

A group of hard-working administrators, on reading in a newspaper of an attack on Imperialism by a British MP, defend their
presence in India by emphasising the inability of local princes to rule
properly:

> 'I'd give a month's pay' says Lowndes of the Civil Service, on
> special duty in the political department, 'to have that gentleman
> spend one month with me and see how the free and
> independent native prince works things.' Old Timbersides –
> this was his soubriquet for an honoured and decorated feudatory
> prince – has been wearing my life out this week past for money.
> By Jove, his latest performance was to send me one of his
> women as a bribe' (in Maugham (ed.), 1952, p. 71).

He goes on to characterise native despotism by referring to the
prince's attitude to his harem:

> 'The darlings haven't had any new clothes for nearly a month,
> and the old man wants to buy a new drag from Calcutta –
> solid silver railings and silver lamps, and trifles of that kind.
> I've tried to make him understand that he played the deuce
> with the revenues for the last twenty years and must go slow.
> . . . I've known the taxman wait by a milch-camel till the foal
> was born and then hurry off the mother for arrears' (ibid., p. 71).

It is such misrule that the English are in India to prevent. Kipling's John Chinn so captures the imagination of the Bhils that they become his 'children', accepting his word as law, confessing their misdeeds, and abandoning their evil ways. But if the Chinn family ever stops providing the tribe with leaders 'and the little Bhils are left to their own imaginings, there will be fresh trouble in the Satpuras' (in Maugham (ed.), 1952, p. 68). So incompetent are the natives at organising their own affairs that even a pair of English 'loafers' can go up to the hills of Afghanistan and be accepted as kings. They plan to go to a place where there are thirty-two heathen idols with whom they can claim kinship, and so be adopted as numbers thirty-three and thirty-four. The tribes are constantly fighting each other, and the basis of the take-over is that the Englishmen can drill them and provide them with British rifles. They go to a valley where there are many tribes, on the principle that 'the more tribes the more they'll fight, and the better for us' (ibid., p. 179); with a show of rifle-power that kills twenty men they win the natives over, and with the aid of the ritual of Freemasonry they establish their position at the top of the local hierarchy. They use this power to bring peace to the area, teaching the tribes to plant and sow, and training a native army for protection: 'Nobody is going to be shot or speared any more, so long as he does well' (ibid., p. 192).

As the boys in *The Coral Island* expect to rule the natives, Allan Quatermain also takes over Zu-Vendiland only a year after arriving, and Sanders is beloved of his people, despite his occasional harshness. Indeed one chief, whom he had punished harshly, later dies to save Sanders's life; in Kipling some Bhils come back from a heavy beating by John Chinn 'warmed, sore but happy'. The natives themselves respect British rule and accept their punishment with the wise stoicism of the English public school boy.

But there is another despot ruling the lives of 'pre-social' man – the innate conservatism of those with closed minds who are subject to the tyranny of custom. That 'primitive' man blindly followed the lead set by his ancestors was an inevitable adjunct of the theory that he could not think for himself. And Henry Maine's assertion that early society begins with the group not the individual, and that custom and habit precede conscious legislation, gave the idea learned authority. Many travellers and writers took the concept out of context and expected to find all 'primitive' peoples the slaves of custom. Lucy Mair, in a recent popular anthropological work, still feels obliged to assert that 'primitive' men are not 'too dull-witted and superstitious to question the rule of conduct' (Mair, 1962, p. 18). The gullibility of the native is a constant theme in the literature and it is supported by accounts of what happens to those occasional sceptics who refuse to be taken in by their society's conventions.

When a thinking man appears among one of Sanders's tribes, his people throw him out; slaves to their old conventions, they cannot understand his new ideas (Wallace, 1912, p. 99). Andrew Lang's short story on this theme presents the current image of 'primitive' man in order to satirise it and to suggest that the Victorians look nearer home before condemning the conservatism of other societies. Why-Why questions the 'body of strange and despotic customs' which rule his tribe and discovers that supernatural sanctions are not so powerful as his fellow savages believe:

> He went against the law forbidding members of the serpent clan to kill a snake, yet the earth did not open for him; he spoke to his sister despite the law forbidding it and his companions immediately executed and ate her; he complained that the witch doctor, far from curing his mother, had frightened her to death and, with all these experiences behind him, came to realise that radical social reforms were desirable (Lang, 1886, p. 187).

After many revolutionary incidents he is driven out by the tribe and finally killed, whereupon they realise their loss and raise a memorial to him. The point that Lang is making is not just that 'primitive' society is hidebound by custom, as most of his contemporaries assumed, but that his own society is equally conservative. Thus Shelley, scorned in his life-time, is worshipped after his death like Why-Why, since society only recognises a radical's true worth when he is safely dead.

In this image of the political life of the 'savage', the chief custom to which he was supposed to be subject was 'superstition', and the chief sanction, the supernatural. Their use of 'humbug' to control the natives made white travellers realise the possibility that it was also being used by native leaders, for example those witch-doctors of popular literature who are really cynical politicians taking advantage of the superstitions of their people.

Evans-Pritchard notes, in addition, the rationalist, atheistic attitude of mind of many early anthropologists which made them see all religion as an illusion used by the ruling classes as an 'opium of the masses':

> Implicit in their thinking were the optimistic convictions of the
> 18th century rationalist philosophers that people are stupid
> and bad only because they have bad institutions and they have
> bad institutions only because they are ignorant and superstitious
> and they are ignorant and superstitious because they have been
> exploited in the name of religion by cunning avaricious priests
> and the unscrupulous classes which have supported them!
> (Evans-Pritchard, 1965, p. 15).

He argues that the intellectuals used this analysis of 'primitive' religions to discredit Christianity; but on the other hand, missionaries also used it to emphasise the need for converting the native to Christianity and freeing him from the superstitions which made him such an easy prey of the wily politician. The superiority of the British political system was assumed to be inextricably bound up with the Christian religion. Superiority was ultimately vested in those who were 'British, Christian and White' (Cairns, 1965, ch. VI) and the qualities were interdependent. Thus the inferiority of 'primitive' political systems could be attributed to superstition and paganism, while the democratic principles of England could be attributed to the prevalence there of the 'true' religion.

The depiction of 'primitive' political life as exploitation of superstition by wily priests and unscrupulous chiefs is characteristically explicit in Edgar Rice Burroughs: when Mbonga, the native chief, observes Tarzan making a fool of his witch-doctor, he is very concerned:

> Wise old patriarch that he was, he never had more than half
> believed in witch doctors, at least since greater wisdom had
> come with age; but as a chief he was well convinced of the
> power of the witch doctor as an arm of government, and often
> it was that Mbonga used the superstitious fears of his people
> to his own ends, through the medium of his medicine man
> (Burroughs, 1919, p. 73),

The chief and the witch-doctor share the spoils; so it is in the interests of the politician to support the official religious hierarchy, and this is why he is worried when Tarzan discredits the head of the church;

> The old chief's interest in the matter was due solely to that
> age-old alliance which exists between church and state. . . .
> As Mbonga received, as chief, a certain proportion of the
> witch doctor's fees . . . his heart and soul were, quite naturally,
> wrapped up in the orthodox church (ibid., p. 102).

The terminology deliberately refers the reader to the Christian religion and its relations with the British Government. All religion is seen as a political weapon, and the 'savage' is only a more superstitious precursor of his equally gullible European counterpart.

Rider Haggard's detailed descriptions of native religion and politics also suggest a comparison with European practice, but he believes in the superiority of the Christian religion and so compares the exploitation common in 'primitive' life only with abuses in European history. In *Allan Quatermain* he devotes a whole chapter to detailed ethnography of the Zu-Vendi tribe, going well beyond the exigencies of the story to show his concern for the facts of native life. The priesthood has a more sophisticated political power than have the witch-doctors in Burroughs's tales. They are nominated by the state but cannot be deposed; they have secret rules which enable an order from a high priest to be carried out unhesitatingly hundreds of miles away; they are the judges of the land with 'practically unlimited jurisdiction over religious and moral offences, together with a right of excommunication which, as in the faiths of more highly civilised lands, is a very effective weapon' (Haggard, 1887a, p. 154); and they have a virtual monopoly of learning, particularly of astronomy 'which enables them to keep a hold on the popular mind by predicting eclipses and even comets'. Thus 'it is scarcely too much to say that they really rule the land' (ibid., p. 155).

Such a detailed analysis of the institutions by which a 'primitive' society is ordered is rare in the anthropological fiction of the day, and Haggard deserves more credit than he is usually accorded for setting this example. The theoretical framework in which he places this detailed knowledge, however, is that of contemporary academics. Religion is seen as political exploitation of native superstition and slavery to custom, though in practice it is more like that of corrupt medieval Europe than the wild and grotesque witch-doctor scenes customary in such literature.

In Mitford's *The King's Assegai* there is a picture of the archetypal

witch-doctor, dressed in 'cow-tails, entrails and hideous paraphernalia' (1894, p. 55), but the horror of his external appearance
is balanced by the insight the novel provides into his life, his feelings
and the thoughts that lie behind his political activities. Mitford
describes the Zulu custom of witch-doctors 'smelling out' the king's
enemies, and shows how it is used with political acumen by king
and witch-doctor alike. Our knowledge of the characters as individuals, however, makes them less stereotyped than the picture
would suggest.

Haggard probes even deeper behind the superficial trappings of
skulls and rattles by presenting one of his Zulu stories, *Nada the
Lily*, through the eyes of a witch-doctor. This man tells of his life
during the time of Chaka, the great Zulu leader, and how he influenced
the political events of that time. We learn that he became a witch-
doctor because he was more intelligent than most, and saw this
career as the best way to use that intelligence to advantage. Thus he
acquiesces in the king's use of religion for political purposes, 'smelling out' the king's enemies as witches for execution and taking great
care to leave his friends in peace. But ultimately he uses religion for
his own purposes, not those of the king, cleverly balancing the
political factions of Zululand to give himself maximum power without having to assume the vulnerable mantle of office itself, in the
tradition of the king-makers in Shakespeare's history plays. Having
persuaded Chaka's two brothers to kill the king, he 'weighs them
both in the balance, for I would know which was the most favourable
to me' and he has his favourite murder the other (Haggard, 1892,
p. 176). The witch-doctor is cast as the power behind the throne,
as Archbishops of Canterbury have been in English history. Haggard's
account of these intrigues helps to dispel the image of primitive man
as always involved in bloody warfare, lacking the subtlety to solve
his disputes in any other way. Mopo tells Umslopogaas 'there are
more ways of killing a man than by assegai' (ibid., p. 195) and he
works by 'filling the land with rumours, prophecies and dark sayings'
– 'and I worked cunningly on the minds of many chiefs that were
known to me' (ibid., p. 245).

The selection of particular aspects of 'primitive' political life by
nineteenth-century observers was also conditioned by contemporary
historical events; and the tendency of popular literature to present
half truths with authority mean that the representation of political
institutions, though based on the writer's own limited experience or

on popular knowledge of political events, seemed to be true for all 'primitive' societies. Thus the Mahdist wars reinforced the image of 'primitive' politics as religious exploitation by showing how a religious leader could rouse emotions to a pitch of fanaticism where various Arab groups would bury their differences in a holy war. The impact of this can be seen in various novels which describe a native religious leader combining peoples who were otherwise divided.

In *The Four Feathers*, A. E. W. Mason describes in romantic terms how religious fanaticism foments political revolt; Mohammed Ahmed

> marched . . . preaching with the fire of a Wesley the coming of
> a saviour. The passionate victims of the Turkish tax gatherer
> had listened, had heard the promise repeated in the whispers
> of the wind in the withered grass, had found the holy names
> imprinted even upon the eggs they gathered up (Mason, 1902,
> p. 25).

Mason is attempting to show the political appeal of religion to ordinary persons as Mitford interpreted the origins of mob frenzy in *John Ames*, and in doing so he perpetuates the image of 'primitive' political life as dominated by war and religion. Attempts by Henty and others to make imaginative capital out of the Mahdist wars, the death of Gordon and the Egyptian campaigns, which had captured the public imagination in the 1880s, inevitably emphasised this theme, while the more mundane aspects of African political activity received less publicity. This is understandable in fiction, but what was selected for dramatic purposes in fiction could easily be regarded as typical of primitive politics as a whole. How particular events in one part of the Empire could be used to colour the popular image of life throughout the colonies is evident in Buchan's account of a native uprising in *Prester John*. Seeing the connection between native religion and nationalism through the eyes of the white colonist in fear of being pushed back into the sea, he over-emphasises the political implications of African religious sects and thereby over-simplifies the actual situation. The English in the story are in constant fear that the Africans will one day combine together to throw them out. While they remain divided, the English can rule South Africa and many colonists believe they will not rise 'because they cannot find a leader with the proper authority and they have no common cause to fight for' (Buchan, 1910, p. 78). But one of the settlers,

Wardlaw, whose views are given authority by continual references
to his wide education and reading, believes they might find a leader:

> 'He has been reading a lot about Ethiopianism which educated
> American negroes had been trying to preach in South Africa.
> He did not see why a kind of bastard Christianity should not
> be the motive of a rising. 'The Kaffir finds it an easy job to
> mix up Christian emotion and pagan practice' (ibid., p. 59).

He accepted that most African leaders, 'fat men with top hats and
old frock-coats, who live in dirty locations' (ibid., p. 58), posed no
threat to the British, but he was afraid that this religious movement
might provide a leader.

Captain Arcoll is another learned man:

> 'It has taken me years to decipher it, and, remember, I've been
> all my life at this native business. . . . So what I tell you you
> can take as gospel for it is knowledge that was not learned in
> a day' (ibid., p. 76).

He traces back the legends of Prester John, a 'pagan Christian' who
founded a great African empire based on Ethiopia. After his death
the centre of authority moved south. Many native empires were
founded which claimed to be 'the successors of Prester John' (ibid.,
p. 77), and carried a fetish with them that was a symbol of his power.
The Zulus from the north 'brought with them the story of Prester
John, but by this time it had ceased to be a historical memory and
had become a religious cult' (ibid.). Chaka had owed his power to
the possession of the symbol and its associations with Prester John,
but after him it had disappeared. Now it seems to have reappeared,
borne by John Laputa, a native missionary who has been preaching 'Africa for the Africans' and who might provide a focus for a
religiously oriented nationalist revolt under the title of 'Ethiopianism'.

The movement that came to be known as 'Ethiopianism' originated
in South Africa in the 1870s when black converts to Christianity,
despised and segregated in the white churches, began to set up their
own missions under black ministers. The sectarianism of the Christian religions and their emphasis on the future life provided a model
for native millenarian sects, and by the 1890s there were great
numbers of them. They derived their title from taking Ethiopia as
their ideal, since it was an African state still ruled by the natives,
and from the sixty-eighth Psalm, 'Ethiopia shall soon stretch out

her hands to God'. The religious movement became more directly
political when the Abyssinians defeated the Italians at Adawa in
1896. Its adherents thus came to stand for 'religious African nationalism which always threatened to boil over into revolt against European
rule' (Shepperson and Price, 1958, p. 72).[1]

In 1897 Joseph Booth, a mission-educated African, wrote 'Africa
for the Africans', whose title became a rallying-cry for the black
inhabitants and a justification for alarmist fears. It is used by Buchan's
crusading minister. Booth suggested three courses to ease the lot of
the oppressed Negro: a Christian Union, the Negro colonisation of
Africa, and self-supporting industrial communities. Towards the
second of these ends he began to bring American Negroes to Africa
so that their education would help bridge the gap of opportunity
he saw between white and black, starting a plantation south of
Blantyre with American Negro labour.

The British press became worried and began to attack Booth for
introducing 'Ethiopianism' under the cover of the mission station,
and a wave of minor hysteria spread through Southern Africa. The
Natal newspapers felt that 'Ethiopianist' American Negroes might
soon cause 'a general native uprising' and the *Central African Times*
carried a correspondence referring to these fears and from Booth
defending his mission.[2] In 1901 Buchan arrived in South Africa to
serve as Milner's secretary in the 'Milner Kindergarten', so that
Wardlaw's 'reading' is based partly on Buchan's own experiences in
trying to deal with the situation. When he arrived, the 'Ethiopianism' scare was at its height and there were many examples of secessionist churches led by black ministers for him to recall in later
years and use for his novel.

One notable example was the Mzimba sect. Pambani T. Mzimba
had been ordained at the Lovedale mission headed by James Stewart,
and was such a model priest that Stewart sent him abroad in 1893
to attend the jubilee of the Free Church of Scotland. At this time
Buchan was eighteen years old and attending Glasgow University
(Buchan, 1940, p. 32), and can hardly have failed to hear of this great
gathering. His autobiography tells of a youth spent wild and free in
the hills and countryside of Scotland, interspersed with the Sunday
ritual of sermons. This background provides the basis for the novel
in which John Laputa, a black minister who has come to Scotland
to preach at the Free Kirk and gather money for his work, is discovered by the roaming boys of the parish performing African rites

on the beach. Mzimba did, in fact, collect a great deal of money for his mission. On his return to Lovedale he wanted to spend it on his own missionary ideas; so in 1892 he seceded to found the Presbyterian Church of Africa, taking with him his congregation and the church property. The Church of Scotland took the case to the African Supreme Court and it was still being debated when Buchan arrived in Africa, to provide yet another strand to the theme of a secessionist black missionary returning from Scotland.

The educated African as a focus for general discontent among his brethren; the influx of American Negroes to help the cause; the belief that the African could only be educated up to a certain point and would then relapse into savagery; the examples of secessionist black missionaries and the Bambuta Revolt of 1906 – all these elements were focused on the term 'Ethiopianism', which the European community applied to any independent African religious movement. Shepperson and Price (1958) point out that these movements, with their highly factional character, in fact served as safety valves for discontents which might otherwise have been channelled into more dangerous activities. White fears were often exaggerated or directed at the wrong people.

Two letters to *The Times* in England during this period demonstrate that not all such movements were political. One letter, from W. M. Cameron, 'lately chaplain to the Bishop of Grahamstown for the Ethiopian Mission', complained that there were two branches of 'Ethiopianism' which had been confused. One branch, coming under the influence of the African Methodist Episcopal, an American Negro group, was violently anti-white and 'dangerous'; the other was loyal to the extent that its leaders subscribed entirely to the English church and accepted its authority and that of its civilian counterparts, while retaining the ideals of self-reliance and dignity under the title of the 'Order of Ethiopia'.[3]

On 19 July this letter was followed by another from Charles E. Grahamstown emphasising the extent to which the 'Order of Ethiopia' was subject to white religious and political authority, happily 'rendering unto Caesar the things that are Caesar's . . .'. Grahamstown also objects to the confusion of this movement with the nationalist fervour of those dominated by American Negro influences.

John Buchan disregards such distinctions and complexities; his black minister leads an 'Ethiopianist' movement dedicated to throwing the white man into the sea; and thus his novel perpetuates only the alarmist fears of the settlers in South Africa in the early 1900s. Even the prophetic similarity of history to the Nyasaland Rising of 1915 fails to capture the human qualities of the reality. According to Shepperson and Price, this rising had 'an intimate drama that Buchan's *Prester John*, for all its great pageantry of African revolt, lacks; and which makes its leader, the Rev. John Chilembwe, so much more of a puzzle than Buchan's Rev. John Laputa' (1958, p. 4).

The review of *Prester John* in *The Times* says of Laputa; 'To paint a simple noble savage and at the same time to Europeanize his brain was the feat that Mr Buchan set himself' (25 August 1910, 303e). Janet Smith in her biography claims that it took 'a rare imaginative sympathy to conceive Laputa – a man of mystery and power of fineness and nobility beside his savagery' (Smith, 1965, p. 141). Despite the 'racism' of the book, she says, Buchan treats Laputa with humanity and the conflict is not between white and black but between 'civilised and savage'. It is exactly the confusion of these sets of categories that makes Buchan's book so much part of the tradition of anthropological fiction. Laputa is black, so, however 'civilised' he becomes, there will always be the danger that his inherent 'savagery' will come to the surface in times of stress.

Buchan, like Haggard, cannot escape the romantic tradition, and Laputa inevitably retains features of the noble savage. But, since in the conflict between primitivism and progress European faith in progress is always stronger, the elements of 'fineness and nobility' in Laputa do not contradict the notion of European superiority, for they represent the beginnings of the 'better culture'. The conflict in Laputa's character thus derives less from Buchan's 'imaginative sympathy' than from the conflicts and prejudices of his age. The result is never in doubt. When the native armies are defeated and their leader is killed, Davie puts the events into perspective in terms of Buchan's own imperialism:

> I knew then the meaning of the white man's duty. He has to
> take all the risks, recking nothing of his life or his fortunes
> and well content to find his reward in the fulfilment of his
> task. That is the difference between white and black, the gift
> of responsibility, the power of being in a little way a king;
> and so long as we know this and practise it, we will rule not in

Africa alone but wherever there are dark men who live only
for the day and their bellies (Buchan, 1910, p. 215).

Thornton, writing of the 'Imperial Idea', realises the role played
in it by such works of fiction which 'embalm for ever the atmosphere
that so kindled the imaginations of the age that has gone '(Thornton,
1959, p. 92). 'Buchan' he writes:

> the Scottish 'outsider' with his idealised admiration for the
> closed circle of English power, where everyone knew everyone
> else, where everyone knew where everything was – 'the pass
> on the right as you go over into Ladakh' – and where everything
> and everyone not so known was not worth knowing, painted
> a better romantic picture of Empire than Disraeli. . . . His
> books set a standard to which imperialists should conform;
> a straight a simple standard, but one which only genuine
> white men were able to follow (ibid., p. 92).

Buchan's account of the importance of religion in 'primitive'
political life is thus coloured by the perspective from which he
viewed all 'primitive' life; and the description of 'Ethiopianism',
which appears so authoritative in the novel and which seemed to
be vindicated by the events of the Chilembwe Rising, ignores the
complexity of the actual situation.

Buchan's concern with religion in 'savage' life can be seen in the
way he adapts the same theme in *Greenmantle* to the situation in the
Middle East during the First World War. Islam, Richard Hannay
hears, is to be united for a holy war by means of a symbol and, if
the Arab states rise, British troops will have to be deployed from
the European front, thus weakening the opposition to Germany.
The rising of Islam thus becomes relevant to life in Britain and, as
in *Prester John*, Buchan relates it to a central symbol, a fetish which
would act as a sign for a general religio-political uprising. The fetish
is the prophet's green mantle, possessed by a beautiful white woman
who will come to lead the rebellion; and the hero's job is to inter-
cept her, since without her and the symbol (as without Laputa and
his fetish) the revolt will fail.

The political interpretation of religious movements is part of the
attempt in the late nineteenth century to read some meaning into the
seemingly irrational customs reported from other parts of the world.
Many institutions, it was realised, though they failed to fulfil their

ostensible purpose, such as appeasing the gods, nevertheless served some useful purpose in helping to maintain social order. This approach was fostered by the work of John Stuart Mill. Rejecting the utilitarian deductive philosophy of applying universal principles to consciously determined ends in all societies, he advocated instead an inductive approach, studying the evidence of history, daily experience and the particular social situation. He thus provided a model for a functional study of society, by putting emphasis on the way different aspects of social life are integrated (cf. Burrow, 1966). Although it was turned into a crude empiricism by Macaulay and others, this approach enabled the European to look for significance, even if unconscious, in customs which seemed at first sight irrational and meaningless.

Thus Tabu Dick notes of the 'savage' religion, 'True it is that some of their tabus are based on foolish superstitions; still tabus govern their moral and civil code. Destroy them, give them nothing to take their place and – . . .' (Greene, L. P., 1935a, pp. 75–6). And Mason notes in *The Drum* that 'foolish beliefs can be wisely used' (1937, p. 49). Likewise the interpretations of South African millenarian cults, of the witch-doctor practices of the Zulu or the fiery preaching of the Mahdi, are based on the assumption that strange religious practices have a political function, that 'primitive' religious life consists largely of political exploitation by those natives who understand its functions.

The application of the functional approach, however, helped to break down some of the stereotypes created by popular fiction; for it entailed taking into account more of the details of 'primitive' life, acknowledging the effect of one institution on another and so refining the image of the savage as in a continual state of anarchy or as ruled by tyrants. Other influences on social control were recognised – for example the importance of a king's retainers as checks on his power, and the use of consensus in deciding local conflicts. These details were incorporated into novels which also perpetuated the simpler stereotypes. The result is that the conflicts of the Victorians in the approach to the study of 'primitive' man can be seen in the descriptions of popular novels, and the range of approaches found there.

Wallace, having described the 'big king' as an eye-blinking tyrant, also demonstrates the part played in 'primitive' political life by consensus. He describes native councils where the elders came 'bringing their own carved stools, and sat about the thatched shelter where the chief sat in his presidency' (Wallace, 1911, p. 162). The kinds of problems these councils has to deal with suggest at least some desire for order in 'primitive' life. When a certain man goes mad, the elders of his family meet to decide what to do with him, and by consensus and debate agree to a test to see if he is really mad (Wallace, 1912, p. 91). When a man who has paid a quantity of salt as bridewealth is deserted by his wife, he brings his demand for recompense to the chief (Wallace, 1911, p. 18). On numerous other occasions problems of litigation are described, particularly concerning the price of wives and compensation for desertion, and the 'savage' is shown coping with them in a manner reasonable to European eyes. Much of this, it is implied, is due to British influence, but nevertheless it is suggested that 'primitive' man uses debate and consensus as well as force and superstition to solve his conflicts, and the 'palaver' assumes the importance for Africa that the 'pow-wow' has for North America in popular fiction.

The despotism of the chiefs described in popular fiction is also sometimes tempered by reason and sympathy. Umzilikasi, head of a breakaway section of Zulus in Mitford's *The King's Assegai*, can kill his enemies at will, and employs witch-doctors to 'smell' them out and thus give him the authority of religion, but he is also shown as heeding a good defence made by one spirited offender (Mitford, 1894a, p. 25). He spares a brave witch-doctor who refused to flinch when thrown on burning stones (ibid.); he accepts a clever argument by which the hero justifies his transgression on the grounds that it revealed his bravery (ibid., p. 79); and he insists on being informed of every detail of kraal life, so that his rule will be wise and just (ibid., p. 190). The story is concerned with Umzilikasi's secession from Chaka and the political intrigues of large empires. As in Haggard's Zulu stories, a comparison is suggested with European practice and despotism is qualified, even if by intrigue.

In India the intrigues and lengthy consultations loved by local princes are as much part of the stereotype as despotism and anarchy are in Africa. In *The Broken Road* Mason describes long political discussions between the British and the Pathans who demand a drawn-out debate, much beating about the bush and much ceremonial on such occasions. The description appeals to the exotic sense of readers accustomed to smile patronisingly at the seemingly artificial rhetoric of Indian princes. The 'ceremonious preliminaries' are followed by hours of talk, of bowing and other such little courtesies and the English, impatient to get down to the political matter in hand, have to be restrained by a wise colonial officer who realises the important function of this form of debate (Mason, 1907, p. 25). Others are less tolerant, and Kipling describes the political life of a native state as 'the gay-coloured tag-rag and bobtail of an old-fashioned Hindu court' (in Maugham (ed.), 1952, p. 274). By describing alien political institutions in exotic terms, the writer implies that they are not to be taken as seriously as the more sober and serious day-to-day work of the English civil service. When Umzilikasi sits on a 'carved block of wood, covered with Leopard skin and surrounded by a body guard' (Mitford, 1894a, p. 105), and the West African chiefs bring their own carved stools and sit in a thatched shelter, or when gaily clad Pathans talk with rhetorical grandeur, the importance of what they are saying is overwhelmed for the observer by the way in which they are saying it and the setting in which the discussion takes place.

The everyday problems that have to be solved in the jungles of Africa as much as in the cities of Europe are described in detail by Edgar Rice Burroughs in the Tarzan stories. Tarzan becomes chief of a tribe of apes whom Burroughs designates as the ancestors of man, revealing in simple form the institutions and habits which 'modern' man has refined. As chief he has to solve numerous domestic problems. When Gunta's wife, for instance, refuses to scratch her back she bites him and Tarzan has to decide who is in the wrong and what has to be done. Burroughs summarises these legal functions of the chief in terms which might also apply to those supposed to be modern man's more recent predecessors, the 'savages'. 'And so it goes, little family differences for the most part which, if left unsettled, would result finally in greater factional strife and the eventual dismemberment of the tribe' (Burroughs, 1917, p. 97). The litigation also contributes to social cohesion, and the tribe is kept together by more than coercive force. This is the 'mass of orderly life' which Conrad noted was so often misrepresented.

As anthropology became more sophisticated and 'primitive' institutions came to be studied in their own terms, popular writers began to incorporate the subtler details of 'savage' life into their novels and to suggest the function of alien customs. The academic interest in kinship and in divine kingship was added to the interests in custom, despotism, the political function of religion and consensus which had already become a regular feature of Victorian fiction.

SIL—L

The widespread custom that an aging king must relinquish his post to a youthful successor when he becomes infirm is incorporated by Ballantyne and Haggard into their novels, in different ways. In Ballantyne the boys discover the tradition that a dead chief's wives are traditionally buried with him. When they hear that the old chief has died they rush to his house to save the women. But the women are already dead. The chief is not yet dead and his son is pacing up and down waiting for a grave to be dug so that the old man can be buried alive. Ralph then recalls

> having heard that it is a custom among the Feejee islanders
> that when the reigning chief grows old or infirm, the heir to
> the chieftainship has a right to depose his father; in which
> case he is considered dead and is buried alive (Ballantyne, 1858,
> p. 207).

Frazer, in *The Golden Bough*, refers to such a custom in Fiji; he notes there the practice of suicide by old men, who voluntarily asked to be buried alive by their family because they want to enter Elysium with some faculties left and because of the scorn of weakness among a martial people (Frazer, 1890, p. 11). Frazer 'explains' this custom according to the principle of Divine Kingship, which his book popularised. The king is identified with the land by his people. When he becomes infirm, it is assumed the land will likewise decline, the crops will die and the country become infertile. So he must be killed, and a young man must take his place so that the land will be fertile again. Frazer links this with 'primitive' men's concern with 'sympathetic' magic and their obsession with fertility rites since they live in close contact with nature. Ballantyne, however, is less concerned to 'explain' such customs, by whatever theory, and merely adduces them as an added example of the inhuman savagery of heathens. Ralph is horrified: 'Oh, my heart groaned when I saw this! and I prayed to God to open the hearts of these poor creatures, as He had already opened mine' (Ballantyne, 1858, p. 207).

Haggard, more influenced by current anthropology than was Ballantyne, describes a Zulu custom by which the physical prowess of the king is identified with the fertility of the land, in more sympathetic terms and with more concern for what it might mean to the people themselves.

Umslopogaas meets a tribe whose chief is he who holds 'Groan-Maker', a great axe. Each year he can be challenged by any comer, and the winner becomes chief. This ensures that the chief remains virile as Frazer believed he should. This does not mean, however, that chiefship is the prerogative merely of the strongest man in the tribe, that might is right; Haggard explains that the axe has remained in the hands of the same family for years, passed on from unconquered father to son, since whoever is holding the axe 'has always been unconquerable' (Haggard, 1892, p. 128). The axe thus provides a means of stability in the succession of chiefship, while ensuring that the chief does not become idle or gross. Umslopogaas explains its function as a symbol of the stability of the tribe; 'by virtue of the axe I bear I rule alone. If I am seen without the axe then any man may take my place who can, for the axe is chieftainess of the People of the Axe, and he who holds it is its servant' (ibid., p. 231). Thus each individual ruler is secondary to the office he holds, and the symbol of that office, the axe, ensures the unity of the tribe, their common allegiance and the obligation owed them by their chief, who is thus ultimately not a despot but a servant, a point of view not dissimilar to that of some modern anthropological interpretations.

This analysis is not particularly sophisticated, but its application to a 'primitive' tribe, particularly in a popular novel, is a considerable advance on the ethnocentric conception of alien customs represented by Ballantyne. Frazer's awareness, in a book published two years earlier than Haggard's, of the continuity of kingship office above the transience of its individual holder, had showed that 'primitive' institutions were worthy of scholarly interest, and had provided an authoritative example of what could be made of such data. With regard to the Zulus, he records an account by a traveller to Chaka's court, who had aroused the king's interest with an oil to get rid of wrinkles and grey hairs. The Zulu king wanted to try this treatment because of the custom, in his tribe, that when a chief exhibited 'those proofs of having become unfit and incompetent to reign' he was forced 'to make his exit from the sublunary world' (Frazer, 1890, p. 272). Frazer uses Chaka's concern with physical prowess as further proof of his theory of Divine Kingship and the association of the king with the fertility of the land.

Haggard, it is evident, had learnt of a particular tribal custom in Zululand and to his audience it must have seemed in keeping with the general theory made popular by Frazer two years before. Although there is no specific reference to Frazer in *Nada the Lily*, and Haggard's interpretation is not based on Frazerian Divine Kingship, nevertheless the very fact of Haggard's interest in the symbolic nature of chiefship arose from the climate of thought that writers like Frazer were creating at the time. The great appeal of works like *The Golden Bough* was that they provided a scheme into which interesting customs from exotic lands could be fitted. Once the technique had been authoritatively established it could be used at all levels of society. 'Primitive' customs were no longer to be merely described as strange or horrific, they were to be 'explained' by some theory borrowed from a well-known scholar, or made up by the author himself. D. H. Lawrence used this licence in *The Plumed Serpent* particularly to give his own interpretations authoritative support, borrowing from the scholars as he saw fit. As for the descriptions of 'primitive' political life in the popular novel, the prevalence of anthropological theory meant that many writers paid more attention to the details and functions of political institutions and attempted to 'explain' strange customs in the way contemporary scholars were doing.

On the one hand, then, the novels represent the contemporary framework of thought which saw all 'primitive' customs as racially determined and as earlier stages towards the development of European custom. Writers were concerned to portray the 'pre-social' state within which it was assumed social control was either non-existent or dependent on force, or unnecessary, or was a despotism resulting from the exploitation of naïve superstitions by unscrupulous priests. On the other hand, the growing preference for the 'inductive' method led to a functionalism that could be used by the popular novelist for his own ends as well as by the scholar. More attention was paid to the details of 'primitive' life, and some explanation was sought for what seemed at first sight unintelligible. These 'explanations' were often based on or borrowed from contemporary anthropological works; the functions of consensus, Divine Kingship and kinship in 'primitive' political life were introduced, albeit tentatively, into some popular novels, along with the traditional stereotypes, and often in conflict with them. These novels translate into dramatic form the theoretical conflicts of the day as to how the information being brought back from 'primitive' lands could be interpreted and classified. And, while the writers inevitably draw on the collective representations of their own society with regard to 'primitive' peoples, and classify them according to that society's system of classification, individual authors are able to make something new, imaginative and creative out of the information available to them, so that the representation is both perpetuated and significantly altered.

Chapter 7

'Primitive' religion in popular literature

The general image of 'primitive' man which derived from the opening up of Africa and the extension of colonial rule in the later nineteenth century and which was influenced by contemporary theories of literature, race and politics, underwent a significant change as the discipline of anthropology developed a specific body of ideas that could be applied to all 'primitive' phenomena. These ideas were absorbed into popular literature which, in turn, created an expectation and demand for them in future works, so that scholarly anthropological theories gained the popular currency which psychological theories have in present-day literature. They were not necessarily incorporated in full academic dress, however. Rather, oddments were added to an already considerable wardrobe of ideas from other sources. Threadbare academic theories were hung up beside long-held prejudices with which they often clashed.

In the field of 'primitive' religion these old prejudices were crystallised in the word 'superstition', used to account for any custom or belief that seemed irrational or out of the ordinary. Indeed so strange were some 'superstitions' that they hardly merited the title of 'religion', which would have suggested that they were comparable with the infinitely 'superior' morality of European life. Jasper Rose in *The Merchandise of Light*, attempting to show the impact of the New Knowledge on English thought in the seventeenth century and after, describes the arguments as to whether 'primitive' man believed in God. Where many early travellers, he claims, were Christians and attributed their own beliefs to 'savages' too, others overcame this initial bias and 'came to admit that certain peoples had no belief in God whatsoever' (Rose, 1954, p. xxvii).[1] Locke, for instance, quoted the Hottentots, the Brazilians and the Chinese as having no such belief, and so cut the ground from under the deists' feet. This argument continued into the nineteenth century and coloured many accounts of the 'beliefs' of 'savages'. Sir Samuel Baker, talking to the Ethnological Society of London in 1866, said of the Nilotic tribes of the Sudan:

> Without any exception, they are without a belief in Supreme
> Being, neither have they any form of worship or idolatry;
> nor is the darkness of their minds enlightened by even a ray of
> superstition. The mind is as stagnant as the morass which
> forms its puny world (Baker, S. W., 1867, p. 231).

Evans-Pritchard has pointed out the sophistication of the beliefs of these peoples, whom he himself lived with and described in detail in such anthropological classics as *The Nuer*. He warns of the dangers of talking about 'religious' 'beliefs':

> Statements about a people's religious beliefs must always be
> treated with the greatest caution, for we are then dealing with
> what neither European nor native can directly observe, with
> conceptions, images, words, which require for understanding
> a thorough knowledge of a people's language and also an
> awareness of the entire system of ideas of which any particular
> belief is part, for it may be meaningless when divorced from the
> set of beliefs and practices to which it belongs (1965, p. 6).

Writers of popular fiction felt no such qualms at the end of the nineteenth century and glibly dismissed 'primitive' beliefs as 'mere pagan error' (Curtin, 1965, p. 23). Gilson writes that the pygmies have 'no religion' at all (1919, p. 23), though he later describes a 'superstitious' belief in the forest as a god (ibid., p. 61). Most of his contemporaries disagree with Baker in attributing some 'ray of superstition' to the native. Long before Baker, travellers had elaborated on the nature of these 'superstitions'. Bishop Heber, in the early nineteenth century, disturbed that the idyllic surroundings of the 'heathen' did not seem to elevate his mind, had described the 'idolatrous worship' of nature:

> What though the spicy breezes
> Blow soft o'er Ceylon's isle;
> Though every prospect pleases,
> And only man is vile;
>
> In vain with lavish kindness
> The gifts of God are strown;
> The heathen in his blindness
> Bows down to wood and stone.
> ('From Greenland's Icy Mountains')

The writers of exotic novels in the later nineteenth century are still disturbed by such 'idolatry' and dismiss it with scorn and horror. Kipling describes the religious beliefs of a Burmese girl in terms similar to Heber, though the style and the tone suggest disdain rather than indignation:

> By the old Moulmein Pagoda, lookin' eastward to the sea,
> There's a Burma girl a-sittin', and I know she thinks of me; ...
>
> An' I seed her first a-smokin' of a whackin' white cheroot,
> An' a-wastin' Christian kisses on an 'eathen idol's foot.
> ('Mandalay')

The beliefs of the native are thus debased. The ordinary British soldier's view of native religion, as represented here, is not far removed from that held in more intellectual circles. No attempt is made in either case to understand the religious significance of such activities for the natives themselves.

Similarly, in the Tarzan stories 'primitive' beliefs are devalued by being made fun of. Tarzan creeps unseen into the native village to overturn a cauldron and place a skull on top of a pile of clothes, and the inhabitants resort to leaving out an offering of food to propitiate this spirit of the jungle. Tarzan, though, takes the food, and this disturbs the natives even more:

> 'for it was one thing to put out food to propitiate a god or devil, but quite another thing to have the spirit come into the village and eat it. Such a thing was unheard of and it filled

their superstitious minds with all manner of strange fears'
(Burroughs, 1917, p. 95).

Burroughs thus satirises the natives both for being superstitious
and for not having faith in their superstitions.

The gullibility of the 'savage', the ease with which he can be taken
advantage of, stems from his superstitious nature, and thus every
example of 'humbug' is a further debasement of the seriousness of
his beliefs. In one of Wallace's stories, for instance, an Arab manages
to persuade the gullible natives that they should pray in a different
place every night. Each night they move farther and farther away
from the village so that the Arab can return to steal their goods;
and when Sanders finds them, they are still moving away every night
in a confused and pathetic way (Wallace, 1912, p. 203).

Missionary travellers, however, had a vested interest in describing
the 'fallacies' of heathen practice and did not stop at merely making
fun of it. Cairns notes how their reports were determined by the
need to collect money and encourage more recruits from home:

> The more degraded, backward and immoral the non-Christian
> world could be painted, the greater would be the difficulty of
> refuting the arguments for missionary expansion. The dramatic
> contrasts of the worst features of heathenism with the most
> exalted aspects of Christianity exaggerated the distinctions
> between the Christian west and the non-Christian world
> (Cairns, 1965, p. 99).

Ballantyne's account of the religious life of the 'heathens' on
Coral Island, compared with the benefits brought to the Christian
converts there, rigidly reproduces this pattern. Native religion is a
long succession of horrors. Apart from throwing babies to a snake
god, burying old chiefs alive and dancing gleefully round human
sacrifices, the islanders conduct a procession to a temple in a ceremony so grotesque that the native missionary feels he cannot
attend: 'I must not go to the heathen temples and witness their
inhuman rites, except for the purposes of condemning their wicked-
ness and folly' (Ballantyne, 1858, p. 213). The boys, however, take
a morbid interest in the spectacle and adopt the dubious plan of
'mingling', white faces, European clothes and all, with a crowd of
naked, black women at the rear of the procession.

The bodies and faces of the natives are painted in 'hideous' fashion

as they carry a number of dead men from the battle to a temple full
of skulls and knife-toting priests. Here the bodies are pulled about
by everyone before being baked in a fire. Then a live prisoner is
placed in a hole in the ground and a pole and earth placed on him
so that he becomes a foundation stone. The boys are 'sick with
horror', yet fascinated by curiosity and 'fear it is all a dreadful
dream'. Afterwards they are told that this 'was a *ceremony* [*sic*]
usually performed at the dedication of a new temple, or the erection
of a chief's house!' (ibid., p. 215). The italics and exclamation mark
suggest what they think of attaching the word 'ceremony' to such
'horrors'.

It is because of these 'pagan' rites that the Christian missionaries
are so necessary. Conversions are achieved with remarkable ease,
an encouragement to prospective recruits. A few prayers from the
missionary often suffice to bring a tearful chief to his hut with all the
pagan gods and effigies to be burnt, and many are the orgies of
destruction by Christian priests. The burning of the Christian gods
in D. H. Lawrence's *The Plumed Serpent* is a deliberate portrayal of
the reaction to this. But the difference between Christianity and
paganism is emphasised in *The Coral Island* mainly by the character
of their respective villages. Those which are converted become
peaceful and civilised. They are now safe anchorages for European
trading vessels and are laid out in a neat and beautiful manner compared with the squalor of pagan villages;

> Everything around this beautiful spot wore an aspect of peace
> and plenty; and as we dropped anchor within a stone's cast
> of the substantial coral reef, I could not avoid contrasting it
> with the wretched village of Emo, where I had witnessed so
> many frightful scenes. When the teacher afterwards told me
> that the people of this tribe had become converts only a year
> previous to our arrival and that they had been living before
> that in the practice of the most bloody system of idolatry,
> I could not refrain from exclaiming 'What a convincing proof
> that Christianity is of God' (Ballantyne, 1858, p. 202).

Similarly, in a short story by John Russell, 'The Witch Woman',
the religion of the natives of Mololo is described with horror and
repulsion, but eventually peace and virtue are brought to the island
through the work of the English missionary. The sailors who brought
the Rev. Spicer to Mololo watch with interest as they leave him

there alone and take bets on how quickly the natives will attack and then eat him. Spicer is shocked at his first encounter with the natives, so different from his fervent hopes when back in his Broomie Street Congregation; 'Undeniably the darkness of the dark places has a shock to it that no amount of theory will lighten much. And he had picked out a pretty dark place' (Russell, 1923, p. 267). His congregation are described in flippant, scornful tones: 'A fine ripe candidate for a deacon was old Faimungo, petty chief of the bay; soot clad and even sootier with encrusted ceremonial dirt' (ibid.).

That 'primitive' body painting may have considerable symbolic and religious significance is seldom remarked by English writers, who see only 'hideous', distorted daubings. Greene describes the natives as 'black painted devils' (Greene, L. P., 1935a, p. 11), and in Gilson 'the warriors were smeared with paint' (1919, p. 157), while those Tarzan meets are painted to look 'even more hideous than nature intended' (Burroughs, 1919, p. 44). The reduction of the significance of these important means of symbolising beliefs to 'ceremonial dirt', and the use of such evaluative terms as 'smeared', 'hideous' and 'soot', further debase the religion of 'primitive' peoples. Only later do writers like D. H. Lawrence in his Mexican series attempt to understand the 'meaning' that lies behind body painting, the symbolism of the colours used and its importance to the actors.

Spicer, seeing little beyond this surface of local beliefs, tries to terrify the 'loathly creatures' he has come to convert by appealing to his own god, and Russell notes the impact of this on them – 'When you already have a pantheon of some hundreds of gods – mostly malevolent – when you believe that every stick and tree harbours a blood-drinking deity, you do not lightly offend a new one' (Russell, 1923, p. 269). Such a conception of the religious life of 'primitive' man comes from an inability to understand the meaning of his customs to the 'primitive' himself and Russell admits the barrier that existed for Spicer: 'He could not penetrate these folk. Their thoughts, their habits – all their ways remained an unchanged mystery' (ibid., p. 279). Thus the ceremonies of the natives are 'unspeakable rites', their horror increased for the reader by being left to his imagination. Conrad employs a similar technique in *The Heart of Darkness* where, as Leavis points out, 'the same adjectival insistence upon inexpressible and incomprehensible mystery is applied to the evocation of human profundities and spiritual horrors' (Leavis, 1948, pp. 196–7). The tone and style of such descriptions

are a key to the author's attitude to the 'primitive' customs being
described and, while Conrad uses the technique consciously, if in
some opinions unsuccessfully, to evoke a sense of profundity,
Russell and many like him use it merely to increase the sense of
horror at native customs and to dramatise the position of their
hero.

In Russell's tale the religion of the natives is characterised not
only as mysterious and incomprehensible, but also as bloodthirsty
and savage and in need of Christian enlightenment. After the natives
in Spicer's village have been subjected to the most cruel and bloody
slaughter by those of the next village, he feels a partisan pity for
them and, having killed the enemy chief, becomes leader of the
village, realising the good he can do for 'these groping, wayward
children – these untaught brethren of his neglected by the centuries'
(Russell, 1923, p. 290). When the sailors who brought him return to
see what has happened to the missionary they are astonished at
what they find:

> 'They stared in silence at the Mission building – trim and
> orderly; at the pastoral residence, already lapped in vines;
> at the new church with its walls of delicate sennit-work like
> an airy great bird cage; and the sanded walks and clean
> thatch-tops of the village and the outlying copra sheds that
> bespoke prosperity (ibid., pp. 292–3).

And they remark on the change: 'No more high old, bloody times
in Mololo.' Spicer has succeeded, as did Ballantyne's missionaries,
in 'civilising' the 'savages' by means of Christianity. The peace and
prosperity of the village provides a vivid symbol of the nature of
Christianity compared with the horrors of native 'religion'. These
simplified descriptions of 'primitive' religious life, and these stylistic
techniques reinforcing the ethnocentricism of the age, are the stock-
in-trade of a great many writers about exotic lands in the late
nineteenth century.

This kind of representation of the horrors and ignorance of
primitive religion is typical, too, of the travellers' reports of the time;
so that when anthropologists began to collate and analyse the information brought back about 'primitive' tribes, they had to deal with
data hardly conducive to detached, academic study. The techniques
and attitudes of these students themselves only served to further
emphasise the 'superstitious' nature of 'primitive' thought, and to

suggest that what meaning could be discerned in their 'religion' was merely an irrational concern with the supernatural, which the scientifically-minded Victorians felt they had long ago rejected. Evans-Pritchard notes this tendency in anthropology:

> If a false impression was created by observers of primitive peoples, giving undue prominence to the mystical in their lives, it was embossed by scrap-book treatment, which was dignified by being labelled the 'Comparative Method'. This consisted, with respect to our subject, of taking from the first-hand records about primitive peoples, and willy-nilly from all over the world, wrenching the facts yet further from their context, only what referred to the strange, weird, mystical, superstitious – use which words we may – and piecing the bits together in a monstrous mosaic, which was supposed to portray the mind of primitive man. Primitive man was thus made to appear . . . as quite irrational . . . living in a mysterious world of doubts and fears, in terror of the supernatural and ceaselessly occupied in coping with it (1965, pp. 9–10).

This concept of the mental faculties of 'primitive' man was re-inforced by the racial theories of the day, which assumed that the intellectual power of the 'childlike' races was not as developed as that of the Europeans, being less 'logical', less able to follow a rational argument (this was why the 'savage' was so overawed by those manifestations of the supernatural which the reason of Euro-pean man saw in a more scientific perspective), while Frazer, one of the anthropologists to whom Evans-Pritchard is referring, saw primitive religion as derived from mistaken thinking: 'The flaw – and it is a fatal one – of the system lies not in its reasoning, but in its premises' (1890, p. 263).

In popular literature such ideas were presented in passing as though they were proven 'fact'. Sanders has to 'treat with folk who were, in the main, illogical and who believed in spirits' (Wallace, 1911, p. 48), while Davie, in *Prester John*, returns home from South Africa more sympathetic to the native but no more enlightened: 'I learned much of the untold grievances of the natives, and saw some-thing of their strange, twisted reasoning' (Buchan, 1910, p. 82). The charismatic native leader whom the English have defeated has proved the inferior reasoning power of the 'primitive' mind: 'I said he was an

educated man, but he is also a Kaffir. He can see the first stage of a
thing, and maybe the second, but no more. That is the native mind'
(ibid.).

This exemplifies how the intellectualist theories of 'primitive'
thought are used as an integral part of the popular novel. It is on the
basis of this judgment of Laputa that his defeat is made to seem
realistic to the reader, for the advantage of numbers, enthusiasm
and knowledge of the terrain were on his side and, had he been
white, the reader might have found it less easy to suspend his disbelief at the ease of the British victory over him. The limited reasoning power of the native, adduced as the origin of religion by the
anthropologists, is used in fiction to make realistic for the reader his
lack of success against the British in a dramatic battle.

The superiority of the white man in a jungle setting stems from
his inherited power of reasoning. Tabu Dick, for instance, 'could
think as the natives think, reason as they reason. But he retained the
white man's ability to take mental short cuts and to make direct
logical conclusions' (Greene, L. P., 1935a, p. 21). It is an advance on
the completely ethnocentric view of 'primitive' customs in Ballantyne
to suggest that 'primitive' man could think and reason at all, but
it is still assumed that the nature of that reasoning is innately
different from that of Europeans. Inevitably the collective representations of different societies involve different categorisation and con-
ceptualisation of experience so that the modes of reasoning may
seem sometimes very different, but nineteenth-century anthropologists
were claiming more than this. They claimed that these differences
derived from racial heritage and many of them, like Hunt, believed
they were permanent, rather than merely different expressions of a
common human capacity. Lévy-Bruhl maintained that 'primitive'
thought was 'pre-logical', 'caractérisée par son orientation mystique;
par un certain nombre d'habitudes mentales, et spécialement par
la loi de participation, qui y existe avec les principes logiques'
(Lévy-Bruhl, 1931, p. 26). Evans-Pritchard (1933, p. 41) has pointed
out the weakness of these arguments and few anthropologists today
would make such distinctions, especially as groups such as 'primitive'
and 'civilised' do not lend themselves to formal definition. But in
the nineteenth century the evolutionary model was still applied to
all areas of experience, including thought processes, and it was
assumed that 'primitive' thought represented an early stage of
development. It was thus 'mystical', and unable to make the logical

steps of European thought. 'Primitive' man was dominated by a superstition that he had not the mental ability to see through.

Thus in popular literature 'primitive' religion is characterised as 'hedged about with tabus of superstition' (Greene, L. P., 1935a, p. 40). 'Because they were surrounded by "tabu" and "ju-ju", because their every waking action is ruled by spirits, Africa's children are very ready to accept the supernatural' (ibid., p. 117). This is continually brought out by examples of the native's inability to discern the 'reality' that lies behind seemingly mystical events. Tabu Dick, for instance, effects a 'vanishing trick' by jumping up into the branches of a tree when all eyes are on the ground and the natives, inevitably, put down his disappearance to the 'supernatural', whereas the white man can see what 'really' happened: 'And yet the explanation, as were the explanations of all Tabu Dick's seemingly supernatural powers, was a very simple one' (ibid., p. 261). All explanations of the 'supernatural', it was assumed, were 'simple' to those with the ability to reason. 'Primitive' man's fear of the 'supernatural' was thus assumed to stem from an inability to reason. Popular writers, by arguing their point so forcefully and with such concrete examples, are engaging in an academic debate, the theoretical suppositions of which they have accepted as given 'fact'.

Much of the academic debate accepted the assumptions of what the anthropologists once called the 'if I were a horse' approach. The Victorian gentleman assumed that he could 'understand' 'primitive' thought by imagining how he himself would act if he lived in those conditions and had that 'limited' reasoning power. At its worst this approach merely involved working out what his reactions and thoughts would be and assuming that those of the 'savage' would be the same. Hence it could be assumed that 'primitive' man would judge his own practices, such as cannibalism, body painting or polytheism by the same standards as a white Christian gentleman. Since a white Christian gentleman could only do those things by abandoning his moral code, it was assumed this was what 'primitive' man had done, as though European morality conformed to 'natural', universal law. This aspect of the 'if I were a horse' approach traps the observer in his own ethnocentrism and prevents him from ever understanding how other people view their actions.

A more fruitful aspect of this approach, and one lying nearer modern anthropological practice, was already well documented in

the 1880s in the Sherlock Holmes stories. Conan Doyle's scientifically-minded detective consciously attempts to put himself inside the
mind of others not so much as he thinks but as they think. In order
to 'understand' a criminal he clears his mind of all preconceptions
and reasons backwards from the person's actions, from what the
anthropologist would call the 'ethnography'. He explains this to
Dr Watson in the first story in which he appears, *A Study in Scarlet*
(1887):

> Most people, if you describe a train of events to them, will tell
> you what the result would be. They can put those events
> together in their minds and argue from them that something
> will come to pass. There are few people, however, who, if you
> told them a result, would be able to evolve from their own
> inner consciousness what the steps were which led up to that
> result. This power is what I mean when I talk of reasoning
> backwards or analytically (Doyle, 1887, p. 138).

Dealing with the Lauriston Gardens mystery he describes how he
put this theory into practice:

> Now this was a case in which you were given the result and
> had to find everything else for yourself. Now let me endeavour
> to show you the different steps in my reasoning. To begin
> at the beginning. I approached the house, as you know, on
> foot and with my mind entirely free from all impressions (ibid.).

He recounts his systematic and careful search for clues and how he
deduced that the victim had been poisoned. He applied a combination of knowledge of similar cases, 'The forcible administration of
poison is by no means a new thing in criminal annals' (ibid., p. 139);
general understanding of human nature, 'Men who died from heart
disease or any sudden natural cause, never by any chance exhibit
agitation upon their features' (ibid., p. 179); and by eliminating
other possibilities, 'By the method of exclusion, I had arrived at this
result, for no other hypothesis would meet the facts' (ibid., p. 179).
This process is now the stock-in-trade of all fictional (and many
'real') detectives, and is not unlike the attempts of the anthropologist
who returns from the 'field' and tries to explain the equally mysti-
fying practices of other societies.

   Holmes's assumptions, of course, are those of his own society.
His generalisations about human nature are really generalisations

about nineteenth-century Englishmen. The general truth for other
societies of such statements as, 'Political assassins are only too glad
to do their work and to fly. . . . It must have been a private wrong,
and not a political one, which called for such a methodical revenge'
(ibid., p. 140) must be called into question as we learn more about
other ways of life. Holmes, though, does take such possibilities into
account, where he knows of 'foreign' customs: 'Now a real German
invariably prints in the Latin character, so that we can safely say
that this was not written by one, but by a clumsy imitator who
overdid his part' (ibid., p. 142). In order to persuade the reader
to a 'willing suspension of disbelief', such cross-cultural details would
have to be presented more often and in a more sophisticated way as
knowledge of other cultures increased in quantity and sophistication.

Holmes sometimes stretches his readers' credibility even when
dealing with his own society. He claimed 'by a momentary expression,
a twitch of a muscle or a glance of an eye, to fathom a man's inmost
thoughts' (ibid., p. 22). But his emphasis on detailed observation of
even the trivia of social life reflects the increasing rigour of contemporary anthropological and sociological enquiry:

> By a man's finger-nails, by his coat sleeve, by his boot, by his
> trouser-knees, by the callouses of his forefinger and thumb,
> by his expression, by his shirtcuffs – by each of these things
> a man's calling is plainly revealed. That all united should fail
> to enlighten the competent enquirer in any case is almost
> inconceivable (ibid., p. 22).

While there is an element here of that assumption, examined
earlier, that internal features can be deduced from external ones,
which eventually led to racism, the attention to detail and concern
with understanding the context of all the elements involved, argues
a more fair-minded and truly scientific attempt to understand others.
Whenever Holmes tells Watson to think as a criminal would think
and not as he himself would; whenever he advocates judging
'strange' practices only in their total context; and whenever he
attempts to clear his mind of all preconceived impressions, then
Doyle's detective is remarkably close to the ideals of the twentieth-
century anthropologist. When he adduces as general features of
human nature what are, in fact, the assumptions of a nineteenth-
century Englishman and when he proposes a universal key to all
human activity, he is more like the 'armchair anthropologist' of his

own period. When Watson exclaims, 'But do you mean to say that without leaving your room you can unravel some knot which other men can make nothing of, although they have seen every detail for themselves' and Holmes replies confidently, 'Quite so. I have a kind of intuition that way' (p. 24) we are reminded of Sir James Frazer, sitting in his library in Cambridge and receiving travellers from all over the world, whose strange tales he claims to 'explain'. Holmes, however, believes in field work: 'Now and again a case turns up which is a little more complex. Then I have to hustle and bustle about and see things with my own eyes' (ibid.). The modern anthropologist usually sees things with his own eyes while young and then remains at home later in life, applying his special 'intuition' to the knowledge brought back by others. He works in many ways according to the principles laid down by the detective of Baker Street, and his training is aimed at freeing him from the blinkered vision of Holmes's companion and foil Dr Watson, who cannot imagine how others think, as the detective and anthropologist must.

The attempts at detection by nineteenth-century anthropologists, however, tended to be very culture-bound – more like that of Watson than of Holmes. The reasoning deduced from the religious practices of 'primitive' man, for instance, is more often that of the educated Englishman than what was actually going on in the minds of the devotees. This is the case when E. B. Tylor, in *Primitive Culture*, asks his readers to imagine the thought of the 'ancient savage philosophers' (1871, p. 428) about the difference between a living body and a dead one, and with regard to dreams. Working his way step by step through these 'primitive' thoughts, he arrives at the idea of a soul or spirit which animates all natural phenomena and which is held 'among the lower races'. The theory of 'animism' is then used to 'explain' all 'primitive' religious life. Nature myths, for instance, stem from this rather than from metaphor and language alone, as Muller had claimed. Muller (1870), adopting the same technique of sympathising with the thoughts of 'savage' man, from his European drawing room, had concluded that the deities of 'primitive' religion were personified natural phenomena. Knowledge, he claimed, is acquired through the senses and reasoning is based on them; so the intangible and majestic phenomena of nature, such as the sun and the moon, inspire in the 'primitive' mind a notion of the infinite which is transposed into concrete form as deities. The infinite is described by metaphor and symbols of majesty taken from nature, and these symbols are then personified and worshipped in their own right as gods. In this sense religion is a 'disease of language', a phrase which Muller coined in a rash moment and which has obscured the issue ever since. It does, however, indicate Muller's method of tracing the origin of religions by following the etymology of god names back to names for natural phenomena. Every deity has his origins in the observation of nature.

Both Tylor and Muller, then, gave academic authority to the assumption that the origin of deities was to be discovered by conjecturing the thought of 'primitive' man about natural phenomena, whether he was overawed by them or philosophical about them. Modern detailed studies of 'primitive' societies have demonstrated the number of different modes of thought regarding deities, and it is evident that the awe, personification, animism and 'mistaken reasoning' that Tylor, Muller and others attributed to primitive peoples belonged in fact to the thinking processes of their own society. They were generalising from their own thoughts and speculations rather than discovering what others thought.[2] Such matters are ideal subjects for popular literature, and much fiction concerning 'primitive' tribes at the time has passages relating how and why the natives worship the sun, or the moon or some other dramatic natural phenomena. Haggard, for instance, can 'understand why primitives worship the sun if the conditions of life render them liable to exposure' (1887a, p. 42), and in *King Solomon's Mines* he introduces the names of the gods and attempts to trace them back. The travellers come across three 'colossi' which obviously represent deities carved by some advanced culture and they are curious to know their origins. Quatermain speaks their thoughts. Contemplating these 'Silent Ones', as the Kukuanas called them:

> an intense curiosity again seized us to know whose were the
> hands that had shaped them, who it was that had dug the pit
> and the road. Whilst I was gazing and wondering, it suddenly
> occurred to me (being familiar with the Old Testament) [*sic*]
> that Solomon went astray after strange gods, the names of three
> of whom I remembered – Ashtoreth, the goddess of the
> Zidonians, Chemosh the god of the Moabites, and Milcom
> the god of the children of Ammon – and I suggested to my
> companions that the three figures before us might represent
> these false divinities (1885, p. 209).

Although the source of Quatermain's theory is the First Book of Kings (I Kings 11: 5, 7), the practice of tracing the origin of deities in this way was being made currently popular by the anthropologists and classicists. Indeed, Muller himself uses this particular reference to make a similar point. Referring to those Hebrew gods which do not belong to the whole of the Semitic family but each to their own branch of it, he conjectures;

> They either started into existence after the first Semitic Separation, or at all events they became in after times the peculiar gods of their own peculiar people, such as Chemosh of the Moabites, Milcom of the Ammonites, Ashtoreth of the Sidonians.
> (1882, p. 119).

Haggard, attempting to lend an air of scholarship to his work, takes Muller's technique even further and traces one of the gods back through history to some natural phenomenon. Sir Henry Curtis replies to Quatermain's suggestions:

> 'Hum,' said Sir Henry, who was a scholar, having taken a high degree in classics at college, 'there may be something in that; Ashtoreth of the Hebrews was the Astarte of the Phoenicians, who were the great traders of Solomon's time. Astarte, who afterwards was the Aphrodite of the Greeks, was represented with horns like the half-moon and there on the brow of the female figure are distinct horns' (Haggard, 1885, p. 209).

Again, the source of this practice, and perhaps even of the particular examples used, lies in contemporary anthropology. Muller, tracing deities back to natural phenomena, pays considerable attention to Ashtoreth:

> Another female goddess is Ashtoreth or Ashtaroth (plural) [sic] . . . and she was worshipped, not only by the Carthaginians, Phoenicians and Philistines, but likewise by the Jews. . . . The Phoenicians called her Astarte, and by that ominous name she became known to Greeks and Romans. She may have been a moon-goddess (1882, pp. 116–17).

As the gods in Haggard's novel belong to the ancient civilisation which once lived where now there are only ignorant and superstitious 'savages', his description contributes less to the image of 'primitive' religion itself than to making the framework of thought within which it was discussed more familiar to a wider public.

In *She* he is also concerned with tracing the classical origins of a particular deity. 'She-who-must-be-obeyed' is the reincarnation of an Egyptian princess, Amenartes, waiting through thousands of years for her lover Kallikrates to return to her, similarly reincarnated. She is able to talk with Holly, another classical scholar travelling in Africa, about the various civilisations and religions since her first existence and thus to realise the relativity of all religion: 'All great Faiths are the same, changed a little to suit the needs of passing times and peoples.' And she traces her own particular religion back to natural phenomena: 'Isis is Nature's soul, the secret spirit of the world' rather than a god (Haggard, 1887c, p. 125). Religion is thus traced back to a worship of nature, and the names of the gods can be found in personifications such as Isis, the spirit of nature. Muller's theory is used as the source for a tale of majesty, love and awe which haunted many in Haggard's time. Morton Cohen, attempting to unravel some of the 'anthropological, cultural and ethnic ingredients' of *She*, cites many South African tribes in whose religion and myth a goddess figures and suggests that Haggard's own experience in Africa contributed to the story. Cohen also suggests that this is an early form of religion and 'with the advent of civilisation, people's concept of the deity becomes more complex' (1965, p. 104). If this is the significance attributed to Haggard's treatment of 'primitive' religion in 1960, after most anthropologists had abandoned the evolutionary framework some forty years before, it is not surprising that Haggard's works helped to establish this image in the 1890s when the theory was still respectable in academic circles.

If we can sometimes trace specific references in the romances of the time back to specific anthropological writings, more often we find the general themes of current anthropology used as background to a romantic setting which may be entirely fictional, or derived from some dubious traveller's report. It is in the use of academic theories as a framework for popular fiction, rather than in specific borrowing, that scholarly ideas are given general currency, especially since the examples which illustrate them are usually more vivid and hence memorable than those of the anthropologists themselves. A discussion of the origin of religion as derived from dreams, for instance, appeals more to the public imagination when related as an integral part of an exciting Tarzan adventure than does the same theory expressed in the works of Spencer or of Tylor.

The Tarzan stories, in fact, weave together the threads of many academic theories of the time about primitive religion and thought. The young white man, born in the jungle, but still imbued with the qualities of a Victorian gentleman, begins to think about the existence of God as he grows up; his development represents a speeded-up version of that of all mankind, from the earliest 'primitive' ideas to 'civilised' religion, so that the progress of religious thought can be followed through. The evolutionary scheme is applied to 'spiritual' progress, and the advance from childlike to mature thought in the individual is used as a model for that of society. Tarzan is able to demonstrate the processes of 'pure' thought because 'he was not handicapped by the second-hand and often erroneous, judgments of others' (Burroughs, 1919, p. 35); the course of progress is assumed to be 'natural', and his life is regarded as something approximating to a controlled experiment. The vivid descriptions of 'primitive' life in popular literature are often treated by the authors themselves as laboratory experiments deliberately intended to prove a theoretical point.

Tarzan finds the word 'God' in the books he is attempting to read, and deduces that it is always associated with ideas of a great 'all-powerful individual', perhaps a different form from himself. On asking his fellow apes he is told: 'The power which made the lightning and the rain and thunder came from Goro the moon' (ibid., p. 64). The reason put forward for this theory is that 'The Dum-Dum always was danced in the light of Goro' (ibid.). This is the first stage of Muller's theory that knowledge comes from the senses and from reasoning from what they show, so that cosmic phenomena like the sun and the moon give rise to the idea of the infinite. Muller then assumed that words attached to these concepts of the infinite became separated and were themselves personified into deities. Tarzan moves in this direction when he invents his own language and applies it to the notion of God: 'Unlike the apes he was not satisfied merely to have a mental picture of the things he knew he must have a word descriptive of each' (ibid., p. 65).

But, being a white man, and having inherited European culture, he soon rejects the moon as God and searches for Him elsewhere. The apes suggest he asks the near-by natives, so he goes to them and sees the awe in which they hold a witch-doctor. This, he thinks, must be God, so he drops into the native enclosure and questions this worthy who, along with his fellows, turns and bolts. Tarzan overtakes him and pins him to the ground, whereupon he realises that this is a very poor version of the deity: 'So this was what he had thought was God! Tarzan's lip curled in an angry snarl. . . . "If you be God, then Tarzan is greater than God"' (ibid., pp. 72–3). The natives, then, do not provide him with a satisfactory explanation of divinity, a view shared by many travellers at the time. 'Primitive' religion is brought further into disrepute by being inadequate to the questioning of an 'impartial' observer.

Tarzan returns, instead, to his own mental processes, which he has inherited from Victorian culture and retained despite his savage surroundings. The strange things he finds around him gradually seem to have some link: his action in sparing the native chief's life; the she-ape's courage in attacking a snake of which she was usually terrified, in order to save her baby; the opening and closing of flowers; the differences between people, animals and trees – all are linked by the notion of 'creation'. They are all 'good' forces in the world and were all made from nothing, he deduces, so God must be all-powerful, creative and good. This is a European Christian concept, but it is suggested that it is one the thinking man would 'naturally' arrive at; and the very symbols of the Christian religion are described as though they were 'natural' – all things in the jungle, but especially Tarzan, hate the snake, though none can say why; and when Tarzan begins to question the presence of evil in the world, in the true Augustinian tradition, he embodies the problem in the traditional Biblical symbol, 'Who made Histah, the snake?' (ibid., p. 83).

Having followed his cultural inheritance to this extent, Tarzan then reverts to his role at an earlier stage of the evolutionary process. He has a dream in which a lion climbs a tree after him and other normal patterns of life are disturbed, so that he finds it difficult to separate the real from the illusory. This gives rise to a new feeling for Tarzan, fear:

A knowledge which Tarzan awake had never experienced, and perhaps he was experiencing what his early forebears passed through and transmitted to posterity in the form of superstition first and religion later; for they, as Tarzan, had seen things by night which they could not explain by daylight standards of sense perception or of reason, and so had built for themselves a weird explanation which included grotesque shapes, possessed of strange and uncanny powers, to which they came finally to attribute all those inexplicable phenomena of nature which, with each occurrence filled them with awe, with wonder or with terror (ibid., pp. 179–80).

The idea that 'primitive' man's dreams are the origin of religion was given authority by Herbert Spencer (1882), who supposed that when a dead person appeared in dreams a man assumed the person still existed in another life, in the form of spirit, and that these ghost figures of ancestors were worshipped as gods. Thus religion derives from ancestor worship, which derives from fallacious reasoning about dreams. Tylor's theory of animism involved the same idea, only with less emphasis on ancestors:

> What then is this soul or life which thus goes and comes in sleep, trance and death? To the rude philosopher the question seems to be answered by the very evidence of his senses. When the sleeper awakens from his dream he believes he has really been away somehow, or that other people have come to him. . . . As it is well known that men's bodies do not go on these excursions, the natural explanation is that every man's living self or soul is his phantom or image which can go out of his body and be seen itself in dreams. . . . Here then in a few words, is the savage and barbaric theory of souls, where life, mind, breath, shadow, reflection, dream, vision come together and account for one another in some such vague, confused way as satisfies the untaught philosopher (Tylor, 1881, p. 243).

Tarzan grapples with this problem in the same way as Tylor's 'primitive philosopher'. The life of his dreams is so real that he is unable to distinguish it from his waking life, and he thus grins sardonically at a real gorilla which he thinks to be a dream, as it attacks him: 'If this was a sleep adventure, what then was reality? How was he to know the one from the other? How much of all that had happened in his life had been real and how much unreal?' (Burroughs, 1919, p. 184). The 'if I were a horse' method of reasoning is used to explain why 'primitive' man is so much at the mercy of superstitious fears. It is because he cannot distinguish between the dream world and the real one, between spirits and inanimate objects.

To conclude that 'primitive' religion derives from mistaken reason-

ing is an advance on the accounts which claim it derives from lack
of reasoning and which portray it as blind 'superstition' and horror.
It represents a movement from a totally ethnocentric viewpoint to
one which, though ultimately ethnocentric too, at least makes an
attempt at understanding alien customs in their own terms. Thus
Burroughs follows Tarzan's reasoning, representative of that of
'primitive' man at an early stage, as he moves step by step towards
a conception of God. Tarzan notices the difference between night
and day and sees also that the sun shines by day and the moon by
night. He then takes the additional step of assuming that the sun
and the moon influence the conditions with which they correspond
and, having already learnt to attribute personalities to inanimate
things, he assumes that the sun and moon conduct their operations
consciously:

> Sometimes he thought that as colours and forms appeared to
> differ by night from their familiar daylight aspects, so sounds
> altered with the passage of Kudu [the sun] and the coming of
> Goro [the moon], and these thoughts roused within his brain
> a vague conjecture that perhaps Goro and Kudu influenced
> these changes. And what more natural that eventually he came
> to attribute to the sun and the moon personalities as real as
> his own? The sun was a living creature and rules the day.
> The moon, endowed with brains and miraculous powers, rules
> the night. Thus functioned the untrained man-mind, groping
> through the dark night of ignorance for an explanation of the
> things he could not touch or smell or hear and of the great,
> unknown powers of nature which he could not see (ibid.,
> pp. 232–3).

The intellectualist theories of 'primitive' religion are thus given a
popular currency and are explained by specific memorable examples.
Since the native is assumed to be childlike, his attempts to make
sense of the physical universe are like those of a child. 'Imagine, if
you can', says Burroughs, 'a child filled with the wonders of nature,
bursting with queries and surrounded only by the beasts of the
jungle to whom his questionings were as strange as Sanskrit would
have been.' Likewise Tarzan: 'In childhood he had wanted to know,
and denied almost all knowledge, he still in manhood, was filled
with the great unsatisfied curiosity of a child' (ibid., p. 237). Thus it is
with primitive man as he gropes in the dark to explain the universe.

He places great weight on physical correspondences between phenomena, which leads him to an illogical but intellectually worked out theory of religion. What he cannot see he explains by what he can see.

The way in which the character of an inanimate object leads the 'primitive' philosopher to compare it, by analogy, with an animate being that has similar qualities, is shown so 'logically' in one incident in the tales as to enable the reader to sympathise with Tarzan's attempts to bring down the stars with his bow and arrows. Tarzan sees, one night, a group of natives in a clearing light a fire to keep away the lions and other predators. A vivid scene is depicted with the blazing light of the fire inside a thorn fence and numerous pairs of sparkling savage eyes twinking just outside. But when the fire dies down, a lion jumps the fence and carries off an unfortunate native. A little later that night, as Tarzan lies thinking about the universe, there springs to his fertile imagination an explanation of the moon and the stars in terms of this unhappy incident. He rushes excitedly to his ape mate, Taug, pointing towards the stars, and exclaims:

> 'See the eyes of Numa and Sabor, of Sheeta and Dongo. They wait around Goro to leap in upon him for their kill. See the eyes and the mouth of Goro. And the light that shines upon his face is the light of the great fire he has built to frighten away Numa and Sabor and Dongo and Sheeta.
>
> 'All about him are the eyes, Taug, you can see them! But they do not come very close to the fire – there are few eyes close to Goro. They fear the fire! It is the fire that saves Goro from Numa. . . . Some night Numa will be very hungry and very angry – then he will leap over the thorn bushes which encircle Goro and we will have no more light after Kudu seeks his lair – the night will be black with the blackness that comes when Goro is lazy and sleeps late into the night, or when he wanders through the skies by day, forgetting the jungle and its people' (ibid., p. 238).

Tarzan's prediction, of course, comes true, as do all predictions of eclipses in popular literature. The apes look up to the sky and seeing the moon begin to disappear, recall Tarzan's words, 'Numa has sprung through the trees and is devouring Goro'. They send to Tarzan for help, and he climbs a high tree with a bow and arrow and attempts to shoot the stars as he would have shot at a lion. After many arrows have been shot a cry goes up from the apes:

> 'Look! Look! . . . Numa is killed. Tarzan has killed Numa! See! Goro is emerging from the belly of Numa' and sure enough the moon was gradually emerging from whatever had devoured her, whether it was Numa the lion, or the shadow of the earth; but were you to try to convince an ape of the tribe of Kerchak that it was aught but Numa who so nearly devoured Goro that night, or that another than Tarzan preserved the brilliant god of their savage and mysterious rites from a frightful death, you would have difficulty (ibid., pp. 249–50).

Contained within this variation on the eclipse theme are the current anthropological theories of magic, 'primitive' thought and mythology, all given a new lease of life in the pages of fiction. The association that Tarzan makes between the stars and the eyes of the lion is typical of contemporary ideas of the way the 'primitive' mind worked. Frazer, in explaining his theory of magic, writes, 'Man sees the uniformity of nature and assumes that it is due to the similarity of cause and effect' (1890, p. 11). 'Primitive' thought thus stems from an illogical law of contact, by which things act on each other through some invisible medium, giving rise to the theory of magic, by which man believed he could control the forces of nature by using the same processes. The first principle of magic is that 'like produces like, or that an effect resembles its cause', which Frazer calls homoeopathic magic. Thus Tarzan believes that, since his arrows can kill a lion on the ground, they can also kill Numa of the skies. And Tarzan's association of Numa with the stars stems from current intellectualist and emotionalist theories of 'primitive' religion, by which it was assumed 'primitive' man went in awe of natural phenomena and attributed spirits to inanimate things.

The notion that there was evolution in religious ideas as well as in technology meant that the rituals of 'primitive' man were adduced by anthropologists as the origin of contemporary Christian practice, a theory which was sacrilege to those described in Ballantyne. Robertson Smith (to whom Frazer dedicated *The Golden Bough*) wrote about the similarities of Christian and 'savage' practice, in his analysis of the clan system of the ancient Semites. Each clan, he claimed, had a material representation in some animal, its totem, and the unity of the clan was annually reasserted and revitalised by partaking of the flesh of this animal, which was otherwise forbidden: the origin of primitive religion thus lay in the communion ceremony by which the god of the clan, having been ritually sacrificed, was consumed by members of the clan. Frazer, in his analysis of the importance of Robertson Smith, points out the significance of his theories for the Christian religion. For the sacrifice he describes in 'primitive' societies is that also of Christian countries, a fact which many members of those countries found very disturbing:

> Among the many questions which it raises, the one which will
> naturally interest Christians most deeply is, How are we to
> explain the analogy which it reveals between the Christian
> Atonement and Eucharist on the one side, and the mystical
> or sacramental sacrifices of the heathen religions on the other?
> Robertson Smith's answer to this question was that the mystical
> sacrifices of the heathen foreshadowed in a dim and imperfect
> way the Christian conception of a divine Saviour who gives his
> life for the world (Frazer, 1927, pp. 288–9).

The passage in which Robertson Smith draws this analogy, however, is omitted in the second revised edition of the book, published posthumously in 1894, a measure of the feeling still aroused by such statements.

Frazer, himself, in *The Golden Bough*, provided even more convincing proof of the relation between 'pagan' practice and Christianity. Writing of 'Our Debt to the Savage', he claims that we should not scorn his early, if misguided, attempts at reasoning; for it is from them that our own conception of the nature of life is derived:

> We stand upon the foundation reared by generations that have
> gone before, and we can but dimly realise the painful and
> prolonged efforts which it has cost humanity to struggle
> up to the point, no very exalted one after all, which we have
> reached (1890, p. 263).

He cites the custom among many 'primitive' people of associating the virility of the king-god with the fertility of the land, so that when his strength begins to fail he must be deposed and a new virile leader take his place. The dates of these festivals of 'renewal' in many parts of the world coincide, and he notes that the Christian festival of Easter is celebrated on the same date and season, the vernal equinox, on which the ancient European resurrection of Attis was celebrated. With evidence from other Christian ceremonies which have replaced the time and form of 'pagan' festivals, he claims that it is more than just coincidence that 'the Christian and the heathen festivals of the divine death and resurrection should have been solemnised at the same season and in the same place' (ibid., p. 360). This he puts down partly to the shrewdness of Christian missionaries seeking converts, modifying their own religion 'so as to accord in some measure with the prejudices, the passions and the superstitions of the vulgar' (ibid., p. 362). He traces the gods Osiris, Adonis and Attis back to 'personifications of the great yearly vicissitudes of nature, especially of the corn', and shows how they are related to the Christian symbols and rituals concerning Christ.

The Golden Bough was read as literature at the turn of the century, by an enthusiastic public haunted by its style and inspired by the range and significance of its theory. And in 1920, in *The Waste Land*, T. S. Eliot made a number of specific references to it which ensured that future generations of literary students would perpetuate Frazer's notion of 'primitive' religion as concerned with fertility rites. The poem was largely incomprehensible to a generation that had inherited Victorian patterns of language, and found it difficult to cope with the seemingly illogical, neo-metaphysical juxtapositions of words and ideas that Eliot was forcing on them. But the 'Notes' which he appended to the poem were written in straightforward prose, and the reader of the time would recognise the references to *The Golden Bough*. Eliot writes there that he is indebted to a work of anthropology 'which has influenced our generation profoundly; I mean *The Golden Bough*; I have used especially the two volumes Adonis, Attis, Osiris. Anyone who is acquainted with these works will immediately recognise in the poem certain references to vegetation ceremonies.' These are the books in which Frazer's conception of the fertility of the Divine King is related to Christianity, and in another note Eliot specifically relates 'The Hanged God of Frazer' with 'the hooded figure in the passage of the disciples to Emmaus', which is, of course, Christ.

Having accepted that 'primitive' religion is concerned with fertility rites, and particularly with the connection between the virility of the king and fertility of the land, Eliot uses the idea to dramatise his feeling about the present state of Europe. Europe has become a 'waste land', symbolised in the poem by 'dry bones', 'limp leaves

waiting for rain' and the 'arid plain'; the Fisher King, symbol of the
fertility of the land contemplates the waste land:

> I sat upon the shore
> Fishing, with the arid plain behind me
> Shall I at least set my lands in order?
>
> (*The Waste Land*, ll. 423–5)

And, with his fondness for a wide and learned range of reference
to provide the symbols and metaphor for his ideas, Eliot uses also
the Arthurian legend to describe the condition of the waste land.
Jessie Weston, in *From Ritual to Romance*,[3] had based on Tylor's
theory of survivals an account of the incorporation into literature
and 'romance' of what had once been the important religious ceremony and 'ritual' of 'primitive' peoples. The major ritual she follows
is that of the association of the king-god with his land, which she
traces as it develops into the European chivalric tradition in which
Sir Launcelot and his peers ride out to free waste lands from aging,
withered rulers. The Fisher King of European romance is associated
with the Dying God of classical and primitive myth and ritual, and
Eliot is able to use this complex detail and symbol as metaphor in
his own exploration of the theme and its relevance for contemporary
Europe. By doing so he gives it new imaginative life, makes it seem
more significant to his contemporaries and their condition, and makes
it part of the literary furnishings of the English-speaking world for
generations to come. Short, compressed references to the 'chapel',
and the 'hanged man', pregnant with literary and anthropological
meaning and range of reference, give a new significance to descriptions of spring ('April is the cruellest month, breeding/Lilacs out of
the dead land'), water, dust, dry bones and aridity. All are linked
with the current image of 'primitive' religion and used as vivid means
of making a symbolic statement about the current condition of
Western man. Even though the notes may now be considered less
seriously than in Eliot's time, their significance lies still in the
specific relationship they point out as existing in the poem, between
anthropological theory of 'primitive' religion, the more traditional
range of literary reference on which European authors were accustomed to draw, and the problems of contemporary life.

But, if *The Waste Land* helped to make 'primitive' religion worthy
subject matter for the poet and man of letters in the style indicated
by Frazer, it also helped to perpetuate the particular image of

'primitive' religion set out by the anthropologist. Modern Christian ritual was seen as a development out of 'primitive' practices which were more crude, erroneous and, often, 'savage'! (Frazer, 1890, p. 357). Frazer demonstrated this process in terms of the Divine King. Robertson Smith, as we have seen, was undertaking the same task with regard to totemism and taboo. He argues that the consumption of the clan totem by 'primitive' peoples in annual sacred rites is related to the 'advanced' Christian communion ceremony. During the rest of the year the people are forbidden to eat the totem, and the purpose of taboo is thus to preserve its sacred character. The self-conscious concern of popular writers with presenting such facts and the theories that lay behind them to the general public can be seen in the references to the practice of totemism and taboo in popular literature at the time.

Thus, when the travellers in *Allan Quatermain* see the natives conducting a wholesale slaughter of sacred hippos, the author is at hand with a footnote to explain to the reader the theories of which Quatermain and his like are unaware. Quatermain attempts an explanation:

> I may as well explain at once that the inhabitants of Zu-Vendi are sun-worshippers, and that for some reason or other the hippopotamus is a sacred animal among them. Not that they do not kill it, because at a certain season of the year they slaughter thousands -- which are specially preserved in large lakes up the country -- and use their hides for armour for soldiers; but this does not prevent them from considering these animals as sacred to the sun (1887a, p. 157).

Haggard is able to clear up Quatermain's uncertainty with a scholarly reference he may well have derived from Andrew Lang:

> Mr. Quatermain does not seem to have been aware that it is common for animal-worshipping people to annually sacrifice the beasts they adore. See Herodotus, ii, 42. – EDITOR, (ibid., p. 141).[4]

Thus the academic theory that links sacrifice and totemism is consciously added to the story, demonstrating the influence of anthropologists on fiction, while the character of the average hunter/explorer as describing only superficially and without analysis, is preserved.

In another African tale Bertram Mitford describes the totemic aspect of religion from the native's point of view. The hero, a member of a breakaway Zulu tribe, is conducting an illicit relationship with his loved one in the woods near his kraal, when they see two serpents creeping towards them. The serpent is their tutelary deity and their guardian spirit, so they cannot kill them and are forced to retreat. A few minutes later, a group of warriors searching for them crosses the very clearing in which they lay before being driven away by the snakes, and this group, itself awed by the appearance of the totems, returns to the kraal. The lovers are saved, as it seems to them, through the intercession of their guardian spirit in the form of the totem; for they would have been discovered had they broken the taboo about killing it. The sanction of taboo and the rewards for observing it are used as an integral part of an exciting adventure.

Other writers, however, cannot indulge even such a romantic view of 'primitive' beliefs and condemn taboos as foolish, and often horrific, 'superstitions'. Ballantyne, for instance, continues the current practice of incorporating the details of 'primitive' beliefs in fiction, but his explanation of them is less relativist than those of Eliot or Haggard. When the native chief sits down and has to be fed by one of his wives, Ralph wonders at such arrogance, but his companion explains:

> They've a strange custom among them, Ralph, which is called 'tabu', and they carry it to great lengths. If a man chooses a particular tree for his god, the fruit of that tree is tabued to him; and if he eats it, he is sure to be killed by his people, and eaten of course, for killing means eating hereaway.
> Then you see that great mop o' hair on the chief's head?
> Well, he has a lot o' barbers to keep it in order; and it's a law that whoever touches the head of a living chief or the body of a dead one, his hands are tabued, so in that way the barber's hands are always tabued, and they daren't use them for their lives, but they have to be fed like big babies, as they are, sure enough (Ballantyne, 1858, pp. 163–4).

Shorn of references to 'mops o' hair', cannibalism, 'big babies' and the arbitrary choosing of a god by the native, this is a typical description of the relationship between totem and taboo as understood at the time, and of the belief in 'mana' found in Melanesia.[5] But whereas strange incidents in Tarzan stories, such as shooting arrows at the stars, are sometimes explained in terms of how the actors themselves are assumed to understand them, the strange hair styles and eating habits of South Sea islanders are described merely as exotic curiosities by Ballantyne. Likewise Russell, in 'The Witch Woman' (1923, p. 715), reduces the complexity of such beliefs to 'totems that leered with a monstrous welcome'.

The ease with which 'primitive' man 'chooses' his gods, and thus the implication that his religion need not be taken seriously, is perpetuated in *Tabu Dick*, where the taboo which protects the trader's young boy is placed on him by a native servant as she dies (Greene, L. P., 1935a, p. 15) while Dick himself glibly contemplates making another 'tabu' when the old one weakens (ibid., p. 76).

But about the 'truth' of the taboo itself Greene remains mysterious. One character tries to explain it in psychological terms; if a native broke Dick's taboo he 'would die because he believed he'd die . . . I had a nigger once who said zebra meat was tabu to him. And I fooled him into believing he'd eaten some. He was dead in a couple of days' (ibid., p. 81). This treatment of 'primitive' people as the subject of interesting laboratory experiments for testing current anthropological theory was common at the time. Dick and his author, however, disagree with the theory and, for all their use of 'superstition' for political purposes, they also have some faith that he who breaks a taboo will eventually be punished by some supernatural agency. Hatteras, seeing the result of the taboo in his growing son, reflects that

> the tabu upon Dick had been more than a ruse. It went deeper than a play upon heathen superstition. It seemed to him that the tabu had invoked the aid of a divinity, for the boy had escaped the usual childish ailments. He had not known a day's sickness (ibid., p. 22).

And whenever anyone does break the taboo and touch Dick, he inevitably dies. Marfwe, who had touched him in order to test the taboo, dies to save Dick's life, but in doing so convinces the natives of the strength of the taboo: 'He broke the tabu. . . . And therefore he died. It is just' (ibid., p. 93). Two white men, who break the taboo about touching a sacred necklace, likewise die and in doing so confirm Dick's faith: 'Do you call that luck? I call it the justness of the jungle' (ibid., p. 124).

Greene thus suggests not only that 'superstition' can serve a useful function (the subject of Frazer's *Psyche's Task*, 1909) but also that there may be some mysterious truth in the 'tabus' it creates, defended by some all-seeing divine justice. This, of course, serves the purpose of the book in creating atmosphere and suspense and in giving Dick the support a hero needs from the gods. But it also gives to the English colonist, shouldering the white man's burden, something of the Divine Right of Kings. It perpetuates notions of the black man's continent as alien and mysterious, and it dramatises current conceptions of 'primitive' religion. Greene attempts to grasp what their beliefs mean to the natives by making his readers accept them too. He thus explains taboo in its own terms where many descriptions pass it off in European terms as merely foolish and horrific.

There are thus some differences in the attitudes of popular authors to 'primitive' man. In the main the customs of other peoples were seen in very Europocentric terms; their beliefs being mere 'superstition', their appearance 'hideous' and their religious rites 'horrific'. Novels represent these feelings in a dramatic and often bloodthirsty manner. However, a feeling for relativity can be discerned even in some ethnocentric descriptions. The evolutionary framework of thought enabled the European to accept the unity of mankind without the intellectual discomfort of ascribing to 'primitive' customs the same value and significance as to those of Europe. An evolutionary relativism accommodated 'primitive' peoples at an earlier stage of development than the European, with institutions sharing the characteristics of European institutions in much less sophisticated form. Thus the 'superstitions' of 'primitive' man were not always to be dismissed as unreasoning, bestial ignorance; they could also be seen as childlike attempts to make sense of the universe. The anthropologist also had started to try, at least, to 'understand' the meaning of 'primitive' customs 'in their own terms'.

This kind of 'relativism' in popular 'writings' depends still on the premises of European thought, and on the categories and system of classification given the student by his own culture, particularly the racial and evolutionary frameworks which anthropologists have since rejected. But the evolutionary relativism of much of nineteenth-century popular fiction was gradually replaced by a more functional relativism, whereby the institutions of other cultures were studied 'in their own terms' and with regard to their function within the total context. Still accepting the theory of the unity of mankind, the adherents of this kind of relativism tried to relate the functions

of seemingly irrational customs in other societies to the functions
that were known for customs in their own society, and thus arrive
at universal principles of human nature. Haggard is constrained,
reluctantly, to pay lip service to this approach, though his work
does not always bear it out:

> It is a depressing conclusion, but in all essentials the savage
> and the child of civilisation are identical. I dare say that the
> highly civilised lady reading this will smile at an old fool of a
> hunter's simplicity when she thinks of her black-bedecked sister.
> . . . And yet, my dear young lady, what are those pretty things
> round your own neck? – they have a strong family resemblance,
> especially when you wear that *very* low dress, to the savage
> woman's beads. Your habit of turning round and round to the
> sound of horns and tom-toms, your fondness for pigments
> and powders, the way in which you love to subjugate yourself
> to the rich warrior who has captured you in marriage; and the
> quickness with which your taste in feathered head-dresses varies
> – all these things might suggest touches of kinship; and
> remember that in fundamental principles of your nature you
> are quite identical (1887a, pp. 4–5).

In the exposition of functional relativism by popular writers,
fashion is very frequently cited as a universal feature of human
society. Even Sanders, for instance, realises that, however much he
may dislike the practice of enlarging the lips for beauty, to the
natives the European fashion for small lips is equally distasteful,
and Lang satirises the Victorians for not admitting the relation
between some of their fashions and those of 'primitive' peoples.
'Young ladies are still forbidden to call young men at large by their
Christian names. . . . The teeth of boys are still knocked out at
public schools' and modern society has its martyred radicals to
compare with the 'primitive' Why-Why (Lang, 1886, p. 209).

With the rejection of social evolution as a framework for understanding other societies and the adoption of Malinowski's example
of living in and with a society for a period of time and learning their
language, anthropologists laid themselves open to total relativism.
Abandoning the arm-chair for the 'field' they claimed, rightly for
the most part, to be adopting a more empirical approach to social
data and to have eschewed the theoretical errors of their predecessors.
But, inevitably, they were subject to the collective representations of

the society from which they came and future generations of anthropologists will no doubt find contemporary historical bias in their work as in that of the Victorians.

Nevertheless, there are some tests of a more enduring truth. Evans-Pritchard's development of the Durkheimian idea of 'collective representations' provides a useful indication of how the field worker may know whether he has 'understood' the collective representations of another culture:

> Beliefs are co-ordinated with other beliefs and with behaviour into an organised system. Hence it happens that when an anthropologist has resided for many months among a savage people he can foresee how they will speak and act in any given situation. I have tested this fact again and again in Central Africa where I found that my questions to the people among whom I carried out ethnological research eventually became more and more formalities since I was able to supply the answers to my questions before I asked them, often in almost identical phraseology in which the replies were afterwards given (1934, p. 48).

This analysis can be applied to our understanding of the collective representations of the Victorians. After studying a number of these representations in the pages of popular fiction, we may predict even something of the very phraseology which the Victorian writer would have used. The reader has only to select at random a novel or story of the period to test whether or not it reproduces the patterns of representation of other cultures here outlined both in style and in content.

Notes

Chapter 2   The English abroad

1 Cf. Malcolm X, writing of his treatment by a white couple who adopted him in America, notes that this attitude is still prevalent today:

> What I am trying to say is that it just never dawned on them that I could understand, that I wasn't a pet, but a human being. They didn't give me credit for having the same sensitivity, intellect and understanding that they would have been ready and willing to recognise in a white boy in my position. But it has historically been the case with white people in this regard for black people, that even though we might be *with* them we weren't considered *of* them. Even though they appeared to have opened the door, it was still closed. Thus they never did really see me. (Extract from his *Autobiography* quoted in *Westside*, vol. 2, no. 2, March, 1970, p. 16.)

Cf. also the attitude of John in Rider Haggard's *Jess* to the Hottentot servant Jantje who goes with him on a long journey. John complains of the loneliness of the journey, with 'only the birds for company'.

Chapter 3   Evolution and race in popular literature: classification, scientific and fictitious

I Camper's method proved too unwieldy in practice and was replaced during the second half of the nineteenth century, by the 'Cephalic Index' invented by A. Retzius in 1840. According to this system, the proportion

of the length to the breadth of the head became an index of classification;
dolichocephals and brachycephals (short-headed people) were compared
as groups inherently more or less intelligent than each other.

2 Joyce Cary's novels of Africa deal more directly with the problems of
'race relations' and thus show the change of treatment evident in some
later works. For this reason, they are not dealt with in detail here.

3 Lecture by Dr R. G. Lienhardt, St Antony's College, 1969.

4 Cf. the fear inspired by the aeroplane in the same story (pp. 40,173), and
the use of dynamite by Tabu Dick.

5 When red coats are worn by natives, it is a sign of their childish pleasure
in bright things; when English soldiers wear them it is a mark of dignity
and grandeur.

6 Cf. C. A. W. Monckton, *Last Days in New Guinea*, London, 1922, p. 100:

> Many writers of books of travel in New Guinea seem to take a
> delight in depicting the natives they have met as of a childish
> form of intelligence. This quite likely may be right of the men the
> writer of the book has met and talked with, just as a hypothetical
> visitor from Mars might try and discuss foreign politics with a
> Sussex yokel, or the higher mathematics with a costermonger, and
> then report to the Martians that the inhabitants of the earth were
> all fools.

The author in the same book, also espouses many of the 'principles' of
Sanders of the River.

7 Conversations today with those who read *The Coral Island* in childhood
suggest that their preconceptions were not upset at that time, since their
memories are mostly of the idyllic conditions on the island rather than
of the 'atrocities' committed by its savage inhabitants.

8 Montesquieu, arguing that environment affected the thickness of the skin,
claimed you would have to flay a Russian very hard to make him feel.

9 E. Lucas Bridges, *The Uttermost Part of the Earth*, 1948, quoted in
Lienhardt, 1964, p. 11.

**Chapter 4   Evolution and race in popular literature: hierarchy and
racial theory**

1 Tylor noted the difficulty of finding
among a list of twenty items of art or knowledge, custom or
superstition, taken at random from a description of any uncivilised
race, a single one to which something closely analogous may not
be found elsewhere among some other race, unlike the first in
physical characters, and living thousands of miles off' (Tylor, 1865,
pp. 361–3).

2 'Not, however, till the expeditions of Sir Henry Stanley were the pygmy
races of the equatorial regions scientifically examined' (Gilson, 1919,
p. 16).

3 Haggard acknowledges his debt in *Allan Quatermain* to J. Thomson's

Through Masai Land and to his brother, the consul at Madagascar (1885, p. 303).

4 In 1930 an anthropologist, I. Schapera, described the social organisation of the Bushman in considerable detail (*The Khoisan Peoples of South Africa: Bushmen and Hottentots*, Routledge). Earlier accounts, by concentrating on a people's place in the scale and seeing them only in terms of European values, failed to present the detail and the dignity of other ways of life.

5 Mastery of environment was a common criterion for man's place on the scale. Cf. Stanley, *How I Found Livingstone*, pp. 69, 108.

6 Creation was variously attributed to the years 3928 B.C., 4004 B.C., 5411 B.C., etc. Cf. Banton, 1967, p. 28.

7 A special number of *Popular Magazine of Anthropology* was published in 1866 to record a meeting of the Anthropological Society of London at St James's Hall, London, at which Commander Bedford Pim spoke on 'The Negro and Jamaica'. He argued for slavery and claimed that the revolt would never have happened if politicians had listened to the Hunt school of anthropologists.

8 Dr Seemann also claimed at this meeting that study of the cranium alone was not enough for racial classification, the 'soft parts' must be observed and, to facilitate this, an 'anthropological garden . . . something on the same principle as the Zoological gardens, might be set up with live specimens from different races' (*Anthropology Review, I*, vol. 1, p. xxiii).

9 'The object of our present undertaking is to endeavour to keep pace with the rapid development of science and to supply to the masses of the reading public an account of some of the more important discoveries in anthropology' (Introduction, vol. 1, no. 1, 1866, p. 2).

Chapter 5 Heredity and environment

1 Cf. Penniman, 1935, pp. 79–81. He claims that Prichard's interest in 'local influences' led him to a more Lamarckian position which earlier he had refuted.

2 Cf. Gilson; Aarden, marooned in the jungle for many years, has a 'magnificent, manly beauty and is worshipped as a god' (1919, pp. 128–30).

3 Cf. *The Sioux at St. Jude's* and the Billy Bunter stories.

4 The stereotype is perpetuated in the recent cartoon depicting two cannibals eating a third man; one turns to his companion and says, 'The food was better at LSE.'

5 One letter, for instance, to the *Popular Magazine for Anthropology* in 1862 reports that the natives in Australia had donned whites' clothes for so long that, when they returned to the bush without them, they had lost their immunity to the cold and died off in thousands. The writer asks that no more supplies of clothes be sent for the natives.

Chapter 6   'Primitive' politics in popular literature

1 This book has a useful bibliography on Ethiopianism.
2 Cf. Shepperson and Price, 1958, p. 134; also *The Times*, 1 June 1906, 13f; Ethiopianism is 'fully reported in the native press in . . . South Africa'.
3 *The Times*, 13 June 1904, 16e, 'Ethiopianism in South Africa'.

Chapter 7   'Primitive' religion in popular literature

1 Rose himself seems to believe that some 'primitives' have no religious beliefs. Cp. p. xxvi.
2 Cf. the 'Emotionalist' school who put down 'primitive' religion to 'awe', for example, Marrett, R. R., *The Threshold of Religion*, Methuen, 1909, and Crawley, A. E., *The Mystic Rose*, A. & C. Black, 1902; Evans-Pritchard, 1965, ch. 2.
3 Cf. Hodgen, 1936, pp. 125–9, for a discussion and brief bibliography of the use in comparative literature of the 'anthropological method', tracing literature back to the religious life of 'primitive' man.
4 Lang, too, quotes Herodotus ii, 42, in his explanation of totemism in *Custom and Myth* (1884, p. 107). He writes, 'tribes abstained religiously (except on certain sacrificial occasions) from the flesh of the animal that gave them its name.'
5 Cf. Frazer, 1890, pp. 233, 203. He describes such customs in Fiji and all over the world and explains them as 'a special application of sympathetic magic'.

Bibliography

I. General

Dates in brackets refer to the first edition; where this differs from the edition used, the more recent date is noted after.

ADAMS, G. H. (n.d.), *The Life and Adventures of Dr. Livingstone*, Blackwood.

ALLPORT, G. (1954), *The Nature of Prejudice*, Addison-Wesley.

ARNOLD, MATTHEW (1869), *Culture and Anarchy*, Cambridge University Press, 1969.

ARTHUR, SIR GEORGE (1938), *Not Worth Reading*, Longman.

BAILEY, J. O. (1947), *Pilgrims through Space and Time*, Argus Books, New York.

BAKER, E. A. and PACKINAN, J. (1932), *A Guide to the Best Fiction*, Routledge & Kegan Paul, 1967.

BAKER, S. W. (1867), 'The Races of the Nile Basin' in *Transactions of the Ethnological Society of London*, p. 231.

BAKER, S. W. (1898), *Albert Nyanza*, Macmillan.

BANTON, M. (1959), *White and Coloured*, Jonathan Cape.

BANTON, M. (1966), 'Race as a Social Category', Inaugural Lecture, University of Bristol, in *Race*, VIII, I, 1966.

BANTON, M. (1967), *Race Relations*, Tavistock Publications.

BARZUN, J. (1937), *Race – A Study in Superstition*, Harper & Row, New York, 1965.

BATHO, E. and DOBREE, E. (1938), *The Victorians and After*, Cresset Press.

BAUDET, H. (1965), *Paradise on Earth: some thoughts on European images of non-European man*, Yale University Press.

BEATTIE, J. (1964), *Other Cultures*, Cohen & West.

BENDYSHE, T. (1865a), 'The History of Anthropology' in *Memoirs of the Anthropological Society of London*, pp. 335–458.

BENDYSHE, T. (1865b), ed., *The Anthropological Treatises of J. F. Blumenbach*, Publications of the Anthropological Society of London.

BIERSTEET, R. (1966), *Emile Durkheim*, Weidenfeld & Nicolson.

BLAVATSKY, H. P. (1888), *The Secret Doctrine*, Theosophical Society, London, 1897.

BLAVATSKY, H. P. (1910), *Isis Unveiled*, Theosophical Society, London.

BLUMENBACH, J. F. (1795), 'On the Natural Variety of Mankind' in Bendyshe (1865b).

BOAS, G. (1948), *Essays on Primitivism and Related Ideas*, Oxford University Press.

BODELSEN, C. A. (1924), *Studies in Mid-Victorian Imperialism*, Heinemann, 1960.

BOTT, ALAN (1931), *Our Fathers*, Heinemann.

BOWRA, G. M. (1962), *Primitive Song*, Weidenfeld & Nicolson.

BRIDGES, E. L. (1948), *The Uttermost Part of the Earth*, Hodder & Stoughton.

BRIGGS, A. (1954), *Victorian People*, Odhams. Penguin, 1970.

BUCHAN, J. (1909), *The African Colony*, Blackwood.

BUCHANNAN, W. and CANTRIL, H. (1953), *How Nations See Each Other*, University of Illinois Press.

BURROW, J. W. (1966), *Evolution and Society*, Cambridge University Press.

CAIRNS, A. C. (1965), *Prelude to Imperialism*, Oxford University Press.

CARLYLE, T. (1849), 'Occasional Discourse on the Nigger Question', *Fraser's Magazine*, XL, pp. 670–90, December, 1849.

CARLYLE, T. (1841), *On Heroes and Hero-Worship*, intro. by W. H. Hudson in Everyman 278, Dent, 1908.

CAZAMIAN, M. L. (1923), *Le Roman et les idées en Angleterre*, vol. 1, 'L'Influence de la science', vol. 3, 'Les Doctrines d'action and d'aventure 1850–1914', University of Strasbourg, 1923. Oxford, Milford, 1955.

CAZAMIAN, M. L. and LEGOUIS, E. (1926), 'Modern Times', vol. 2 of *A History of English Literature*, Dent, 1933.

CAZANEUVE, J. (1963), *Lucien Lévy-Bruhl – Sa Vie, son oeuvre*, Philosophes, Presses Universitaires de France.

CERAM, C. W. (1952), *Gods, Graves and Scholars*, Sidgwick & Jackson.

CHAILLU, P. DU (1866), *Equatorial Africa and the Country of the Dwarfs*, John Murray, 1890.

CHANCELLOR, V. E. (1970), *History for their Masters – Opinion in the English History Textbook 1800–1914*, Adams & Dart.

CHAPMAN, E. M. (1910), *English Literature in Account with Religion*, Houghton, Mifflin, Boston.

CHESTERTON, G. K. (1913), *Studies in Victorian Literature*, Oxford University Press.

CHURCH, R. (1951), *The Growth of the English Novel*, Methuen.

Church Times (28 November 1825), 'Jamaica Massacre', London.

CLARK, J. P. (1968), 'The Legacy of Caliban', *Black Orpheus*, vol. 1, no. 2, February.

COCKSHUTT, A. O. J. (1964), *The Unbelievers*, Collins.

COLLINGWOOD, R. G. (1938), *The Principles of Art*, Oxford University Press, 1960.

COLLINGWOOD, R. G. (1946), *The Idea of History*, Clarendon Press.

COUNT, E. W. (1950), *This is Race*, Henry Schuman, New York.

CRUSE, A. (1935), *The Victorians and their Books*, Allen & Unwin.

CURTIN, P. (1965), *The Image of Africa*, Macmillan.

CURTIS, L. P., Jun. (1968), *Anglo-Saxons and Celts*, New York University Press.

DARLINGTON, C. D. (1969), *The Evolution of Man and Society*, Allen & Unwin.

DALZIEL, M. (1957), *Popular Fiction 100 Years Ago*, Cohen & West.

DARTON, F. J. H. (1932), *Children's Books in England*, Cambridge University Press.

DARWIN, C. (1858), *Origin of Species*, John Murray, 1889.

DARWIN, C. (1871), *The Descent of Man*, John Murray, 1889.

DARWIN, C. (1872), *Expressions of the Emotions in Man and Animals*, John Murray.

DAVIDSON, B. (ed.), (1964), *The African Past*, Longman.

DE LA MARE, W. (1930), *The Eighteen-eighties*, Cambridge University Press.

DÉGERANDO, J. M. (1800), *The Observation of Savage Peoples* (trans. F. G. T. Moore, Routledge & Kegan Paul, 1969).

DOBZHANSKY, T. (1964), *Heredity and the Nature of Man*, Signet, New York.

DORSON, R. M. (1968a), *Peasant Customs and Savage Myths*, Routledge & Kegan Paul.

DORSON, R. M. (1968b), *The British Folklorists*, Routledge & Kegan Paul.

DOWDEN, E. (1878), 'The Scientific Movement in Literature' in *Studies in Literature*, Kegan Paul, Trench.

DURKHEIM, É. (1893), *The Division of Labour in Society*, Paris (trans. G. Simpson, Macmillan, New York, 1933).

DURKHEIM, É. (1895), *The Rules of the Sociological Method*, Paris (trans. Sarah A. Solvey and John H. Mueller, Free Press, Chicago, 1938).

DURKHEIM, É. (1897), *Suicide*, Paris (trans. J. A. Spaulding and G. Simpson, Routledge & Kegan Paul, 1947).

DURKHEIM, É. (1912), *The Elementary Forms of the Religious Life*, Paris (trans. J. Swain, Allen & Unwin, 1915).

DURKHEIM, É. and MAUSS, M. (1903), *Primitive Classification* (trans. R. Needham, Cohen & West, 1963).

DUVIGNAUD, J. (1965), *Durkheim – Sa Vie, son oeuvre*, Philosophes, Presses Universitaires de France.

DYKES E. B. (1942), *The Negro in English Romantic Thought*, Associated Publishers, Washington.

EARLE, A. (1832), *Journal of a Residence in Tristan da Cunha* (ed. E. H. McCormick, Oxford University Press, 1966).

EDWARDS, M. (1968), *Glorious Sahibs*, Eyre & Spottiswoode.

ELLIMANN, R., ed. (1959), *Edwardians and Victorians*, English Institute Essays, Columbia University Press.

ELMSLIE, W. A. (1899), *Among the Wild Ngoni*, Oliphant.

EVANS-PRITCHARD, E. E. (1934), '*Lévy-Bruhl's theory of primitive mentality*', *Bulletin of the Faculty of Arts*, Cairo, vol. II, Part I (reprinted in *Journal of the Anthropological Society of Oxford*, vol. 1, no. 2, 1970).

EVANS-PRITCHARD, E. E. (1965), *Theories of Primitive Religion*, Oxford University Press.

FAIRCHILD, H. N. (1928), *The Noble Savage: a study in romantic naturalism*, Oxford University Press.

FORD, E. B. (1931), *Mendelism and Evolution*, Methuen.

FORTUNE, R. E. (1947), 'Law and force in Papuan societies', *American Anthropologist*, 49, no. 2.

FRAZER, J. G. (1890), *The Golden Bough*, Macmillan, abridged 1963.

FRAZER, J. G. (1909), *Psyche's Task*, Macmillan.

FRAZER, J. G. (1927), *The Gorgon's Head*, Macmillan.

FRIERSON, W. C. (1932), *The English Novel in Transition*, Cooper Square, New York.

FURNAS, J. C. (1957), *Goodbye to Uncle Tom*, Secker & Warburg.

GARDINER, A. G. (1914), *Prophets, Priests and Kings*, Dent.

GEORGE, K. (1958), 'The civilised West looks at primitive Africa', *Isis*, XLIX.

GIEDION, S. (1948), *Mechanisation Takes Command*, Oxford University Press.

GOBINEAU, J. A. DE (1853), *The Inequality of Human Races*, Paris. Heinemann, 1915.

GOLDTHORPE, J. H. (1969), 'Herbert Spencer' in T. Raison, *The Founding Fathers of Social Science*, Penguin, 1969.

GRAY, W. F. (1912), 'Books That Count' (*A Dictionary of Standard Books*), A. & C. Black.

GREEN, L. (1935), *Great African Mysteries*, Hutchinson.

GREENE, J. C. (1954), 'Some Early Speculations on the Origins of the Human Races', *American Anthropologist*, 56, pp. 31–41.

GROSS, J. (1969), *The Rise and Fall of the Man of Letters*, Weidenfeld & Nicolson.

GROSS, S. and HARDY, J. F., eds (1966), *Images of the Negro in American Literature*, University of Chicago Press.

HACKETT, A. (1945), *Fifty Years of Best Sellers (1895–1945)*, A. R. Barker, New York.

HACKETT, A. (1949), *Ideas and Beliefs of the Victorians*, BBC Publications.

HANKE, L. (1959), *Aristotle and the American Indians*, Hollis & Carter.

HANSEN, A. (1934), *Twentieth Century Forces in European Fiction*, American Library Association.

HARRISON, J. (1911), *Ancient Art and Ritual*, Williams & Norgate.

HARRISON, J. (1912), 'A study of the Social Origins of Greek Religion', thesis, Cambridge University.

HAYS, H. R. (1958), *From Ape to Angel*, Methuen.

HEARNSHAW, F. J .L. (1935), *Social and Political Ideas of Some Representative Thinkers of the Victorian Age*, Harrap.

HENDERSON, W. (1937), *Victorian Street Ballads*, Country Life.

HENKIN, L. J. (1940), *Darwinism in the English Novel 1860–1910*, Russell & Russell, New York.

HERSKOVITS, M. (1967), *The Myth of the Negro Past*, Beacon Press, Boston.
HILL, D. (1949), 'Imperialism in English Literature of the Late 19th Century', Ph.D. thesis, University of Illinois.
HILL, W. (1930), *The Overseas Empire in Fiction*, Oxford University Press.
HODGEN, M. (1936), *The Doctrine of Survivals*, Allenson & Co.
HODGEN, M. (1964), *Early Anthropology in the 16th and 17th Centuries*, University of Pennsylvania Press.
HOME, H. (Lord Kames) (1774), *Sketches of the History of Man*, W. Strahan & T. Cadell, 2nd edn 1778.
HOWE, S. (1949), *Novels of Empire*, Columbia University Press.
HUNT, J. (1863), 'On the Negro's Place in Nature', *Anthropology Review*, III, p. 386.
HUXLEY, J. and HADDON, A. C. (1935), *We Europeans – A Survey of Racial Problems*, Jonathan Cape.
HUXLEY, T. H. (1910), *Man's Place in Nature and Other Essays*, Watts.
IRVINE, W. (1955), *Apes, Angels and Victorians*, Readers' Union edn, 1956.
JAMES, L. (1963), *Fiction for the Working Man. 1830–1850*, Oxford University Press.
JAMES, W. (1902), *Varieties of Religious Experience*, Longmans.
JANOWITZ, M. and BETTLEHEIM, B. (1950), *The Dynamics of Prejudice*, Harper & Row.
JARVIE, I. C. (1964), *The Revolution in Anthropology*, Routledge & Kegan Paul.
JOHNSON, H. (1927), *Anthropology and the Fall*, Blackwell.
JONES, E. (1965), *Othello's Countrymen*, Oxford University Press.
JORDAN, W. (1969), *White Over Black*, Johns Hopkins University Press, Baltimore.
KAMM, J. (1957), *Men Who Served Africa*, Harrap.
KAUVAR, G. and SORENSON, G. (1969), *The Victorian Mind*, Cassell.
KEITH, A. (1931), *New Discoveries Relating to the Antiquity of Man*, Williams & Norgate.
KERR, W. M. (1886), *The Far Interior*, Sampson, Low.
KETTLE, A. (1951), *An Introduction to the English Novel*, Hutchinson.
KIERNAN, V. G. (1969), *The Lords of Human Kind*, Weidenfeld & Nicolson.
KILLAM, G. D. (1968), *Africa in English Fiction 1874–1939*, Ibadan University Press.
KNOX, R. (1850), *The Races of Men: a fragment*, Renshaw.
KOESTLER, A. and SMYTHIES, (1969), *Beyond Reductionism*, Hutchinson.
Lancet (1865), 'Race Antagonism', Editorial, 2 December 1865.
LANG, A. (1884), *Custom and Myth*, Longmans.
LANG, A. (1887), *Myth, Ritual and Religion*, Longmans.
LANG, A. (1894), *Cock Lane and Common-Sense*, Longmans.
LEAVIS, F. R. (1948), *The Great Tradition*, Chatto & Windus, 1967.
LESTER, J. A., Jun. (1968), *Journey Through Despair*, 1880–1914, Princeton University Press.
LÉVI-STRAUSS, C. (1962), *Race and History*, UNESCO, Paris.
LÉVY-BRUHL, L. (1931), 'La mentalité primitive', Herbert Spencer Lecture, Oxford.

LIENHARDT, R. G. (1964), *Social Anthropology*, Oxford University Press, 1967.

LILJEGREN, S. B. (1961), *Studies on the Origin and Early History of English Utopian Fiction*, Lundequistska Bokhandeln, Uppsala.

LIPS, J. E. (1937), *The Savage Hits Back*, Universe Books, 1966.

LITTLE, K. (1947), *Negroes in Britain*, Kegan Paul, Trench, Trubner.

LIVINGSTONE, D. (1857), *Missionary Travels*, John Murray.

LLOYD, A. B. (1899), *In Dwarf Land and Cannibal Country*, Unwin.

LOCKHART, J. G. (1933), *Cecil Rhodes*, Duckworth.

LONG, E. (1774), *A History of Jamaica*, J. T. Lowndes.

LOVEJOY, O. (1936), *The Great Chain of Being*, Harvard University Press.

LOVEJOY, O. and BOAS, F. (1935), *Documentary History of Primitivism and Related Ideas*, Oxford University Press.

LYONS, A. (1970), 'The Genesis of Scientific Racism' in *JASO*, vol. 1, no. 2, Oxford.

MCCARTHY, J. (1897), *A History of Our Own Times*, Chatto & Windus.

MCLELLAND, E. M. (1967), *Comparative Studies in Sociology and History*, vol. IX, no. 4, July.

MCLEOD, A. L. ed. (1961), *The Commonwealth Pen*, Oxford University Press.

MAINE, H. (1862), *Ancient Law*, Everyman edn, Dent.

MAIR, L. (1962), *Primitive Government*, Penguin.

MALINOWSKI, B. (1922), *Argonauts of the Western Pacific*, Routledge.

MANNONI, O. (1956), *Prospero and Caliban – The Psychology of Colonisation* (trans. P. Poweslomi, Methuen).

MARCUS, S. (1966), *The Other Victorians*, Weidenfeld & Nicolson.

MARRETT, R. R. (1936), *Tylor*, Chapman & Hall.

MARRIOT, J. (1940), *English History in Fiction*, Blackie.

MASSINGHAM, H. J. and H. (eds) (1932), *The Great Victorians*, Nicholson & Watson.

MAUNIER, R. (1932), *The Sociology of Colonies*, trans. E. O. Lenmer, Routledge & Kegan Paul, 1949.

MIDDLETON, J. (1960), *Lugbara Religion*, International African Institute, London.

MONTAGU, A. ed., (1964), *The Concept of Race*, Free Press, 1969.

MOONEY, J. (1896), *The Ghost-Dance Religion and the Sioux Outbreak of 1890*, ed. A. Wallace, University of Chicago Press, 1965.

MOORHEAD, A. (1969), *The Fatal Impact*, Hamish Hamilton.

MPHALELE, E. (1958), *The African Image*, Praeger & Rye, 1962.

MULLER, M. (1870), *Introduction to the Science of Religion*, Longmans, 1882.

MURRAY, G. G. (1912), *Greek and English Tragedy*, Oxford University Press.

MURRAY, G. G. (1912), *Four Stages of Greek Religion*, Frowde.

MYRES, J. (1911), *The Dawn of History*, Oxford University Press.

NATHAN, M. (1925), *South African Literature*, Juta, Cape Town.

NUTTAL, Z. (1901), *The Fundamental Principles of Old and New World Religions, Archeological and Ethnological Papers of the Peabody Museum*, Harvard University, vol. II.

ORWELL, G. (1940), 'Boys' Weeklies', in *Inside the Whale and Other Essays*, Penguin, 1957.

PEARCE, R. H. (1965), *The Savages of America*, Johns Hopkins University Press, Baltimore.

PELLING, H. (1960), *Modern Britain 1855–1955*, Nelson.

PENNIMAN, T. K. (1935), *A Hundred Years of Anthropology*, Duckworth, 1952.

PERHAM, M. and SIMMONS, J. (1943) *African Discovery – an Anthology of Exploration*, Faber.

PETHERICK, J. (1861), *Egypt, the Soudan and Central Africa*, Blackwood.

PIM, B. (1866), *The Negro and Jamaica, Popular Magazine of Anthropology* (Special Issue).

POCOCK, D. (1961), *Social Anthropology*, Sheed & Ward.

Popular Magazine of Anthropology, vol. 1, January, vol. 2, April 1966.

PORTER, B. (1969), 'Critics of Empire', *Times Literary Supplement*, 1 January.

RAISON, T. (1969), *The Founding Fathers of Social Science*, Penguin.

ROBINSON, R. and GALLAGHER, J. (1961), *Africa and the Victorians*, Macmillan.

ROLLINGTON, R. (1913), *A Brief History of Boys' Journals*, H. Simpson, Leicester.

ROSE, J. (1954), 'The Merchandise of Light; A Study of the Impact of the New Knowledge of the Non-European World on Some Aspects of English Thought in the Seventeenth Century', dissertation submitted for a prize Fellowship at King's College, Cambridge.

ROYAL ANTHROPOLOGICAL INSTITUTE (1892), *Notes and Queries on Anthropology*.

RUNCIMAN, H. (1960), *The White Rajahs*, Cambridge University Press.

ST HILAIRE, GEOFFREY DE (1835), 'Classification anthropologique', *Memoirs de la Société Anthropologique de Paris*.

SAINTSBURY, G. E. (1892), *The English Novel*, Dent.

SANDISON, A. (1967), *The Wheel of Empire*, Macmillan.

SARGANT, E. B. and WHISHAW, B. (1891), *A Guide-book to Books*, Frowde.

SELOUS, F. C. (1893), *Travel and Adventures in East Africa*, R. Ward.

SHEPPERSON, G. and PRICE, T. (1958), *Independent African – John Chilembwe*, Edinburgh University Press.

SIMPSON, G. E. and YINGER, J. M. (1953), *Racial and Cultural Minorities*, Harper & Row.

SMITH, B. (1960), *European Vision in the South Pacific (1768–1850)*, Clarendon Press.

SMITH, J. (1965), *John Buchan*, Rupert Hart-Davis.

SPENCER, H. (1876–96), *Systems of Synthetic Philosophy*, vols. 6, 8, 'Principles of Sociology', Williams & Norgate.

SPROAT, G. M. (1868), *Scenes and Studies of Savage Life*, Smith & Elder.

STANLEY, H. M. (1872), *How I Found Livingstone*, Sampson Low.

STEVENSON, L. (ed.) (1964), *Victorian Fiction*, Harvard University Press.

STOCKING, G. (1968), *Race, Culture and Evolution*, Free Press.

STREET, B. V. (1969), 'Stereotypes in science and literature', *JASO*, vol. 1, no. 1.

STREET, B. V. (1973), 'In the shadow of the Golden Bough', *JASO*, vol. 4, no. 3.

STREET, B. V. 'D. H. Lawrence and anthropology', pending publication.
STREET, B. V. 'Joseph Conrad and anthropology', pending publication.
THOMSON, J. (1878, 1881), *To the Central African Lakes and Back*, (2 vols), Low.
THOMSON, J. (1887), *Through Masai Land*, Low.
THORNTON, A. P. (1959), *The Imperial Idea and Its Enemies*, Macmillan.
TINDALL, W. Y. (1947), *Forces in Modern British Literature (1885–1946)*, Random House.
TREVELYAN, G. M. (1944), *Illustrated English Social History*, Penguin, 1964.
TREVELYAN, G. M. (1949–51), *British History in the Nineteenth Century*, Longmans.
TYLOR, E. B. (1865), *Researches into the Early History of Mankind and the Development of Civilisation*, John Murray.
TYLOR, E. B. (1871), *Primitive Culture*, John Murray, 1891.
TYLOR, E. B. (1881), *Anthropology: An Introduction to the Study of Man and Civilisation*, Macmillan.
VAN DEN BERGHE, P. (1967), *Race and Racism*, John Wiley, New York.
WADDINGTON, C. H. (1969), 'The Theory of Evolution Today', in Koestler and Smythies, 1969.
WAKE, C. S. (1868), *Chapters on Man, with Outlines of a Science of Comparative Psychology*, Trübner.
WAKE, C. S. (1878), *The Evolution of Morality; being a History of the Development of Moral Culture*, Trübner.
WAKE, C. S. (1888), 'The Classification of the Races of Mankind', read before the Hull Literary Club, 18 October 1888 (Private).
WALLACE, A. R. (1898), *The Wonderful Century: its Successes and its Failures*, Sonnenschein.
WELLECK, R. (1941), *The Rise of English Literary History*, University of North Carolina Press.
WEYGANDT, C. (1925), *A Century of the English Novel*, Century, New York.
WHITNEY, L. (1934), *Primitivism and the Idea of Progress in English Popular Literature of the Eighteenth Century*, Oxford University Press.
WILLEY, B. (1949), *Nineteenth Century Studies*, Penguin.
WILLIAMS, R. (1958), *Culture and Society 1780–1950*, Penguin, 1966.
WOLFF, K. H., ed. (1960), *Émile Durkheim*, Ohio State University Press.
YONGE, C. (1888), *What Books to Lend and What to Give*, National Society.

II. Authors (texts)

Dates in brackets refer to the first edition; where this differs from the edition used, the more recent date is noted after. This selection of texts is in no way intended to be comprehensive or full.

BALLANTYNE, R. M. (1858), *The Coral Island*, Nelson.
BALLANTYNE, R. M. (1861), *The Gorilla Hunters*, Nelson.
BALLANTYNE, R. M. (1880), *The Lonely Island*, Nelson.
BEST, H. (1937), *Flag of the Desert*, Blackwell.

BORROW, G. (1851), *Lavengro*, Macmillan, 1896.
BORROW, G. (1857), *The Romany Rye*, Macmillan.
BOWEN, E. S. (1954), *Return to Laughter*, Natural History Library, 1964.
BOYES, J. (1911), *John Boyes, King of the Wa-Kikuyu*, ed. C. Bulpett, Methuen.
BUCHAN, J. (1910), *Prester John*, Pan, 1950.
BUCHAN, J. (1916), *Greenmantle*, Hodder & Stoughton, 1923.
BUCHAN, J. (1940), *Memory Hold the Door*, Hodder & Stoughton.
BURROUGHS, E. R. (1917), *Tarzan of the Apes*, Methuen, 1964.
BURROUGHS, E. R. (1919), *Jungle Tales of Tarzan*, Methuen.
CONRAD, J. (1912), *A Smile of Fortune*, Dent.
CURWOOD, J. O. (1925), *The Black Hunter*, Hodder & Stoughton.
DARLEY, H. (1925), *Slaves and Ivory*, Mellifont Press.
DOYLE, A. C. (1887), *A Study in Scarlet*, John Murray.
DOYLE, A. C. (1898), *The Tragedy of the Korosko*, John Murray, 1958.
DOYLE, A. C. (1912), *The Lost World*, John Murray, 1964.
ELIOT, T. S. (1922), *The Waste Land*, Faber & Faber, 1961.
ELIOT, T. S. (1932), *Selected Essays*, Peregrine, 1953.
ELIOT, T. S. (1934), *After Strange Gods*, Faber & Faber.
ELIOT, T. S. (1948), *Notes Towards a Definition of Culture*, Faber & Faber, 1962.
ELLIOTT, W. A. (1910), *Gold from the Quartz*, London Missionary Society.
ELLIS, E. S. (1885), *The Lost Trail*, Cassell, 1897.
FAWCETT, B. (ed.) (1924), *Exploration Fawcett*, Arrow, 1963.
FITZPATRICK, J. P. (1896), *The Transvaal From Within*, Heinemann, 1900.
FITZPATRICK, J. P. (1907), *Jock of the Bushveldt*, Longmans.
FLEMMING, L. (1933), *A Fool on the Veld*, A. C. White, Bloemfontein.
FORESTER, C. S. (1935), *The African Queen*, Heinemann.
FORESTER, C. S. (1948), *The Sky and the Forest*, Michael Joseph.
FORESTER, F. B. (n.d.), *The Indian Vengeance*, Partridge
FORSTER E. M. (1924), *A Passage to India*, Edward Arnold.
GALE, M. (1920), *The Isle of Treasures*, London Missionary Society.
GILSON, C. (1919), *In the Power of the Pygmies*, Milford.
GILSON, C. (1920), 'The Fire Gods', *Boy's Own Paper*.
GILSON, C. (1934), *Taboo*, Warne.
GOGERLY, G. (1871), *The Pioneers – A Narrative of the Bengal Mission*, John Snow.
GREEN, R. L. (1946), *Tellers of Tales*, Edmund Ward, Leicester.
GREENE, L. P. (1935a), *Tabu Dick*, Hamilton.
GREENE, L. P. (1935b), *The Splendid Exile*, Hamilton.
HAGGARD, H. R. (1884), *The Witches Head*, Collier & Son, New York, Longmans, 1894.
HAGGARD, H. R. (1885), *King Solomon's Mines*, Penguin, 1968.
HAGGARD, H. R. (1887a), *Allan Quatermain*, Longmans.
HAGGARD, H. R. (1887b), *Jess*, Smith, Elder.
HAGGARD, H. R. (1887c), *She*, Hodder & Stoughton, 1953.
HAGGARD, H. R. (1892), *Nada the Lily*, Longmans.
HAGGARD, H. R. (1893), *Montezuma's Daughter*, Longmans.

HAGGARD, H. R. (1896), *Heart of the World*, Longmans.

HAGGARD, H. R. (1900), *Black Heart and White Heart*, Longmans.

HAGGARD, H. R. (1905), *Ayesha*, Ward, Lock.

HEATH, F. G. (1889), *Illustrations – A Pictorial Review of Knowledge*, monthly magazine, W. Kent & Co.

HENTY, G. A. (1902), *With Kitchener in the Sudan*, Blackie.

HENTY, G. A. (ed.) (n.d.), *Stirring Adventures Afloat and Ashore*, Ward, Lock & Bowden.

HIGGINSON, J. A. (1919), *A Boy's Adventures Round the World*, The Religious Tract Society.

HILTON, J. (1933), *Lost Horizon*, Macmillan 1937.

HORN, A. A. (1927), *The Life and Works of Aloysius Horn*, ed. E. Lewis, Jonathan Cape: (1927), vol. 1, *The Ivory Coast;* (1928), vol. 2, *Harold the Webbed;* (1929), vol. 3, *The Waters of Africa.*

HUBNER, M. LE BARON DE (1871), *A Ramble Round the World*, Macmillan.

HUDSON, W. (1893), *Idle Days in Patagonia*, Chapman & Hall.

HUDSON, W. (1904) *Green Mansions*, Everyman, Dent.

HUDSON, W. (1918), *Far Away and Long Ago*, Everyman, Dent, 1960.

'INTELLIGENCE OFFICER, THE' (1902), *On the Heels of De Wet*, Blackwood.

KINGSLEY, C. (1855), *Westward Ho!*, Macmillan, 1880.

KINGSLEY, C. (1901), *Life and Letters*, ed. Mrs Kingsley, Macmillan.

KINGSLEY, C. (1863), *The Water Babies*, Macmillan, 1882.

KINGSTON, W. H. G. (n.d.), *Afar in the Forest*, Nelson.

KIPLING, R. (1888), *Plain Tales From the Hills*, Collected Edition, Macmillan.

KIPLING, R. (1904), *Traffics & Discoveries*, Macmillan, Bombay, 1938.

KIPLING, R. (1922), *Kipling's Poems*, Collected Edition, Macmillan.

KIPLING, R. (1895), *Jungle Book*, Macmillan.

KIPLING, R. (1901), *Kim*, Macmillan.

KIPLING, R. (1920), *Letters of Travel*, Macmillan.

KIRBY, M. and E. (1912), *The World at Home – Pictures and Scenes from Far-Off Lands*, Nelson.

LAMBERT, J. C. (1919), *Missionary Knights of the Cross*, Seeley, Service.

LANG, A. (1886), *In the Wrong Paradise*, Kegan Paul, Trench.

LANG, A. (1880), *Ballades in Blue China*, Kegan Paul, Trench.

LANG, A. (1894), *Cock Lane and Common Sense*, Longmans.

LANG, A. (1891), *Essays in Little*, Whitefriars Library of Wit and Humour.

LEWIS, L. (ed.) (n.d.), *Epics of Empire*, Dean & Son.

MARAN, R. (1922), *Batoula*, Jonathan Cape.

MARRYAT, F. (1844), *Settlers in Canada*, Dean & Son.

MASON, A. E. W. (1902), *The Four Feathers*, Hodder & Stoughton.

MASON, A. E. W. (1907), *The Broken Road*, Hodder & Stoughton.

MASON, A. E. W. (1937), *The Drum*, Hodder & Stoughton.

MAUGHAM, W. S. (1921), *The Trembling of a Leaf*, Heinemann.

MAUGHAM, W. S. (1923), *On a Chinese Screen*, Heinemann.

MAUGHAM, W. S. (ed.) (1952), *A Choice of Kipling's Prose*, Macmillan.

MERRIMAN, H. S. (1898), *In Kedar's Tents*, Smith, Elder.

MILES, A. H. (ed.) (1902), *Captured by Navajo Indians*, Everett.

MITFORD, B. (1891), *The Weird of Deadly Hollow*, Ward, Lock & Bowden.

MITFORD, B. (1894a), *The King's Assegai*, Ward, Lock & Bowden.

MITFORD, B. (1894b), *The Curse of Clement Waynfleete*, Ward, Lock & Bowden.

MITFORD, B. (1900), *John Ames – Native Commissioner*, F. V. White.

'GREY OWL' (1935), *Pilgrims of the Wild*, Peter Davies, 1943.

OLIPHANT, L. (1888), *Episodes in a Life of Adventure*, Blackwood.

ORWELL, G. (1936), 'Shooting an Elephant', in *Inside the Whale and Other Essays*, Penguin, 1957.

PARNELL, E. C., ed. (1928), *Stories of the South Seas*, Oxford University Press.

PATON, J. (1889), *The Story of John G. Paton or Thirty Years Among South Sea Cannibals*, Hodder & Stoughton, 1897.

POLLARD, E. F. (n.d.), *A South African Story*, Partridge.

RAYMOND, G. L. (1900), *The Aztec God and Other Dramas*, Putnam.

REID, M. (1860), *The Rifle Rangers*, C. H. Clarke.

RUSSELL, J. (1921), *Where the Pavement Ends*, Thornton Butterworth, 1932.

RUSSELL, J. (1923), *In Dark Places*, Thornton Butterworth, 1932.

RUSSELL, J. (1929), *Far Wandering Men*, Thornton Butterworth, 1932.

SCHREINER, O. (1881), *The Story of an African Farm*, Hutchinson.

SIENKIEWICZ, H. (1912), *In Desert and Wilderness*, Edinburgh, Polish Book Depot, 1945.

STABLES, G. (n.d.), *For Honour Not Honours, The Story of Gordon of Khartoum*, J. F. Shaw.

STACPOOLE, H. DE VERE (1909), *The Pools of Silence*, Unwin.

STANLEY, H. M. (1872), *How I Found Livingstone*, Sampson Low.

STANLEY, H. M. (1893), *My Dark Companions and their Strange Stories*, Sampson Low.

STEVENSON, R. L. (1878), *Travels With A Donkey*, Everyman, Dent.

STEVENSON, R. L. (1883), *Treasure Island*, Cassell, 1907.

STOWE, H. B. (1852), *Uncle Tom's Cabin*, Hutchinson, U.S.A.

TENNYSON, A. (1850), *In Memorian*, Collected Poems, Routledge, 1904.

TENNYSON, A. (1859), *Idylls of the King*, Collected Poems, Routledge, 1904.

TENNYSON, A. (1886), *Locksley Hall*, Collected Poems, Routledge, 1904.

VANDERCOCK, J. W. (1928), *Black Majesty – The Life of Christophe, King of Haiti*, Harper.

WALLACE, E. (1911), *Sanders of the River*, Ward, Lock.

WALLACE, E. (1912), *The People of the River*, Ward, Lock.

WELLS, H. G. (1903), *Mankind in the Making*, Chapman.

WELLS, H. G. (1909), *A Modern Utopia*, Nelson.

WELLS, H. G. (1920), *Outline of History*, Newnes.

WENTWORTH, W. (n.d.), *The Drifting Island*, Nelson.

WILSON, W. W. (n.d.), *The Sioux of St. Jude's*, Goodship House.

WRIGHT, F. S. (1933), *Dream of the Simian Maid*, Harrap.

YEATS, W. B. (1964), *Selected Poetry*, ed. N. Jeffares, Macmillan.

YOUNG, E. R. (1903), *The English in Egypt – Pictorial Records with a Life of General Gordon etc.*, Frederick Warne.

YOUNG, E. R. (1917), *On the Indian Trail*, The Religious Tract Society.

III. Authors (critical)

Buchan, John

BUCHAN, J. (1940), *Memory Hold the Door*, Hodder & Stoughton.
SMITH, J. (1965), *John Buchan*, Hart-Davis.

Burroughs, Edgar Rice

MEIKIN, E. M. (1963), *Edgar Rice Burroughs*, Antiquarian Bookman Special.

Doyle, Sir Arthur Conan

PEARSON, H. (1943), *Conan Doyle,* Methuen.

Eliot, T. S.

FRYE, N. (1963), *T. S. Eliot*, Oliver & Boyd.

Haggard, Sir H. Rider

COHEN, M. (1960), *Rider Haggard – His Life and Works*, Hutchinson.
COHEN, M. (ed.) (1965), *Rudyard Kipling to Rider Haggard*, Hutchinson.
GREENE, G. (1951), 'H. Rider Haggard' in *The Lost Childhood*, Eyre & Spottiswoode.
HAGGARD, H. R. (1926), *The Days of My Life*, Longmans.
HAGGARD, L. R. (1951), *The Cloak that I Left*, Hodder & Stoughton.

Kipling, Rudyard

CARRINGTON, C. E. (1955), *The Life of Rudyard Kipling*, Doubleday, New York.
CORNELL, L. (1966), *Kipling in India*, St Martin's Press, New York.
GILBERT, E. L. (ed.) (1966), *Kipling and the Critics*, Owen.

Lang, Andrew

GREEN, R. L. (1946), *Andrew Lang – A Critical Biography*, Edmund War.
GROSS, J. (1969), *The Rise and Fall of the Man of Letters*, Weidenfeld & Nicolson.

Tennyson, Alfred Lord

LANG, MRS ANDREW (1925), *The Approach to Tennyson*, Nelson.
LYALL, A. (1905), *Alfred Tennyson*, Macmillan.

Wallace, Edgar

LANE, M. W. (1938), *Edgar Wallace*, Heinemann.

Index

Routledge Social Science Series

Routledge & Kegan Paul   London and Boston
68–74 Carter Lane   London EC4V 5EL
9 Park Street   Boston   Mass 02108

Contents

*Authors wishing to submit manuscripts for any series in
this catalogue should send them to the Social Science Editor,
Routledge & Kegan Paul Ltd, 68–74 Carter Lane,
London EC4V 5EL*

● *Books so marked are available in paperback
All books are in Metric Demy 8vo format (216 × 138mm approx.)*

International Library of Sociology

General Editor John Rex

GENERAL SOCIOLOGY

Barnsley, J. H. The Social Reality of Ethics. *464 pp.*
Belshaw, Cyril. The Conditions of Social Performance. *An Exploratory Theory. 144 pp.*
Brown, Robert. Explanation in Social Science. *208 pp.*
● Rules and Laws in Sociology. *192 pp.*
Bruford, W. H. Chekhov and His Russia. *A Sociological Study. 244 pp.*
Cain, Maureen E. Society and the Policeman's Role. *326 pp.*
Gibson, Quentin. The Logic of Social Enquiry. *240 pp.*
Glucksmann, M. Structuralist Analysis in Contemporary Social Thought. *212 pp.*
Gurvitch, Georges. Sociology of Law. *Preface by Roscoe Pound. 264 pp.*
Hodge, H. A. Wilhelm Dilthey. *An Introduction. 184 pp.*
Homans, George C. Sentiments and Activities. *336 pp.*
Johnson, Harry M. Sociology: *a Systematic Introduction. Foreword by Robert K. Merton. 710 pp.*
Mannheim, Karl. Essays on Sociology and Social Psychology. *Edited by Paul Keckskemeti. With Editorial Note by Adolph Lowe. 344 pp.*
Systematic Sociology: *An Introduction to the Study of Society. Edited by J. S. Erös and Professor W. A. C. Stewart. 220 pp.*
Martindale, Don. The Nature and Types of Sociological Theory. *292 pp.*
●**Maus, Heinz.** A Short History of Sociology. *234 pp.*
Mey, Harald. Field-Theory. *A Study of its Application in the Social Sciences. 352 pp.*
Myrdal, Gunnar. Value in Social Theory: *A Collection of Essays on Methodology. Edited by Paul Streeten. 332 pp.*
Ogburn, William F., and **Nimkoff, Meyer F.** A Handbook of Sociology. *Preface by Karl Mannheim. 656 pp. 46 figures. 35 tables.*
Parsons, Talcott, and **Smelser, Neil J.** Economy and Society: *A Study in the Integration of Economic and Social Theory. 362 pp.*
●**Rex, John.** Key Problems of Sociological Theory. *220 pp.*
Discovering Sociology. *278 pp.*
Sociology and the Demystification of the Modern World. *282 pp.*
●**Rex, John** (Ed.) Approaches to Sociology. *Contributions by Peter Abell, Frank Bechhofer, Basil Bernstein, Ronald Fletcher, David Frisby, Miriam Glucksmann, Peter Lassman, Herminio Martins, John Rex, Roland Robertson, John Westergaard and Jock Young. 302 pp.*
Rigby, A. Alternative Realities. *352 pp.*
Roche, M. Phenomenology, Language and the Social Sciences. *374 pp.*
Sahay, A. Sociological Analysis. *220 pp.*
Urry, John. Reference Groups and the Theory of Revolution. *244 pp.*
Weinberg, E. Development of Sociology in the Soviet Union. *173 pp.*

FOREIGN CLASSICS OF SOCIOLOGY

●**Durkheim, Emile.** Suicide. *A Study in Sociology. Edited and with an Introduction by George Simpson. 404 pp.*
Professional Ethics and Civic Morals. *Translated by Cornelia Brookfield. 288 pp.*
●**Gerth, H. H.,** and **Mills, C. Wright.** From Max Weber: *Essays in Sociology. 502 pp.*
●**Tönnies, Ferdinand.** Community and Association. (*Gemeinschaft und Gesellschaft.) Translated and Supplemented by Charles P. Loomis. Foreword by Pitirim A. Sorokin. 334 pp.*

SOCIAL STRUCTURE

Andreski, Stanislav. Military Organization and Society. *Foreword by Professor A. R. Radcliffe-Brown. 226 pp. 1 folder.*
Coontz, Sydney H. Population Theories and the Economic Interpretation. *202 pp.*
Coser, Lewis. The Functions of Social Conflict. *204 pp.*
Dickie-Clark, H. F. Marginal Situation: *A Sociological Study of a Coloured Group. 240 pp. 11 tables.*
Glaser, Barney, and **Strauss, Anselm L.** Status Passage. *A Formal Theory. 208 pp.*
Glass, D. V. (Ed.) Social Mobility in Britain. *Contributions by J. Berent, T. Bottomore, R. C. Chambers, J. Floud, D. V. Glass, J. R. Hall, H. T. Himmelweit, R. K. Kelsall, F. M. Martin, C. A. Moser, R. Mukherjee, and W. Ziegel. 420 pp.*
Jones, Garth N. Planned Organizational Change: *An Exploratory Study Using an Empirical Approach. 268 pp.*
Kelsall, R. K. Higher Civil Servants in Britain: *From 1870 to the Present Day. 268 pp. 31 tables.*
König, René. The Community. *232 pp. Illustrated.*
●**Lawton, Denis.** Social Class, Language and Education. *192 pp.*
McLeish, John. The Theory of Social Change: *Four Views Considered. 128 pp.*
Marsh, David C. The Changing Social Structure of England and Wales, 1871-1961. *288 pp.*
Mouzelis, Nicos. Organization and Bureaucracy. *An Analysis of Modern Theories. 240 pp.*
Mulkay, M. J. Functionalism, Exchange and Theoretical Strategy. *272 pp.*
Ossowski, Stanislaw. Class Structure in the Social Consciousness. *210 pp.*
Podgórecki, Adam. Law and Society. *About 300 pp.*

SOCIOLOGY AND POLITICS

Acton, T. A. Gypsy Politics and Social Change. *316 pp.*
Hechter, Michael. Internal Colonialism. *The Celtic Fringe in British National Development, 1536–1966. About 350 pp.*
Hertz, Frederick. Nationality in History and Politics: *A Psychology and Sociology of National Sentiment and Nationalism. 432 pp.*

Kornhauser, William. The Politics of Mass Society. *272 pp. 20 tables.*
Laidler, Harry W. History of Socialism. *Social-Economic Movements: An Historical and Comparative Survey of Socialism, Communism, Co-operation, Utopianism; and other Systems of Reform and Reconstruction. 992 pp.*
Lasswell, H. D. Analysis of Political Behaviour. *324 pp.*
Mannheim, Karl. Freedom, Power and Democratic Planning. *Edited by Hans Gerth and Ernest K. Bramstedt. 424 pp.*
Mansur, Fatma. Process of Independence. *Foreword by A. H. Hanson. 208 pp.*
Martin, David A. Pacifism: *an Historical and Sociological Study. 262 pp.*
Myrdal, Gunnar. The Political Element in the Development of Economic Theory. *Translated from the German by Paul Streeten. 282 pp.*
Wootton, Graham. Workers, Unions and the State. *188 pp.*

FOREIGN AFFAIRS: THEIR SOCIAL, POLITICAL AND ECONOMIC FOUNDATIONS

Mayer, J. P. Political Thought in France from the Revolution to the Fifth Republic. *164 pp.*

CRIMINOLOGY

Ancel, Marc. Social Defence: *A Modern Approach to Criminal Problems. Foreword by Leon Radzinowicz. 240 pp.*
Cain, Maureen E. Society and the Policeman's Role. *326 pp.*
Cloward, Richard A., and Ohlin, Lloyd E. Delinquency and Opportunity: *A Theory of Delinquent Gangs. 248 pp.*
Downes, David M. The Delinquent Solution. *A Study in Subcultural Theory. 296 pp.*
Dunlop, A. B., and McCabe, S. Young Men in Detention Centres. *192 pp.*
Friedlander, Kate. The Psycho-Analytical Approach to Juvenile Delinquency: *Theory, Case Studies, Treatment. 320 pp.*
Glueck, Sheldon, and Eleanor. Family Environment and Delinquency. *With the statistical assistance of Rose W. Kneznek. 340 pp.*
Lopez-Rey, Manuel. Crime. *An Analytical Appraisal. 288 pp.*
Mannheim, Hermann. Comparative Criminology: *a Text Book. Two volumes. 442 pp. and 380 pp.*
Morris, Terence. The Criminal Area: *A Study in Social Ecology. Foreword by Hermann Mannheim. 232 pp. 25 tables. 4 maps.*
Rock, Paul. Making People Pay. *338 pp.*
●Taylor, Ian, Walton, Paul, and Young, Jock. The New Criminology. *For a Social Theory of Deviance. 325 pp.*

SOCIAL PSYCHOLOGY

Bagley, Christopher. The Social Psychology of the Epileptic Child. *320 pp.*
Barbu, Zevedei. Problems of Historical Psychology. *248 pp.*
Blackburn, Julian. Psychology and the Social Pattern. *184 pp.*

●**Brittan, Arthur.** Meanings and Situations. *224 pp.*

Carroll, J. Break-Out from the Crystal Palace. *200 pp.*

●**Fleming, C. M.** Adolescence: Its Social Psychology. *With an Introduction to recent findings from the fields of Anthropology, Physiology, Medicine, Psychometrics and Sociometry. 288 pp.*

● The Social Psychology of Education: *An Introduction and Guide to Its Study. 136 pp.*

Homans, George C. The Human Group. *Foreword by Bernard DeVoto. Introduction by Robert K. Merton. 526 pp.*

● Social Behaviour: *its Elementary Forms. 416 pp.*

●**Klein, Josephine.** The Study of Groups. *226 pp. 31 figures. 5 tables.*

Linton, Ralph. The Cultural Background of Personality. *132 pp.*

●**Mayo, Elton.** The Social Problems of an Industrial Civilization. *With an appendix on the Political Problem. 180 pp.*

Ottaway, A. K. C. Learning Through Group Experience. *176 pp.*

Ridder, J. C. de. The Personality of the Urban African in South Africa. *A Thematic Apperception Test Study. 196 pp. 12 plates.*

●**Rose, Arnold M.** (Ed.) Human Behaviour and Social Processes: *an Interactionist Approach. Contributions by Arnold M. Rose, Ralph H. Turner, Anselm Strauss, Everett C. Hughes, E. Franklin Frazier, Howard S. Becker, et al. 696 pp.*

Smelser, Neil J. Theory of Collective Behaviour. *448 pp.*

Stephenson, Geoffrey M. The Development of Conscience. *128 pp.*

Young, Kimball. Handbook of Social Psychology. *658 pp. 16 figures. 10 tables.*

SOCIOLOGY OF THE FAMILY

Banks, J. A. Prosperity and Parenthood: *A Study of Family Planning among The Victorian Middle Classes. 262 pp.*

Bell, Colin R. Middle Class Families: *Social and Geographical Mobility. 224 pp.*

Burton, Lindy. Vulnerable Children. *272 pp.*

Gavron, Hannah. The Captive Wife: *Conflicts of Household Mothers. 190 pp.*

George, Victor, and **Wilding, Paul.** Motherless Families. *220 pp.*

Klein, Josephine. Samples from English Cultures.
1. Three Preliminary Studies and Aspects of Adult Life in England. *447 pp.*
2. Child-Rearing Practices and Index. *247 pp.*

Klein, Viola. Britain's Married Women Workers. *180 pp.*

The Feminine Character. *History of an Ideology. 244 pp.*

McWhinnie, Alexina M. Adopted Children. *How They Grow Up. 304 pp.*

● **Myrdal, Alva,** and **Klein, Viola.** Women's Two Roles: *Home and Work. 238 pp. 27 tables.*

Parsons, Talcott, and **Bales, Robert F.** Family: Socialization and Interaction Process. *In collaboration with James Olds, Morris Zelditch and Philip E. Slater. 456 pp. 50 figures and tables.*

6

SOCIAL SERVICES

Bastide, Roger. The Sociology of Mental Disorder. *Translated from the French by Jean McNeil.* 260 pp.
Carlebach, Julius. Caring For Children in Trouble. *266 pp.*
Forder, R. A. (Ed.) Penelope Hall's Social Services of England and Wales. *352 pp.*
George, Victor. Foster Care. *Theory and Practice.* 234 pp.
Social Security: *Beveridge and After.* 258 pp.
George, V., and **Wilding, P.** Motherless Families. *248 pp.*
●**Goetschius, George W.** Working with Community Groups. *256 pp.*
Goetschius, George W., and **Tash, Joan.** Working with Unattached Youth. *416 pp.*
Hall, M. P., and **Howes, I. V.** The Church in Social Work. *A Study of Moral Welfare Work undertaken by the Church of England.* 320 pp.
Heywood, Jean S. Children in Care: *the Development of the Service for the Deprived Child.* 264 pp.
Hoenig, J., and **Hamilton, Marian W.** The De-Segregation of the Mentally Ill. *284 pp.*
Jones, Kathleen. Mental Health and Social Policy, 1845-1959. *264 pp.*
King, Roy D., Raynes, Norma V., and **Tizard, Jack.** Patterns of Residential Care. *356 pp.*
Leigh, John. Young People and Leisure. *256 pp.*
Morris, Mary. Voluntary Work and the Welfare State. *300 pp.*
Morris, Pauline. Put Away: *A Sociological Study of Institutions for the Mentally Retarded.* 364 pp.
Nokes, P. L. The Professional Task in Welfare Practice. *152 pp.*
Timms, Noel. Psychiatric Social Work in Great Britain (1939-1962). *280 pp.*
● Social Casework: *Principles and Practice. 256 pp.*
Young, A. F. Social Services in British Industry. *272 pp.*
Young, A. F., and **Ashton, E. T.** British Social Work in the Nineteenth Century. *288 pp.*

SOCIOLOGY OF EDUCATION

Banks, Olive. Parity and Prestige in English Secondary Education: a Study in Educational Sociology. *272 pp.*
Bentwich, Joseph. Education in Israel. *224 pp. 8 pp. plates.*
●**Blyth, W. A. L.** English Primary Education. *A Sociological Description.*
1. Schools. *232 pp.*
2. Background. *168 pp.*
Collier, K. G. The Social Purposes of Education: *Personal and Social Values in Education.* 268 pp.

Dale, R. R., and **Griffith, S.** Down Stream: *Failure in the Grammar School.*
108 pp.

Dore, R. P. Education in Tokugawa Japan. *356 pp. 9 pp. plates.*

Evans, K. M. Sociometry and Education. *158 pp.*

●**Ford, Julienne.** Social Class and the Comprehensive School. *192 pp.*

Foster, P. J. Education and Social Change in Ghana. *336 pp. 3 maps.*

Fraser, W. R. Education and Society in Modern France. *150 pp.*

Grace, Gerald R. Role Conflict and the Teacher. *About 200 pp.*

Hans, Nicholas. New Trends in Education in the Eighteenth Century.
278 pp. 19 tables.

● Comparative Education: *A Study of Educational Factors and Traditions.*
360 pp.

Hargreaves, David. Interpersonal Relations and Education. *432 pp.*

● Social Relations in a Secondary School. *240 pp.*

Holmes, Brian. Problems in Education. *A Comparative Approach. 336 pp.*

King, Ronald. Values and Involvement in a Grammar School. *164 pp.*

School Organization and Pupil Involvement. *A Study of Secondary
Schools.*

●**Mannheim, Karl,** and **Stewart, W. A. C.** An Introduction to the Sociology
of Education. *206 pp.*

Morris, Raymond N. The Sixth Form and College Entrance. *231 pp.*

●**Musgrove, F.** Youth and the Social Order. *176 pp.*

●**Ottaway, A. K. C.** Education and Society: An Introduction to the Sociology
of Education. *With an Introduction by W. O. Lester Smith. 212 pp.*

Peers, Robert. Adult Education: *A Comparative Study. 398 pp.*

Pritchard, D. G. Education and the Handicapped: *1760 to 1960. 258 pp.*

Richardson, Helen. Adolescent Girls in Approved Schools. *308 pp.*

Stratta, Erica. The Education of Borstal Boys. *A Study of their Educational
Experiences prior to, and during, Borstal Training. 256 pp.*

Taylor, P. H., Reid, W. A., and **Holley, B. J.** The English Sixth Form.
A Case Study in Curriculum Research. 200 pp.

SOCIOLOGY OF CULTURE

Eppel, E. M., and **M.** Adolescents and Morality: *A Study of some Moral
Values and Dilemmas of Working Adolescents in the Context of a
changing Climate of Opinion. Foreword by W. J. H. Sprott. 268 pp.
39 tables.*

●**Fromm, Erich.** The Fear of Freedom. *286 pp.*

● The Sane Society. *400 pp.*

Mannheim, Karl. Essays on the Sociology of Culture. *Edited by Ernst
Mannheim in co-operation with Paul Kecskemeti. Editorial Note by
Adolph Lowe. 280 pp.*

Weber, Alfred. Farewell to European History: *or The Conquest of Nihilism.
Translated from the German by R. F. C. Hull. 224 pp.*

SOCIOLOGY OF RELIGION

Argyle, Michael and **Beit-Hallahmi, Benjamin.** The Social Psychology of Religion. *About 256 pp.*

Nelson, G. K. Spiritualism and Society. *313 pp.*

Stark, Werner. The Sociology of Religion. *A Study of Christendom.*
Volume I. *Established Religion. 248 pp.*
Volume II. *Sectarian Religion. 368 pp.*
Volume III. *The Universal Church. 464 pp.*
Volume IV. *Types of Religious Man. 352 pp.*
Volume V. *Types of Religious Culture. 464 pp.*

Turner, B. S. Weber and Islam. *216 pp.*

Watt, W. Montgomery. Islam and the Integration of Society. *320 pp.*

SOCIOLOGY OF ART AND LITERATURE

Jarvie, Ian C. Towards a Sociology of the Cinema. *A Comparative Essay on the Structure and Functioning of a Major Entertainment Industry. 405 pp.*

Rust, Frances S. Dance in Society. *An Analysis of the Relationships between the Social Dance and Society in England from the Middle Ages to the Present Day. 256 pp. 8 pp. of plates.*

Schücking, L. L. The Sociology of Literary Taste. *112 pp.*

Wolff, Janet. Hermeneutic Philosophy and the Sociology of Art. *About 200 pp.*

SOCIOLOGY OF KNOWLEDGE

Diesing, P. Patterns of Discovery in the Social Sciences. *262 pp.*

●**Douglas, J. D.** (Ed.) Understanding Everyday Life. *370 pp.*

●**Hamilton, P.** Knowledge and Social Structure. *174 pp.*

Jarvie, I. C. Concepts and Society. *232 pp.*

Mannheim, Karl. Essays on the Sociology of Knowledge. *Edited by Paul Kecskemeti. Editorial Note by Adolph Lowe. 353 pp.*

Remmling, Gunter W. (Ed.) Towards the Sociology of Knowledge. *Origin and Development of a Sociological Thought Style. 463 pp.*

Stark, Werner. The Sociology of Knowledge: *An Essay in Aid of a Deeper Understanding of the History of Ideas. 384 pp.*

URBAN SOCIOLOGY

Ashworth, William. The Genesis of Modern British Town Planning: *A Study in Economic and Social History of the Nineteenth and Twentieth Centuries. 288 pp.*

Cullingworth, J. B. Housing Needs and Planning Policy: *A Restatement of the Problems of Housing Need and 'Overspill' in England and Wales. 232 pp. 44 tables. 8 maps.*

Dickinson, Robert E. City and Region: *A Geographical Interpretation* *608 pp. 125 figures.*
The West European City: *A Geographical Interpretation. 600 pp. 129 maps. 29 plates.*
● The City Region in Western Europe. *320 pp. Maps.*
Humphreys, Alexander J. New Dubliners: *Urbanization and the Irish Family. Foreword by George C. Homans. 304 pp.*
Jackson, Brian. Working Class Community: *Some General Notions raised by a Series of Studies in Northern England. 192 pp.*
Jennings, Hilda. Societies in the Making: *a Study of Development and Re-development within a County Borough. Foreword by D. A. Clark. 286 pp.*
●**Mann, P. H.** An Approach to Urban Sociology. *240 pp.*
Morris, R. N., and **Mogey, J.** The Sociology of Housing. *Studies at Berins-field. 232 pp. 4 pp. plates.*
Rosser, C., and **Harris, C.** The Family and Social Change. *A Study of Family and Kinship in a South Wales Town. 352 pp. 8 maps.*

RURAL SOCIOLOGY

Chambers, R. J. H. Settlement Schemes in Tropical Africa: *A Selective Study. 268 pp.*
Haswell, M. R. The Economics of Development in Village India. *120 pp.*
Littlejohn, James. Westrigg: *the Sociology of a Cheviot Parish. 172 pp. 5 figures.*
Mayer, Adrian C. Peasants in the Pacific. *A Study of Fiji Indian Rural Society. 248 pp. 20 plates.*
Williams, W. M. The Sociology of an English Village: *Gosforth. 272 pp. 12 figures. 13 tables.*

SOCIOLOGY OF INDUSTRY AND DISTRIBUTION

Anderson, Nels. Work and Leisure. *280 pp.*
●**Blau, Peter M.,** and **Scott, W. Richard.** Formal Organizations: *a Compara-tive approach. Introduction and Additional Bibliography by J. H. Smith. 326 pp.*
Eldridge, J. E. T. Industrial Disputes. *Essays in the Sociology of Industrial Relations. 288 pp.*
Hetzler, Stanley. Applied Measures for Promoting Technological Growth. *352 pp.*
Technological Growth and Social Change. *Achieving Modernization. 269 pp.*
Hollowell, Peter G. The Lorry Driver. *272 pp.*
Jefferys, Margot, *with the assistance of Winifred Moss.* Mobility in the Labour Market: *Employment Changes in Battersea and Dagenham. Preface by Barbara Wootton. 186 pp. 51 tables.*

Millerson, Geoffrey. The Qualifying Associations: *a Study in Professionalization. 320 pp.*

Smelser, Neil J. Social Change in the Industrial Revolution: *An Application of Theory to the Lancashire Cotton Industry, 1770-1840. 468 pp. 12 figures. 14 tables.*

Williams, Gertrude. Recruitment to Skilled Trades. *240 pp.*

Young, A. F. Industrial Injuries Insurance: *an Examination of British Policy. 192 pp.*

DOCUMENTARY

Schlesinger, Rudolf (Ed.) Changing Attitudes in Soviet Russia.
2. The Nationalities Problem and Soviet Administration. *Selected Readings on the Development of Soviet Nationalities Policies. Introduced by the editor. Translated by W. W. Gottlieb. 324 pp.*

ANTHROPOLOGY

Ammar, Hamed. Growing up in an Egyptian Village: *Silwa, Province of Aswan. 336 pp.*

Brandel-Syrier, Mia. Reeftown Elite. *A Study of Social Mobility in a Modern African Community on the Reef. 376 pp.*

Crook, David, and **Isabel.** Revolution in a Chinese Village: *Ten Mile Inn. 230 pp. 8 plates. 1 map.*

Dickie-Clark, H. F. The Marginal Situation. *A Sociological Study of a Coloured Group. 236 pp.*

Dube, S. C. Indian Village. *Foreword by Morris Edward Opler. 276 pp. 4 plates.*

India's Changing Villages: *Human Factors in Community Development. 260 pp. 8 plates. 1 map.*

Firth, Raymond. Malay Fishermen. *Their Peasant Economy. 420 pp. 17 pp. plates.*

Firth, R., Hubert, J., and **Forge, A.** Families and their Relatives. *Kinship in a Middle-Class Sector of London: An Anthropological Study. 456 pp.*

Gulliver, P. H. Social Control in an African Society: a Study of the Arusha, Agricultural Masai of Northern Tanganyika. *320 pp. 8 plates. 10 figures.*

Family Herds. *288 pp.*

Ishwaran, K. Shivapur. *A South Indian Village. 216 pp.*

Tradition and Economy in Village India: *An Interactionist Approach. Foreword by Conrad Arensburg. 176 pp.*

Jarvie, Ian C. The Revolution in Anthropology. *268 pp.*

Jarvie, Ian C., and **Agassi, Joseph.** Hong Kong. *A Society in Transition. 396 pp. Illustrated with plates and maps.*

Little, Kenneth L. Mende of Sierra Leone. *308 pp. and folder.*

Negroes in Britain. *With a New Introduction and Contemporary Study by Leonard Bloom. 320 pp.*

Lowie, Robert H. Social Organization. *494 pp.*
Mayer, Adrian,C. Caste and Kinship in Central India: *A Village and its Region. 328 pp. 16 plates. 15 figures. 16 tables.*
Peasants in the Pacific. *A Study of Fiji Indian Rural Society. 248 pp.*
Smith, Raymond T. The Negro Family in British Guiana: *Family Structure and Social Status in the Villages. With a Foreword by Meyer Fortes. 314 pp. 8 plates. 1 figure. 4 maps.*

SOCIOLOGY AND PHILOSOPHY

Barnsley, John H. The Social Reality of Ethics. *A Comparative Analysis of Moral Codes. 448 pp.*
Diesing, Paul. Patterns of Discovery in the Social Sciences. *362 pp.*
●**Douglas, Jack D.** (Ed.) Understanding Everyday Life. *Toward the Reconstruction of Sociological Knowledge. Contributions by Alan F. Blum. Aaron W. Cicourel, Norman K. Denzin, Jack D. Douglas, John Heeren, Peter McHugh, Peter K. Manning, Melvin Power, Matthew Speier, Roy Turner, D. Lawrence Wieder, Thomas P. Wilson and Don H. Zimmerman. 370 pp.*
Jarvie, Ian C. Concepts and Society. *216 pp.*
Pelz, Werner. The Scope of Understanding in Sociology. *Towards a more radical reorientation in the social humanistic sciences. 283 pp.*
Roche, Maurice. Phenomenology, Language and the Social Sciences. *371 pp.*
Sahay, Arun. Sociological Analysis. *212 pp.*
Sklair, Leslie. The Sociology of Progress. *320 pp.*

International Library of Anthropology
General Editor Adam Kuper

Brown, Paula. The Chimbu. *A Study of Change in the New Guinea Highlands. 151 pp.*
Lloyd, P. C. Power and Independence. *Urban Africans' Perception of Social Inequality. 264 pp.*
Pettigrew, Joyce. Robber Noblemen. *A Study of the Political System of the Sikh Jats. 284 pp.*
Van Den Berghe, Pierre L. Power and Privilege at an African University. *278 pp.*

International Library of Social Policy
General Editor Kathleen Jones

Bayley, M. Mental Handicap and Community Care. *426 pp.*
Butler, J. R. Family Doctors and Public Policy. *208 pp.*
Holman, Robert. Trading in Children. *A Study of Private Fostering. 355 pp.*

Jones, Kathleen. History of the Mental Health Service. *428 pp.*
Thomas, J. E. The English Prison Officer since 1850: *A Study in Conflict.*
258 pp.
Woodward, J. To Do the Sick No Harm. *A Study of the British Voluntary Hospital System to 1875. About 220 pp.*

International Library of Welfare and Philosophy

General Editors Noel Timms and David Watson

● **Plant, Raymond.** Community and Ideology. *104 pp.*

Primary Socialization, Language and Education

General Editor Basil Bernstein

Bernstein, Basil. Class, Codes and Control. *2 volumes.*
 1. *Theoretical Studies Towards a Sociology of Language. 254 pp.*
 2. *Applied Studies Towards a Sociology of Language. About 400 pp.*
Brandis, W., and **Bernstein, B.** Selection and Control. *176 pp.*
Brandis, Walter, and **Henderson, Dorothy.** Social Class, Language and Communication. *288 pp.*
Cook-Gumperz, Jenny. Social Control and Socialization. *A Study of Class Differences in the Language of Maternal Control. 290 pp.*
● **Gahagan, D. M.,** and **G. A.** Talk Reform. *Exploration in Language for Infant School Children. 160 pp.*
Robinson, W. P., and **Rackstraw, Susan D. A.** A Question of Answers. *2 volumes. 192 pp. and 180 pp.*
Turner, Geoffrey J., and **Mohan, Bernard A.** A Linguistic Description and Computer Programme for Children's Speech. *208 pp.*

Reports of the Institute of Community Studies

Cartwright, Ann. Human Relations and Hospital Care. *272 pp.*
● Parents and Family Planning Services. *306 pp.*
 Patients and their Doctors. *A Study of General Practice. 304 pp.*
● **Jackson, Brian.** Streaming: *an Education System in Miniature. 168 pp.*
Jackson, Brian, and **Marsden, Dennis.** Education and the Working Class: *Some General Themes raised by a Study of 88 Working-class Children in a Northern Industrial City. 268 pp. 2 folders.*
Marris, Peter. The Experience of Higher Education. *232 pp. 27 tables.*
 Loss and Change. *192 pp.*

Marris, Peter, and **Rein, Martin.** Dilemmas of Social Reform. *Poverty and Community Action in the United States. 256 pp.*

Marris, Peter, and **Somerset, Anthony.** African Businessmen. *A Study of Entrepreneurship and Development in Kenya. 256 pp.*

Mills, Richard. Young Outsiders: *a Study in Alternative Communities. 216 pp.*

Runciman, W. G. Relative Deprivation and Social Justice. *A Study of Attitudes to Social Inequality in Twentieth-Century England. 352 pp.*

Willmott, Peter. Adolescent Boys in East London. *230 pp.*

Willmott, Peter, and **Young, Michael.** Family and Class in a London Suburb. *202 pp. 47 tables.*

Young, Michael. Innovation and Research in Education. *192 pp.*

●**Young, Michael,** and **McGeeney, Patrick.** Learning Begins at Home. *A Study of a Junior School and its Parents. 128 pp.*

Young, Michael, and **Willmott, Peter.** Family and Kinship in East London. *Foreword by Richard M. Titmuss. 252 pp. 39 tables.*
The Symmetrical Family. *410 pp.*

Reports of the Institute for Social Studies in Medical Care

Cartwright, Ann, Hockey, Lisbeth, and **Anderson, John L.** Life Before Death. *310 pp.*

Dunnell, Karen, and **Cartwright, Ann.** Medicine Takers, Prescribers and Hoarders. *190 pp.*

Medicine, Illness and Society

General Editor W. M. Williams

Robinson, David. The Process of Becoming Ill. *142 pp.*

Stacey, Margaret, *et al.* Hospitals, Children and Their Families. *The Report of a Pilot Study. 202 pp.*

Monographs in Social Theory

General Editor Arthur Brittan

●**Barnes, B.** Scientific Knowledge and Sociological Theory. *About 200 pp.*

Bauman, Zygmunt. Culture as Praxis. *204 pp.*

● **Dixon, Keith.** Sociological Theory. *Pretence and Possibility. 142 pp.*

●**Smith, Anthony D.** The Concept of Social Change. *A Critique of the Functionalist Theory of Social Change. 208 pp.*

Routledge Social Science Journals

The British Journal of Sociology. *Edited by Terence P. Morris. Vol. 1, No. 1, March 1950 and Quarterly. Roy. 8vo. Back numbers available. An international journal with articles on all aspects of sociology.*

Economy and Society. *Vol. 1, No. 1. February 1972 and Quarterly. Metric Roy. 8vo. A journal for all social scientists covering sociology, philosophy, anthropology, economics and history. Back numbers available.*

Year Book of Social Policy in Britain, The. *Edited by Kathleen Jones. 1971. Published annually.*

Printed in Great Britain by Unwin Brothers Limited
The Gresham Press Old Woking Surrey
A member of the Staples Printing Group